Practice Tests
for the
TOEFL® iBT

by
Bruce Stirling

TOEFL® is a registered trademark of Educational Testing Service (ETS®), Princeton, New Jersey, USA. This publication is not endorsed or approved by ETS.

2 - Practice Tests for the TOEFL® iBT

Copyright © 2017 by Bruce Stirling. All rights reserved.
First Edition

Test samples by Bruce Stirling.
Graphics and layout design by Bruce Stirling.
Audio written and produced by Bruce Stirling.
Sound engineer Jon Conine.

Editors

Patricia Stirling, Gretchen Anderson, Kateryna Kucher, Renata C. T. Rabacov, Yosra Ben Chikh Brahim, Oussama Bellaleh.

Audio Talent

Patricia Stirling, Gretchen Anderson, Jennie Farnell, Bruce Stirling.

Duplication, distribution or database storage of any part of this work by any means is prohibited without prior written approval of the publisher.

For permission to use material from this text in any form, please forward your request to info@novapress.net.

ISBN-10: 1889057940

ISBN-13: 9781889057941

Published by

NOVA PRESS

P. O. Box 692023
West Hollywood, CA USA 90069
1-310-275-3513
info@novapress.net
www.novapress.net

Contents

ALSO BY BRUCE STIRLING..5
TO THE TEST-TAKER...6
TOEFL iBT FACTS...7
    What is the TOEFL iBT?..7
    What is Educational Testing Service (ETS)?...................................7
    Why TOEFL?..7
    What does the TOEFL iBT test?...7
    What are the topics?..7
    Can I fail the TOEFL iBT?...8
    Task Order..8
    What TOEFL iBT score do I need?..8
    The TOEFL PBT and CBT...9
    How important is TOEFL in the admissions process?......................9
    What is the SAT?...10
    How long is my TOEFL iBT score good for?.................................10
    How do I register for the TOEFL iBT?...10
    How should I prepare for the TOEFL iBT?...................................10
TEST ONE..11
    Reading Section..12
    Listening Section...26
    Speaking Section...44
    Writing Section..55
TEST TWO...59
    Reading Section..60
    Listening Section...76
    Speaking Section...94
    Writing Section..105
TEST THREE..109
    Reading Section..110

Listening Section... 124
Speaking Section.. 142
Writing Section.. 153

TEST FOUR... 157
Reading Section... 158
Listening Section.. 172
Speaking Section.. 189
Writing Section.. 200

ANSWER KEY.. 204

READING: CALCULATING SCORES.. 214
Reading Sections: Raw Scores and Conversion Chart...................... 215

LISTENING: CALCULATING SCORES.. 216
Listening Sections: Raw Scores and Conversion Chart..................... 217

SPEAKING: CALCULATING SCORES.. 218
Speaking Sections: Ratings and Conversion Chart........................... 220
Independent Speaking Proficiency Checklist.................................. 221
Independent Speaking Rating Guide.. 222
Integrated Speaking Proficiency Checklist..................................... 224
Integrated Speaking Rating Guide... 225

WRITING: CALCULATING SCORES.. 228
Writing Sections: Ratings and Conversion Chart............................. 230
Integrated Essay Proficiency Checklist... 231
Integrated Essay Rating Guide... 232
Independent Essay Proficiency Checklist...................................... 234
Independent Essay Rating Guide.. 235

SCORING MULTI-ANSWER QUESTIONS.................................... 237

TEST SCORES... 238

RANGE SCORES... 239
Range Score Conversion Chart.. 240

AUDIO SCRIPTS... 241

ACKNOWLEDGEMENTS.. 292

DOWNLOAD AUDIO FILES.. 293

Also by *Bruce Stirling*

Scoring Strategies for the TOEFL® iBT
- A Complete Guide -
Nova Press, Los Angeles, USA

Speaking and Writing Strategies for the TOEFL® iBT
Nova Press, Los Angeles, USA

Speaking and Writing Strategies for the TOEFL® iBT
Chinese version published by
Foreign Language Teaching and Research Press
Beijing, China

Speaking and Writing Strategies for the TOEFL® iBT
published by Prakash Books, New Delhi, India
available at uRead.com

500 Words, Phrases and Idioms for the TOEFL® iBT
plus **Typing Strategies**
Nova Press, Los Angeles, USA

Got a TOEFL® question? Ask Bruce Stirling

Visit Bruce Stirling TOEFL® Pro on Facebook
and
www.toeflpro.blogspot.com

To the Test-Taker

This book contains four, full-length TOEFL iBT practice tests.

Each practice test...

- reflects the design of the official TOEFL iBT;
- tests English-language proficiency expected of first and second year college and university students in the United States, Canada, Australia, New Zealand, Ireland, Scotland and England;
- provides extra practice before you take the official TOEFL iBT;
- will help you identify those areas of English you need to improve for a higher TOEFL iBT score;
- will give you an unofficial, TOEFL iBT range score within a 10-point range;
- will help you determine: 1) if you need to take a TOEFL iBT preparation class and/or ESL classes to increase your proficiency of academic English required at the TOEFL level, or; 2) if you are ready to take the TOEFL iBT.

When doing each practice test...

- Do not use a dictionary or a grammar checker.
- You may take notes. On test day, you must use test-center paper and pencils.
- Watch the clock. Be consistent and accurate when timing yourself.
- Take a 10-minute break between the listening section and the speaking section. On test day, you will get a 10-minute break between these two sections.
- Do not stop and start when taking a test. Complete each test in one sitting. This will help make you "test-ready."
- Your official speaking and writing responses will be scored by two or more raters. The average of their scores will be your final speaking score and writing score. When practicing for the TOEFL iBT, it is not always possible to get two or more qualified raters to rate, then average, your practice speaking and writing responses. However, you can still rate like an official rater. The raters are trained to identify specific rhetorical elements in your spoken and written responses. Those rhetorical elements are defined in the speaking proficiency checklists (pg. 221 + 224) and the essay proficiency checklists (pg. 231 + 234). These user-friendly checklists and rating guides were designed by the author.
- Type your essays. On test day, you will type two essays using a regular Microsoft keyboard. A regular Microsoft keyboard is not "touch sensitive" like a laptop keyboard.
- When typing your essays, you can cut, paste and copy, and keep track of the word count. Do not use a spell checker or a grammar checker.
- On test day, you will do the TOEFL iBT test on a computer in a secure test center. The computer version of the TOEFL iBT is user-friendly. While these paper practice tests are excellent preparation, do sample computer-based tests as well. For sample TOEFL iBT computer tests, visit www.ets.org/toefl.

TOEFL® iBT Facts

What is the TOEFL iBT?

The TOEFL iBT is an English-language proficiency test. TOEFL means *test of English as a foreign language*. iBT means *internet-based test*.

What is Educational Testing Service (ETS)?

Educational Testing Service designs and implements the TOEFL iBT worldwide. ETS is located in Princeton, New Jersey, USA. When you take the TOEFL iBT, you will use a desktop computer connected to the internet. Your responses will be sent via the internet to ETS to be scored. For more information, visit www.ets.org/toefl.

Why TOEFL?

Many non native English speakers wish to study or practice professionally in English-speaking countries, such as the United States and Canada. To do so, they are required to demonstrate English-language proficiency. Enter TOEFL.

What does the TOEFL iBT test?

The TOEFL iBT tests:

1) your ability to apply academic English across four skill sets: reading, listening, speaking, writing;

2) your ability to learn new material at the academic level, then answer questions about that material in a timed environment.

What are the topics?

The topics used for testing are those found in first and second year university life science and humanities courses, such as biology, economics, art, geology, zoology, literature, and history. The TOEFL iBT does not test applied sciences, such as physics and mathematics, nor does it test current events.

You do not need to study life sciences and the humanities before you take the TOEFL iBT. The TOEFL iBT will teach you all you need to know to answer questions specific to the task. In this way, the TOEFL iBT is a learning test.

Can I fail the TOEFL iBT?

No. You cannot pass or fail the TOEFL iBT. The TOEFL iBT measures your ability to understand and apply academic English on a scale from 0 to 120. The higher your score, the higher your English-language proficiency.

Task Order

The TOEFL iBT is divided into four test sections. You cannot change the task order. You must type your two essays. You may take notes throughout.

Section	Task	Questions	Time	Score
Reading	3-5 passages	12-14 questions each	60-100 minutes	30/30
Listening	2-3 conversations	5 questions each		
	4-6 lectures	6 questions each	60-90 minutes	30/30
BREAK			**10 minutes**	
Speaking	independent	2 tasks	2 minutes	
	integrated	4 tasks	18 minutes	30/30
Writing	integrated	1 task	23 minutes	
	independent	1 task	30 minutes	30/30
TOTAL			**4 hours**	**120/120**

What TOEFL iBT score do I need?

Undergraduate applicants in the U.S. and Canada should aim for at least 80/120. Graduate school applicants should aim for at least 90/120.

The TOEFL score you need is different from the score you want. All test-takers want a perfect TOEFL score. However, if you only need 85 to enter the college of your choosing, then 85 is a good score.

The TOEFL requirements for each school are different. Before you take the TOEFL iBT, contact the school of your choosing and find out their TOEFL requirements. Professional license applicants should consult their licensing agencies for TOEFL requirements.

The TOEFL PBT and CBT

The TOEFL PBT (paper-based test) is the original TOEFL test. It was replaced by the CBT (computer-based test), which was replaced by the iBT (internet-based test). The CBT has been discontinued. The PBT is still offered at select locations. Visit www.ets.org/toefl for PBT test locations. See the chart below for score comparisons.

TOEFL iBT	TOEFL PBT	TOEFL CBT
120	677	300
110	637	270
100	600-603	250
90	577	233
80	550	213
70	523	193
60	497	170

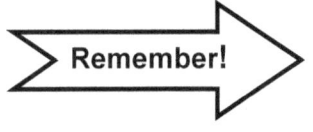

If you are applying for undergraduate or graduate school in the United States or Canada, do not take the PBT. American and Canadian schools want to know if you can communicate verbally at the academic level. The iBT tests speaking proficiency at the academic level. The PBT does not test speaking.

Do not take the PBT simply because you have heard it is easier than the iBT. The TOEFL test you take will depend on the requirements of the school/agency to which you are applying.

How important is TOEFL in the admissions process?

Your TOEFL iBT score is only one part of your university/college application. You will also be required to write a personal essay, submit your official grades, and provide letters of recommendation. You might also be interviewed. Most U.S. and Canadian universities and colleges base admittance on your application as a whole. If you are applying as an undergraduate in the United States, you must also submit an SAT score.

What is the SAT?

SAT means *Scholastic Aptitude Test*. American high school students take the SAT upon graduation. The SAT tests knowledge of high-school reading, writing, and math. A foreign-born student applying as an undergraduate to a U.S. university or college is required to submit an SAT score. Visit www.sat.collegeboard.org for more about the SAT.

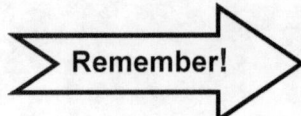 *Ask those schools to which you are applying for their SAT requirements, and for any other test requirements.*

How long is my TOEFL iBT score good for?

Your TOEFL iBT score is good for two years. You cannot renew your score. You must retake the test.

How do I register for the TOEFL iBT?

Register for TOEFL online or by phone. In the United States, the busiest registration times are at the end of each school semester when TOEFL courses end and TOEFL students are ready to take the test. TOEFL is very popular. Register early. For registration information, visit www.ets.org/toefl.

How should I prepare for the TOEFL iBT?

1. Take advanced ESL classes to practice reading, listening, speaking, and writing at the academic level.

2. Take a TOEFL iBT class. By doing so, you will meet test-takers with similar goals and interests. Chances are you will meet someone who has already taken the TOEFL iBT. Learn from his/her experiences.

3. Improve your typing. Classroom experience indicates that a majority of test-takers are not proficient English typists. Poor typing can reduce your writing score.

4. Read. For advanced English speakers, reading English material (novels, essays, newspapers) is the best way to acquire an academic-level vocabulary.

5. Do not take the TOEFL iBT without preparation. Many test-takers have taken the TOEFL iBT without preparation only to realize that the TOEFL iBT was much harder than they had expected.

6. Visit Educational Testing Service's web site (www.ets.org/toefl). Everything you need to know about TOEFL is there. Take "the TOEFL iBT test tour." Also, do the "free TOEFL iBT test samples" and read "TOEFL iBT Test Tips." By doing so, you will familiarize yourself with the TOEFL iBT.

Test 1

Test #1
Reading Section

Directions

For this section, you have 60 minutes to read three passages and answer the questions following each passage. The passages are typical of those found in North American college and university text books.

Answer each question based on what is stated or implied in the passage. You will not lose points for wrong answers. Remember to time yourself.

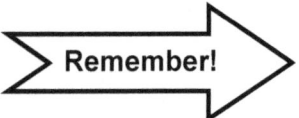

You may take notes. They will not be rated. After the test, calculate your reading score. See pg. 214.

Passage #1 - *The Tulip Bubble*

1 ➔ The seventeenth century is known as the Dutch Golden Age. During this period, the Dutch empire, centered in the port city of Amsterdam, stretched from Manhattan Island in North America to the spice islands in Southeast Asia. The engine that drove the Dutch empire was the Dutch East India Company, a company considered to be the world's first multi-national corporation. Funded by shareholders and the Bank of Amsterdam, the Dutch East India Company was, by 1640, the dominant force in the world economy. Ships arriving in Amsterdam were filled with exotic cargo, such as nutmeg, cinnamon, and pepper from the islands of Indonesia. They also carried silk, tea, and porcelain from China and beaver fur from Manhattan. Dutch merchants became fabulously wealthy. They had their portraits painted by Rembrandt and Vermeer, and sought ways to reinvest their money. One investment opportunity was tulips.

2 ➔ The tulip is a flowering plant that grows from a bulb similar in appearance to an onion. In North America, tulips are one of the first flowering plants to emerge in early spring. In North America, the tulip is as synonymous with Dutch culture as are windmills and wooden shoes. However, the tulip is not native to the Netherlands. The tulip arrived in Holland from the Ottoman Empire sometime in the mid-sixteenth century, the Ottoman empire encompassing present-day Turkey and Iran. ■ Tulip cultivation took off in 1593 when famed Flemish botanist Carolus Clusius started to grow tulips for research. ■ Clusius was interested in "tulip breaking," a natural phenomenon that resulted in multi-colored tulips. ■ His neighbors, so the story goes, were so captivated by Clusius's tulips that they stole some bulbs which they sold. ■ And with that, tulipmania was on.

3 ➔ Dutch tulips were classified according to color. Solid reds, yellows, and white were called couleren while multi-colored, striped tulips were called rosen (red or pink vertical stripes on a white background), violetten, (purple or lilac stripes on a white background), and bizarden (red or purple stripes on a yellow background). Today, botanists know that tulip striping, the thing that made them so valuable in the early seventeenth century, is caused by a virus known as the tulip breaking virus. At the time, however, this fact was not known. What is known is that world's first economic bubble was started by Dutch with the buying and selling of tulip bulbs.

4 ➔ Much like stocks on Wall Street today, Dutch tulips were traded with buyers hoping to turn around and sell their bulbs at much higher prices, prices that had nothing to do with reality. For example, for one tulip bulb, a man traded twelve acres of land while another bought forty bulbs for 100,000 florins. At the time, a skilled laborer earned less than one-hundred-and-fifty florins a year. Perhaps the most outrageous trade was the man who traded for one bulb "a silver drinking cup, a suit of clothes, a complete bed, 1,000 pounds of cheese, two tons of butter, four tons of beer, two barrels of wine, twelve fat sheep, eight fat swine, four fat oxen, four lasts of rye, [and] four lasts of wheat." When the mania reached its peek in the winter of 1636, buyers were no longer willing to plant their bulbs come spring. They deemed it too risky. Instead, the trend was to have parties in which people viewed unplanted tulip bulbs arranged on tables.

5 ➔ In the winter of 1636, every Dutchman it seemed was trying to cash in on the tulip craze. The government could do nothing to stop it. Money kept pouring into the tulip market and prices kept going up with no one actually taking possession of the bulbs they had purchased. Moreover, the Dutch, like Americans and the 1929 stock market, were convinced that the good times were here to stay. By the winter of 1637, however, Dutch tulip traders could no longer find buyers willing to pay such exorbitant prices for their bulbs. Panic erupted when one buyer failed to show up to claim his purchase. Within days, prices plummeted. The tulip bubble had finally burst.

lasts: old Dutch measurement; one last = 1,250 kilograms or 2,750 pounds

1. In paragraph 1, the word dominant is closest in meaning to...

   a) important
   b) commanding
   c) dangerous
   d) wealthy

2. In paragraph 1, to what does they refer?

   a) Dutch merchants
   b) Rembrandt and Vermeer
   c) China and Manhattan
   d) tulips

3. In paragraph 2, why does the author mention windmills and wooden shoes?

   a) to describe what life was like in Holland in 1740
   b) to highlight what people wore back then
   c) to illustrate other popular symbols of Dutch culture
   d) to compare and contrast Holland then and now

4. In paragraph 2, the word captivated is closest in meaning to...

   a) persuaded
   b) allured
   c) captured
   d) fascinated

5. Look at the four squares [■]. They indicate where the bold sentence below could be added to paragraph 2. Select the square where you think the bold sentence could be inserted into the passage.

    Almost overnight, the tulip became a status symbol, a much coveted luxury item sought by rich and poor alike.

    ■ Tulip cultivation took off in 1593 when famed Flemish botanist Carolus Clusius started to grow tulips for research. ■ Clusius was interested in "tulip breaking," a natural phenomenon that resulted in multi-colored tulips. ■ His neighbors, so the story goes, were so captivated by Clusius's tulips that they stole some bulbs which they sold. ■ And with that, tulipmania was on.

6. In paragraph 3, what is NOT TRUE about tulip striping?

    a) Striped tulips were called rosen, violetten, and bizarden.
    b) At the time, botanists did not understand why tulips were striped.
    c) Striped tulips caused the first tulip bubble.
    d) Color was the method used for classifying striped tulips.

7. In paragraph 4, the word outrageous is closest in meaning to...

    a) unique
    b) shocking
    c) courageous
    d) exciting

8. In paragraph 4, what can we infer about the speculation in tulips?

    a) Tulips were not traded for money but for real property.
    b) People bought tulips for the purpose of having parties.
    c) A person was willing to pay almost any price for a prized tulip.
    d) Prices were fairly valued and reflected the Dutch economy as a whole.

9. In paragraph 4, why does the author mention a skilled laborer?

    a) to illustrate how much a common man made at the time in contrast to what others were willing to pay for tulip bulbs
    b) to highlight the dangers of individuals investing in speculative products such as plants
    c) to give an example of someone who lost a lot of money while investing during a bubble
    d) to describe the process of buying and selling tulips at the time

10. In paragraph 5, what does the phrase cash in on mean?

    a) take advantage of
    b) lose control of
    c) think about
    d) turn away from

11. In paragraph 5, why does the author mention Americans and the 1929 stock market?

    a) to draw a comparison between two economic bubbles in two different countries at two different times
    b) to compare and contrast two important historical events that changed the course of world history
    c) to classify economic bubbles and where they occurred and when
    d) to compare the Dutch economic bubble to the American tulip bubble in 1939

12. Which of the following sentences best restates the essential information in the highlighted sentence in paragraph 5? Incorrect choices will change the meaning and omit important information.

    a) No one paid money for tulips because the prices were too high.
    b) The price of tulip bulbs went up while purchases went down.
    c) After a bulb was a bought, the buyer had to wait to possess it.
    d) As prices steadily rose, money changed hands but bulbs did not.

13. Directions: The sentence in bold is the first sentence of a brief summary of the passage. Complete the summary by selecting three answer choices. Your choices will express the most important ideas in the passage. Some choices are not in the passage or do not express important ideas. This is a 2-point question.

    The passage discusses the Dutch tulip bubble.

    -
    -
    -

Answer Choices

1. In sixteenth century Holland, flowers were classified according to color.

2. The Dutch mania for tulips started when bulbs from a botanist's garden were stolen then sold.

3. During the Dutch Golden Age, the speculation in tulips made everyone rich.

4. The price for one tulip bulb was often far more than a common man made in one year.

5. Speculators drove the price of tulip bulbs so high, the market finally collapsed due to a lack of buyers.

6. The Dutch East India company was a major investor in tulip bulbs.

For scoring multi-answer questions, see pg. 237.

Raw Score =   / 14

Add your raw score to Test #1 box pg. 215.

Passage #2 - *The Women of Liberia Mass Action for Peace*

1 ➔ Of all the peace movements in recent years, one in particular stands out: *The Women of Liberia Mass Action for Peace*. In 2003, the movement, through non violent protest, ended the second Liberian civil war and ousted president Charles Taylor. Taylor, a warlord who had overthrown his predecessor, was accused of a plethora of crimes including crimes against humanity for the brutal repression of his fellow Liberians. Rebel groups, supported by neighboring Guinea and Côte d'Ivoire, attempted to overthrow Taylor. In early 2003, the rebels controlled most of the countryside and were laying siege to the capital of Monrovia. Taylor fought back with paramilitary units he called small-boy units. These units marked a new type of warfare. Instead of regular soldiers, small-boy units consisted of war-orphaned boys as young as eight. To entice boys to join his army, Taylor promised gifts and assault weapons. Taylor ordered his small-boy units to terrorize the civilian population using any means possible, including rape and torture. Small-boy units were particularly savage. Because of their lack of maturity, the boys believed that they were invincible thus feared nothing as they terrorized the populace and battled the invading rebels. Peace conferences were held, but the fighting continued with civilians caught in the middle. By 2003, Liberia had been in a state of constant civil war for thirteen years. Finally, one woman said enough. That woman was Leymah Gbowee.

2 ➔ At the age of seventeen, Leymah Gbowee moved from central Liberia where she was born to the capital Monrovia. Trained as a trauma counselor, she helped child soldiers who had fought in Taylor's small-boy units. By doing so, Gbowee witnessed firsthand the physical and psychological damage Taylor had visited upon the people of Liberia. Determined to stop the war, Gbowee brought Christian and Muslim mothers together and formed *The Women of Liberia Mass Action for Peace*. United, the mothers of Liberia believed that "Regardless of whom you pray to, during war our experience as a community and as mothers is the same."

3 ➔ ■ With their numbers growing, the WLMAP forced Taylor to attend peace talks in neighboring Ghana. ■ The talks were held in the presidential palace with Gbowee and a delegation from the WLMAP there to monitor the talks. ■ The talks, however, broke down when the warring parties refused to negotiate. ■ With the delegates threatening to leave, Gbowee and her delegation took action. They blocked the doors and windows of the presidential palace and barred the delegates from leaving without a resolution. In the end, Taylor resigned as president of Liberia and found refuge in Nigeria. With Taylor's exit, Liberia's second civil war came to an end. Elections were held and Ellen Johnson Sirleaf was elected president thus making her the first female head of an African state. These changes would not have been possible if it were not for Leymah Gbowee and her determination to bring peace to Liberia.

4 ➔ The achievements of Leymah Gbowee and the WLMAP are documented in the movie *Pray the Devil Back to Hell* by Gini Reticker and Abigail E. Disney. To date, the film has won many awards while Leymah Gbowee herself has received many prestigious honors including the John F. Kennedy Profile in Courage Award. Leymah Gbowee continues to fight for peace and women's rights as the executive director of the *Women Peace and Security Network, Africa* (WIPSEN), an

organization devoted to building relationships to support and promote women and youth throughout West Africa. In 2011, Leymah Gbowee was awarded the Nobel Peace Prize.

laying siege: The surrounding of a city or town by military force.

1. In paragraph 1, the word ousted is closest in meaning to...

   a) banned
   b) reinstated
   c) removed
   d) elected

2. In paragraph 1, a plethora of is closest in meaning to...

   a) a few
   b) excessive
   c) various
   d) murderous

3. Which of the following sentences best restates the essential information in the highlighted sentence in paragraph 1? Incorrect choices will change the meaning and omit important information.

   a) The boys were so young they thought they were immortal.
   b) The population feared the boys because they were invading rebels.
   c) The boys lacked maturity but were courageous fighters.
   d) The population feared nothing as the boys terrorized the rebels.

4. In paragraph 2, what can we infer about Christian and Muslim mothers?

   a) They were all very young, around the age of seventeen.
   b) They believed that by uniting they would be a stronger peace movement.
   c) Previous to uniting, they had been fighting each other for many years.
   d) They were all from the capital city of Monrovia, like Leymah Gbowee.

5. In paragraph 3, the phrase broke down is closest in meaning to...

   a) failed
   b) slowed down
   c) paused
   d) started

6. In paragraph 3, which of the following is TRUE?

   a) Taylor stepped down as president and found safe haven in Nigeria.
   b) At first, the peace talks in Nigeria were unsuccessful.
   c) Leymah Gbowee became Liberia's first freely-elected female prime minister.
   d) Taylor was invited to the peace talks in Ghana.

7. Look at the four squares [■]. They indicate where the bold sentence below could be added to paragraph 3. Select the square where you think the bold sentence could be inserted into the passage.

Dressed in white, the Christian and Muslim mothers staged daily, non violent protests in the fish market of the capital.

■ With their numbers growing, the WLMAP forced Taylor to attend peace talks in neighboring Ghana. ■ The talks were held in the presidential palace with Gbowee and a delegation from the WLMAP there to monitor the talks. ■ The talks, however, broke down when the warring parties refused to negotiate. ■ With the delegates threatening to leave, Gbowee and her delegation took action.

8. To what does they refer in paragraph 3?

   a) talks
   b) delegates
   c) warring parties
   d) Gbowee and her delegation

9. In paragraph 3, the word barred is closest in meaning to...

   a) encouraged
   b) observed
   c) prevented
   d) bargained

10. In paragraph 3, why does the author mention Ellen Johnson Sirleaf?

    a) to compare and contrast her leadership to Charles Taylor's
    b) to define and further develop her role in the peace movement
    c) to highlight a positive result of Leymah Gbowee's peace efforts
    d) to illustrate the process of electing a female president in an African state

11. In paragraph 4, what can we infer about Leymah Gbowee?

    a) Her efforts have not gone unnoticed.
    b) She wanted to be president of Liberia.
    c) She understands the psychology of war.
    d) She believes that religion can stop war.

12. Directions: The sentence in bold is the first sentence of a brief summary of the passage. Complete the summary by selecting three answer choices. Your choices will express the most important ideas in the passage. Some choices are not in the passage or do not express important ideas. This is a 2-point question.

    The passage discusses the achievements Leymah Gbowee.
    -
    -
    -

    Answer Choices

    1. Leymah Gbowee protested against Liberia's second civil war by organizing peaceful demonstrations in which Christian and Muslim mothers united.
    2. Leymah Gbowee helped soldiers become responsible members of society once again.
    3. She was trained as a trauma counselor specializing in small-boy units.
    4. As a result of Leymah Gbowee's peace efforts, Liberia elected Africa's first female president.
    5. Leymah Gbowee has received many awards, including the Nobel Peace Prize.
    6. Leymah Gbowee's actions at the Ghana peace conference helped end Liberia's second civil war by forcing President Sirleaf to resign.

13. Directions: Complete the following table by indicating which topics go under each topic heading. This is a 4-point question.

Charles Taylor	Leymah Roberta Gbowee
•	•
•	•
•	•
	•

    1. trauma doctor
    2. peace activist
    3. small-boy units
    4. crimes against humanity
    5. born in Monrovia
    6. Nobel-prize winner
    7. helped elect Ellen Johnson Sirleaf
    8. *Pray the Devil Back to Hell*
    9. warlord

    For scoring multi-answer questions, see pg. 237.

    Raw Score =   / 17

    Add your raw score to Test #1 box pg. 215.

Passage #3 - *Crypsis*

1 → ■ Camouflage means hiding by blending in with the environment. ■ An organism that employs camouflage is the tawny frogmouth of Australia. ■ When seen, the tawny frogmouth is often confused with an owl; however, the tawny frogmouth is not an owl but a nightjar. ■ The tawny frogmouth gets its name from its large, wide beak. ■ It is nocturnal and feeds primarily on insects. When sleeping during the day, or when threatened, the tawny frogmouth perches on a branch of a tree that is the same color as the tawny frogmouth's plumage. Camouflaged during the day this way, the tawny frogmouth is virtually invisible to the observer. Blending in with the native environment in such a manner is called cryptic coloration. This is the most common form of crypsis.

2 → Another organism that benefits from cryptic coloration is the flounder. Flounders spend the majority of their time on the ocean floor thus evolution has provided the flounder with a speckled coloration that matches the color of the ocean floor. The flounder's ability to camouflage itself by appearing to look like the ocean floor makes it invisible to predators hoping to make a meal out of the flounder while at the same time allowing the flounder to ambush its prey, such as shrimp and crabs. In the aforementioned tawny frogmouth, camouflage served only one purpose: to protect. With the flounder, however, camouflage serves a dual purpose: to help it survive by avoiding being detected and possibly eaten while at the same time allowing it to hunt. Tigers too rely on cryptic coloration for survival and hunting. The tiger's vertical black and orange stripes allow it to blend in with the environment. Deer and other prey that confuse the tiger's stripes for light and shade more often than not end up on the dinner plate.

3 → Disruptive camouflage is the opposite of cryptic coloration. With disruptive camouflage, an organism tries to confuse the observer by changing shape and color or, as in the octopus's case, by ejecting a cloud of black ink, which disrupts the predator's sight and smell. This allows the octopus to escape. The pufferfish, a small, slow moving fish, employs another type of disruptive camouflage. If threatened, the pufferfish balloons into a ball by filling its stomach with water. At the same time, spikes protrude from its body making the otherwise small pufferfish look like a much larger and more dangerous fish. A predator, looking for a small fish, and not wanting to risk a confrontation with a ballooned pufferfish, would likely move on to easier prey. However, if a predator were to attack, it would run into the pufferfish's second line of defense, the poison tetrodotoxin, a neurotoxin with no known antidote. The only vertebrate whose toxin is more lethal than the pufferfish's is the golden dart frog's.

4 → A second form of crypsis is mimicry. An example is the lo moth. In the center of each wing is a large black dot called an eyespot. When observed, these eyespots look like the eyes of a large predator, such as an owl. In this equation, the mimic, the lo moth, is sharing the characteristics of a different species called the model. By modeling itself after a larger animal, the lo moth sends a signal to the observer that it is a potential threat and should not be eaten. This relationship, one in which a species shares similarities with another species while pretending to be a threat, is called a Batesian mimic. Named after Henry Walter Bates, the English scientist who first observed mimicry in the wild, a Batesian mimic is a sheep in wolf's clothing. Another

example is *Malpolon moilensis* or false cobra. This cobra looks and moves like its more lethal cousin, the hooded cobra, but is innocuous.

1. Look at the four squares [■]. They indicate where the bold sentence below could be added to paragraph 1. Select the square where you think the bold sentence could be inserted into the passage.

   Crypsis, the ability of an organism to avoid being seen by another organism, can be achieved through camouflage and mimicry.

   1 → ■ Camouflage means hiding by blending in with the environment. ■ An organism that employs camouflage is the tawny frogmouth of Australia. ■ When seen, the tawny frogmouth is often confused with an owl; however, the tawny frogmouth is not an owl but a nightjar. ■ The tawny frogmouth gets its name from its large, wide beak.

2. In paragraph 1, what can be inferred about the tawny frogmouth?

   a) It is a lizard.
   b) It is a monkey.
   c) It is a bird.
   d) It is a snake.

3. It refers to what in paragraph 1?

   a) wide beak
   b) name
   c) tawny frogmouth
   d) frogmouth

4. In paragraph 2, ambush is closest in meaning to...

   a) escape to safety
   b) attack with surprise
   c) change color quickly
   d) hide quietly

5. In paragraph 2, why does the author introduce the topic of tigers?

   a) to classify and develop the topic of camouflage and mimicry in nature
   b) to add to and develop the subject of how animals use cryptic coloration
   c) to compare and contrast a bird, a fish and a cat, and how they hide
   d) to illustrate and develop the topic of how tigers hunt during the day

6. In paragraph 3, protrude is closest in meaning to...

   a) stick up
   b) cover up
   c) show up
   d) wrap up

7. In paragraph 3, antidote is closest in meaning to...

   a) a form of therapy
   b) a type of medicine
   c) a solution to a problem
   d) a remedy that reverses

8. Which of the following sentences best restates the essential information in the highlighted sentence in paragraph 3? Incorrect choices will change the meaning and omit important information.

   a) Disruptive camouflage is one way in which an octopus changes shape and hides from predators and prey.
   b) An octopus, when threatened by a predator, will release a jet of black ink in order to confuse a predator's senses.
   c) Disruptive camouflage means changing color whenever an animal feels threatened by an octopus.
   d) Disruptive camouflage is a form of crypsis in which animals, such as an octopus, will use black clouds to confuse predators.

9. In paragraph 4, what is TRUE about the lo moth?

   a) The lo moth employs both mimicry and camouflage to protect itself from predators and, as a result, is rarely eaten or attacked by birds.
   b) The lo moth's wing eyespots, resembling a larger predator's eyes, in this case an owl's, are an example of a Batesian mimic wherein the lo moth pretends to be another more dangerous animal.
   c) The lo moth, an example of a Batesian mimic, pretends to be a different animal in order to eat other animals, such as owls.
   d) The lo moth is, according to Henry Walter Bates, an example of a wolf in sheep's clothing because of how it uses mimicry to hunt and hide.

10. In paragraph 4, why does the author talk about the lo moth and *Malpolon moilensis*?

    a) to provide two Batesian mimics for comparison and contrast
    b) to identify two Batesian mimics that are similar to sheep and wolves
    c) to describe how Batesian mimics might look innocuous but are not
    d) to develop the topic of camouflage with two contrasting examples

11. In paragraph 4, innocuous is closest in meaning to...

   a) harmless
   b) dangerous
   c) innocent
   d) protected

12. Directions: The sentence in bold is the first sentence of a brief summary of the passage. Complete the summary by selecting three answer choices. Your choices will express the most important ideas in the passage. Some choices are not in the passage or do not express important ideas. This is a 2-point question.

   The passage discusses crypsis.

   -
   -
   -

Answer Choices

1. Camouflage and mimicry are types of crypsis.

2. The false cobra looks dangerous but is really a harmless mimic.

3. The tawny frogmouth is an owl that hides by using camouflage for protection.

4. Disruptive camouflage confuses predators.

5. The English scientist Henry Walter Bates first observed mimicry in the wild.

6. To survive, some animals pretend to be larger, more dangerous animals.

13. <u>Directions</u>: Complete the following table by indicating which topics go under each topic heading. This is a 4-point question.

tawny frogmouth	Io moth	octopus
•	•	•
•	•	
•	•	

1. striped
2. disruptive camouflage
3. cryptic coloration
4. eyespots on wings
5. nightjar
6. insect
7. poisonous
8. Batesian mimic
9. nocturnal

For scoring multi-answer questions, see pg. 237.

Raw Score =   / 17

Add your raw score to Test #1 box pg. 215.

Test #1
Listening Section

Directions

The listening section measures your ability to answer questions specific to English conversations and lectures. The conversations and lectures are typical of the North American college and university experience.

After each conversation and lecture, you will answer questions. Answer each question based on what the speakers state or imply. Answer all questions. You will not lose points for a wrong answer.

For some questions, you will see a headset symbol: 🎧
The headset symbol means you will hear part of the conversation or lecture. After you hear part of the conversation or lecture, you will answer a question about it.

Do not look at the answers as you listen. On test day, you will not see the answers as you listen. Remember to time yourself.

> **Remember!** *You have 60 minutes to complete this section.*

> **Remember!** *You may take notes. Your notes will not be rated. After the test, calculate your listening score. See pg. 216.*

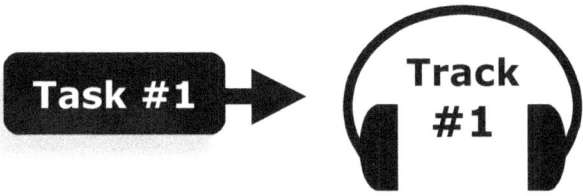

Directions: Listen to a discussion in a geriatrics class, then answer the questions on the next page.

Questions

Directions: Now get ready to answer the questions. Answer each question based on what is stated or implied in the discussion.

#1

What is the discussion mainly about?

A) degenerative diseases in America
B) Alois Alzheimer's disease
C) Alzheimer's Disease
D) the effects of memory loss in an aging population

#2

What is the point of the discussion?

A) to highlight recent advances in memory-related diseases
B) to summarize and give context to what is currently known about AD
C) to help people better understand how aging affects parts of the brain
D) to check the students' homework

#3

Why does the professor say this?

A) to indicate that an aging population will result in more cases of AD
B) to warn that AD is only getting worse
C) to emphasize that more research is needed in this area
D) to compare one generation of AD patients to previous generations

#4

According to the discussion, what don't we know about Alzheimer's Disease? Select two. This is a 1-point question.

A) how it was discovered and by whom
B) why it starts
C) how it can be reversed
D) how it changes the cerebral cortex

#5

According to the discussion, Alzheimer's Disease has four stages. Put the stages in order. This is a 2-point question.

a. early
b. pre-dementia
c. advanced
d. moderate

1. _____
2. _____
3. _____
4. _____

 *Do not replay this question type. On test day, you will hear the replayed segment only once.*

Turn the page for question #6

#6

Complete the chart based on information from the discussion. This is a 3-point question.

	YES	NO
AD is a degenerative disease affecting older populations.		
AD was discovered by Allen Alzheimer, a Bavarian physicist.		
There are four types and three stages of AD.		
In advanced AD, the ability to communicate is greatly reduced.		
Tangled nerve cell fibers and plaque are evidence of AD.		

audio script pg. 241

For scoring multi-answer questions, see pg. 237.

Raw Score =   / 9

Add your raw score to Test #1 box pg. 217.

Task #2 — Track #2

Directions: Listen to a lecture in a biology class, then answer the questions on the next page.

Questions

Directions: Now get ready to answer the questions. Answer each question based on what is stated or implied in the lecture.

#1

What is the topic of the lecture?

A) organizing common life forms
B) biological classification
C) comparing biological classifications
D) the history of classifying nature

#2

According to the lecture, Primates have what? Select three. This is a 2-point question.

A) the ability to walk on two or four limbs
B) the same DNA as chimpanzees
C) stereoscopic vision
D) large brains
E) descended from Old World monkeys

#3

Why does the professor say this?

A) to indicate that the class Amphibia contains Orders based on similarities
B) to illustrate the difference between Amphibia and Orders
C) to compare and contrast Orders and Classes
D) to describe what Amphibians look like

#4

According to Carl Woese, Life is divided into three Domains. What are they? Select three. This is a 2-point question.

A) Bacteria
B) Eukaryotic
C) Archaea
D) Eukarya
E) Biomass

#5

From the lecture, what can we infer about humans and apes?

A) They have the same brain size.
B) Genetically, they are almost identical.
C) They fall under the same Family.
D) They evolved together five million years ago.

Turn the page for question #6

#6 (see answering instructions below*)

The professor mentions **three topics**. Match each **topic** to its corresponding *description*. This is a 2-point question.

a. Class	b. Chordata	c. Order
vertebrates	Mammalia	Primates

* **Note:** This is a matching question. Answer it this way, for example...

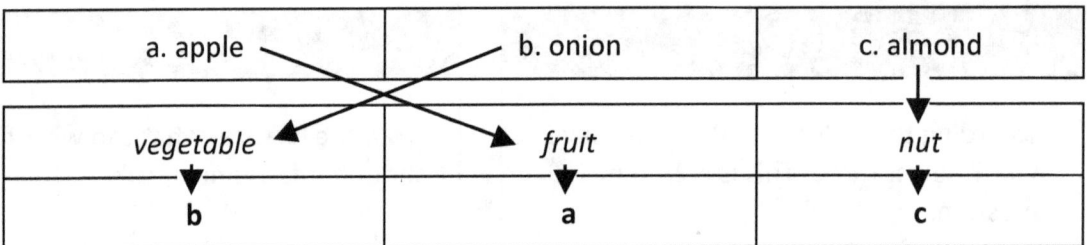

Answers

B A C

Do the same for all matching questions.

audio script pg. 243

For scoring multi-answer questions, see pg. 237.

Raw Score =   / 9

Add your raw score to Test #1 box pg. 217.

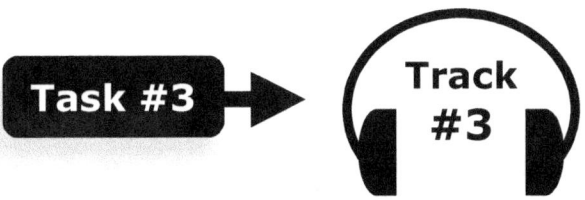

Directions: Listen to a lecture in a history class, then answer the questions on the next page.

Questions

Directions: Now get ready to answer the questions. Answer each question based on what is stated or implied in the lecture.

#1

On what does the lecture mainly focus?

A) a controversial figure
B) the American space program
C) a popular scientist
D) the history of rocket science

#2

Which three astronauts flew to the moon on Apollo 11? Select three. This is a 2-point question.

A) Neil Armstrong
B) Herman Oberth
C) Wernher Von Braun
D) Buzz Aldrin
E) Michael Collins

#3

Why does the professor say this?

A) to highlight the fact that Von Braun's past casts a shadow over his successes
B) to illustrate the pros and cons of Von Braun's scientific achievements
C) to classify how work was done during World War II
D) to describe a process in which slavery benefitted a scientific program

#4

From the lecture, what can we infer about Wernher Von Braun?

A) He was morally unopposed to using slave labor.
B) He believed that his designs would one day change the world.
C) He had no choice but to go along with the Nazi party or risk death.
D) He was morally conflicted.

#5

The professor describes the rockets and missiles Wernher Von Braun designed. Put them in historical order. This is a 2-point question.

a. Jupiter-C
b. Saturn
c. Jupiter
d. V-2

1. _____
2. _____
3. _____
4. _____

#6

What is true about Wernher Von Braun? This is a 3-point question.

	YES	NO
He was born in the spring of 1945 in Wirsitz, Poland.		
He was brought to America under Operation Paperclip.		
His work influenced the Russian and American space programs.		
He wrote a novel exploring the possibilities of going to Mars.		
He designed the V-2, the rocket that took Apollo 11 to the moon.		

audio script pg. 244

For scoring multi-answer questions, see pg. 237.

Raw Score =   / 10

Add your raw score to Test #1 box pg. 217.

Directions: Listen to a lecture in a science class, then answer the questions on the next page.

Questions

Directions: Now get ready to answer the questions. Answer each question based on what is stated or implied in the lecture.

#1

What is the lecture mainly about?

A) flooding and its impact on the natural environment
B) flooding as a double-edged sword
C) flooding and its impact on history
D) flooding and its impact on human evolution

#2

What percentage of the Earth is covered in water?

A) three-quarters
B) seventy percent
C) sixty-five percent
D) eighty percent

#3

Besides agriculture, what else throughout time has benefitted from flooding?

A) lakes and rivers
B) Isis and Osiris
C) silt
D) endemic biomass

#4

Why does the professor say this?

A) to show the steps in a natural process
B) to summarize a cause-and-effect relationship
C) to describe an important historical event
D) to classify early civilizations that depended on flooding for survival

#5

The professor describes the flooding of the Nile during the time of ancient Egypt. Put those steps in order. This is a 2-point question.

a. silt fertilized fields
b. heavy rain fell in equatorial Africa
c. the Nile River flooded its banks
d. flax and wheat were grown

1. _____
2. _____
3. _____
4. _____

#6

The professor mentions three rivers that flood. Match each river to its country. This is a 2-point question.

a. Euphrates	b. Huai	c. Indus
Pakistan	Iraq	China

audio script pg. 246

For scoring multi-answer questions, see pg. 237.

Raw Score =   / 8

Add your raw score to Test #1 box pg. 217.

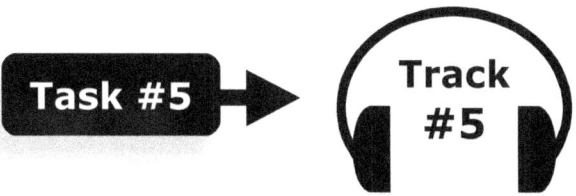

Directions: Listen as a student talks to a professor, then answer the questions on the next page.

Questions

Directions: Now get ready to answer the questions. Answer each question based on what is stated or implied in the conversation.

#1

What is the main topic of discussion?

A) the assignment and why the student wants to postpone it
B) the assignment and why the student wants to do it virtually
C) the assignment and why the student can't do it
D) the assignment and why the student has already completed it

#2

What percentage of the assignment is the student's final grade?

A) 50
B) 25
C) 30
D) 40

#3

Why does the student say this?

A) to emphasize that she is still confused
B) to indicate a moment of realization
C) to stress how much she really dislikes the assignment
D) to indicate that she is saying goodbye and leaving behind her study cards

#4

What does the student's decision imply?

A) She will eventually go to veterinary school.
B) She will not become a vet.
C) After some time off, she will try the course again.
D) She will major in chemistry and biology instead.

#5

Listen again to part of the talk, then answer the question.

What does the student mean when she says this?

A) to make her position clear regarding the assignment
B) to suggest that she will never up give no matter what
C) to request more time to consider her choices
D) to emphasize her belief that hurting animals for research is unethical

Raw Score = _____ / 5

Add your raw score to Test #1 box pg. 217.

audio script pg. 247

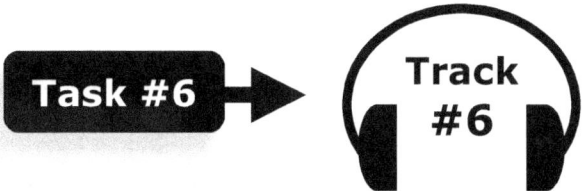

Directions: Listen as a student talks to a campus employee, then answer the questions.

Questions

Directions: Now get ready to answer the questions. Answer each question based on what was stated or implied in the conversation.

#1

To whom is the student speaking?

A) to the professor who recommended that she exhibit her art
B) to an art dealer
C) to the editor of an art magazine
D) to the manager of the school's art gallery

#2

From the conversation, we can infer that the student...

A) regularly buys art supplies
B) never buys art supplies
C) needs money to buy supplies
D) prefers to use only used supplies

#3

How long will the student's exhibition last?

A) a month
B) a day
C) two weeks
D) one week

#4

Who is Karen Goldblatt?

A) a magazine publisher
B) the student's art professor
C) an art expert
D) a famous artist

#5

Listen again to part of the conversation, then answer the question.

Why does the employee say this?

A) He is advising the student to stay calm.
B) He is recommending that the student price her work to sell.
C) He is suggesting that her work has no monetary value.
D) He is telling the student not to be disappointed if only a few people see her paintings.

Raw Score =   / 5

Add your raw score to Test #1 box pg. 217.

audio script pg. 249

10-minute break

Test #1
Speaking Section

Directions

For this section, you have <u>20 minutes</u> to complete six speaking tasks. The first two tasks are independent tasks. The last four tasks are integrated tasks. Begin speaking after the indicated preparation time. Remember to time yourself.

Remember! *You may take notes. Your notes will not be rated.*

Remember! *Record your responses. After the test, calculate your speaking score. See pg. 218.*

Task #1 - *Independent Speaking*

> Prompt   Why do people take photographs? Use examples and reasons to develop your argument.

Preparation Time – 15 seconds

Speaking Time – 45 seconds

proficiency checklist pg. 221 * rating guide pg. 222

add your rating to Test #1 box pg. 220

Task #2 - *Independent Speaking*

Prompt   Do you prefer taking paper-based tests or computer-based tests? Why? Give examples and reasons to support your argument.

Preparation Time – 15 seconds

Speaking Time – 45 seconds

proficiency checklist pg. 221   *   rating guide pg. 222

add your rating to Test #1 box pg. 220

Task #3 - *Integrated Speaking*

Directions: Read the following passage. Shelton University is introducing a new computer policy.

Reading Time – 45 seconds

Announcement from the Dean

Starting next semester, students at Shelton University will not be allowed to use laptop computers during class time. Any student using a laptop computer during class time will be asked to turn it off or leave the room. This policy is in response to complaints saying that increased laptop usage during class time is noisy and distracting. Laptop usage will be permitted in all main campus areas, including libraries and food service areas. If you have any questions regarding this policy, please feel free to contact the Dean. Office hours are Monday-Friday 9 a.m. to 5 p.m.

Directions: Now listen as two students discuss the announcement.

 *Do not look at the reading passage as you listen to the dialogue or when you speak. On test day, after you read the passage, the passage will leave your screen and will not come back.*

Track #7

(This task continues on the next page.)

Now get ready to answer the prompt.

> Prompt The woman expresses her opinion about the new policy. State her opinion and explain the reasons she gives for maintaining that position.

Preparation Time – 30 seconds

Speaking Time – 60 seconds

audio script pg. 250 * proficiency checklist pg. 224 * rating guide pg. 225

add your rating to Test #1 box pg. 220

Task #4 - *Integrated Speaking*

Directions: Read the following passage on the Green Revolution.

Reading Time – 45 seconds

The Green Revolution

The Green Revolution of the 1960's had one goal: to eliminate famine worldwide. It did so by introducing the concept of industrialized agriculture. Prior to the Green Revolution, farming in less developed nations had changed little since man first planted seeds. Crop yields were unpredictable, insects uncontrollable, and disease impossible to fight. At the same time, the world's population was skyrocketing with famine threatening the lives of millions. To feed the world, agronomist engineers, like American Norman Ernest Borlaug, developed high-yielding cereal grains that were also disease resistant. At the same time, scientists developed synthetic fertilizers and pesticides. The result was the Green Revolution, a global revolution in which technology took control of the agricultural process. The results were immediate. Countries like Mexico were soon net exporters of wheat while in Pakistan and India, wheat yields doubled between 1965 and 1970.

Directions: Now listen to a lecture on the same topic.

Do not look at the reading passage as you listen to the dialogue or when you speak. After you read the passage, the passage will leave your screen and will not come back.

_____
_____
_____
_____
_____

(This task continues on the next page.)

Now get ready to answer the prompt.

> Prompt   What is the Green Revolution and what are its short and long term effects?

Preparation Time – 30 seconds

Speaking Time – 60 seconds

audio script pg. 251   *   proficiency checklist pg. 224   *   rating guide pg. 225

add your rating to Test #1 box pg. 220

Task #5 - *Integrated Speaking*

Directions: Listen to a conversation between two students.

(This task continues on the next page.)

Now get ready to answer the prompt.

> Prompt   The students discuss two solutions to the woman's problem. Identify the problem and the solutions, then state which solution you think is best and why.

Preparation Time – 20 seconds

Speaking Time – 60 seconds

audio script pg. 251 * proficiency checklist pg. 224 * rating guide pg. 225

add your rating to Test #1 box pg. 220

Task #6 - *Integrated Speaking*

Directions: Listen to a lecture in a women's studies class.

(This task continues on the next page.)

Now get ready to answer the prompt.

> Prompt   The lecture talks about hormone replacement therapy (HRT). Summarize the recent history of HRT usage in the United States and its impact on women's health.

Preparation Time – 20 seconds

Speaking Time – 60 seconds

---

audio script pg. 252   *   proficiency checklist pg. 224   *   rating guide pg. 225

add your rating to Test #1 box pg. 220

Test #1
Writing Section

Directions

For this section, you have 53 minutes to complete two writing tasks. The first task is the integrated task. This task combines reading, listening, and writing. You have 23 minutes to complete the integrated writing task. Next is the independent writing task. For this task, you will use your experience when writing an independent essay. You have 30 minutes to complete this task. Remember to time yourself.

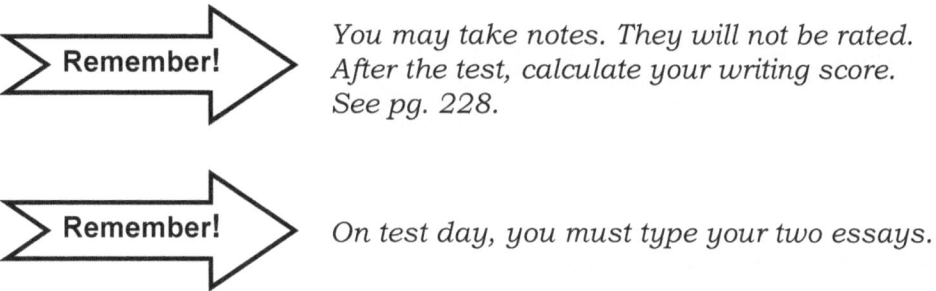

Remember! — *You may take notes. They will not be rated. After the test, calculate your writing score. See pg. 228.*

Remember! — *On test day, you must type your two essays.*

Task #1 - *Integrated Essay*

Directions: Read the following passage, then listen to the lecture and write an integrated essay.

Reading Time – 3 minutes

Cell Phones

Cell phones. It's hard to imagine life without one. They are as ubiquitous as cars. But are cell phones really that safe? A growing body of research says no. Case in point: beneath a cell phone's innocuous exterior lies a complex array of electronics, which produces radio frequency radiation (RF). Research shows that RF can damage genetic material in the blood and cause cancer. In fact, Swedish researchers have evidence indicating that acoustic neuroma, an ear nerve cancer, is more prevalent on the side of the head on which a cell phone is regularly placed.

Distraction is another way that cell phones pose a threat to human safety. How often do you see someone chatting or texting while driving even though most states prohibit it? Yet people still do it despite the danger and the law. The result is that in the year ending 2010, the National Safety Council (NSC) states that 28% of all traffic crashes (1.6 million) were caused by drivers using cell phones while driving. To underscore the danger, a University of Utah report says that a person driving while texting is as impaired as a drunk driver with a .08 blood alcohol level, (.08 g alcohol per 100 ml blood), .08 being the legal limit in all 50 states.

Cell phones are a danger not only to humans, but also to the environment, particularly to honey bees. To prove it, researchers at India's Panjab University put a cell phone on top of a healthy honey bee hive. The cell phone was powered twice each day for fifteen minutes. The results are shocking. After only three months, the bees stopped producing honey while the queen's egg production was cut by half. This sudden and drastic destruction of a bee hive is called Colony Collapse Disorder (CCD). CCD is happening in the wild as well. If action is not taken soon, the British Bee Keepers Association (BBKA) predicts that the honey bee will disappear from Britain by 2018.

(This task continues on the next page.)

Directions: Now listen to a lecture on the same topic.

Now get ready to write your response.

| Prompt | Summarize the points made in the lecture and show how they cast doubt on the points made in the reading. |

 *You can look at the reading passage as you write your essay.*

Writing Time – 20 minutes

___

audio script pg. 252 * proficiency checklist pg. 231 * rating guide pg. 232

add your rating to Test #1 box pg. 230

Task #2 - *Independent Essay*

Directions: Read the following prompt, then write an independent essay.

Prompt   Honesty is the best policy. Do you agree or disagree? Why? Use examples and reasons to support your argument.

Writing Time – 30 minutes

proficiency checklist pg. 234 * rating guide pg. 235

add your rating to Test #1 box pg. 230

Test 2

60 - Practice Tests for the TOEFL® iBT

Test #2
Reading Section

Directions

For this section, you have 60 minutes to read three passages and answer the questions following each passage. The passages are typical of those found in North American college and university text books.

Answer each question based on what is stated or implied in the passage. You will not lose points for wrong answers. Remember to time yourself.

 *You may take notes. They will not be rated. After the test, calculate your reading score. See pg. 214.*

Passage #1 - *Public Education in Early New England*

1 ➔ In America, public education had its genesis in the New England Colonies of Massachusetts, Connecticut and New Hampshire. At the time, circa 1600, these colonies were settled by two main religious groups: the Puritans and the Congregationalists. Both were Protestant, both were fiercely independent, both rejected the centralized power of Catholicism, and both shared the belief that educating children was critical to the survival of their beliefs thus the earliest form of public education in America was funded by the Protestant church with the tenets of Protestantism the core curriculum.

2 ➔ The first publicly supported high school in America, the Boston Latin School, was founded in 1635. Now, I need to be clear here. Publicly supported doesn't mean what it means today: a public school system funded by tax dollars, quite the contrary. Back in 1635, public education meant that church money paid for books and teachers' salaries while students had to pay tuition. These so-called public schools, of which the Boston Latin School was the first, educated an elite, all-male student body in Latin and Greek, the humanities and philosophy with an emphasis on religious studies, for it was assumed that the students would become teachers or ministers espousing the Protestant faith.

3 ➔ At the same time, immigrants were arriving in the New England colonies. These immigrants, many of whom were Catholic, soon came into conflict with the Puritans and the Congregationalists over the issue of public education. The Catholics viewed the English-dominated public education system as simply a way in which the English Protestants could impose their religious views. As a result, the Catholics rejected the Protestant-based, public-school system and created a system of private Catholic schools, a system which survives to this day.

4 ➔ As you can see, the educational system in colonial America was very much a religious conflict. Keep in mind, however, that these schools, for Catholics and Protestants alike, were for the sons of the rich and politically powerful. For those boys on the lower end of the social scale, charity or "common schools" were set up. While public money paid for books and teachers, students still had to pay tuition, money most simply did not have. Instead, most school-age boys became apprentices learning a trade. As for girls, they were educated at home by mothers and grandmothers. Girls learned how to cook and sew with the aim of being good housewives thus the literacy rate among women was very low.

5 ➔ By the early nineteenth century, the common or public school system was in dire straits. The schools were poorly equipped, one-room buildings with poorly paid, poorly trained teachers. Students, if they attended classes, attended in winter and only for a few weeks. The rest of the time they worked in agriculture or in the growing number of factories, for the industrial revolution was picking up steam, particularly in big east coast cities like Boston, New York and Philadelphia.

6 ➔ ■ In 1837, with the public school system hitting rock bottom, Horace Mann, a social reformer and a powerful Massachusetts politician, decided enough was enough. ■ Believing that all children should learn in common schools, he set about

reforming the public school system. ■ He established institutes to train teachers. ■ He increased teacher salaries, increased the school year to six months, and raised money for books and school construction. Mann pursued these reforms because he believed that public education would result in greater economic prosperity for the individual, the state and the country while teaching respect for private property. This, Mann argued, would decrease the crime rate, for the industrial revolution had created a rising class of urban poor. By providing public money for public schools, Mann viewed education as a means of controlling the crime rate. Thus "moral training", as Mann called it, was part of the curriculum along with standardized lessons and classroom drills. This, Mann also argued, would create greater equality for the masses and greater economic prosperity for all.

1. In paragraph 1, genesis is closest in meaning to...

   a) origin
   b) foundation
   c) support
   d) nemesis

2. In paragraph 1, tenets is closest in meaning to...

   a) benefits
   b) principles
   c) people
   d) tenants

3. Which of the following sentences best restates the essential information in the highlighted sentence in paragraph 2? Incorrect choices will change the meaning and omit important information.

   a) These misnamed schools produced proponents who would continue to spread the Protestant message.
   b) These famous schools educated teachers and ministers who espoused the humanities, such as Greek and Latin and the Protestant faith.
   c) These Boston schools were attended by elite boys who were the sons of Protestant teachers and ministers, who strongly believed in religious studies.
   d) These public schools, which were not really private, taught girls and boys how to become teachers and ministers who supported the Protestant faith.

4. What can we infer from the information in paragraph 3?

   a) The Protestant school system was only interested in teaching Catholics.
   b) Public education was controlled by local governments, most of which were controlled by Protestants and Catholics.
   c) The Catholic church rejected private Protestant schools in favor of their own public school system, which survives to this day.
   d) The Protestant school system was one way of limiting the power of the Catholic church in early New England.

5. In paragraph 4, all of the following are TRUE EXCEPT...

   a) Girls were taught domestic duties at home by mothers and grandmothers.
   b) Politically powerful Protestants and Catholics did not send their sons to common schools.
   c) Boys who did not have rich parents, and who were old enough, learned a trade or became apprentices.
   d) Common schools were set up for the purpose of educating all children, especially those on the lower end of the social scale.

6. What can we infer from the information in paragraph 4?

   a) Women never worked outside the home.
   b) Gender roles were clearly defined.
   c) Girls and boys often attended charity schools together.
   d) Mothers and grandmothers taught girls at the same time.

7. In paragraph 5, in dire straits is closest in meaning to...

   a) changing course
   b) acceptable state
   c) awful condition
   d) as directed

8. In paragraph 5, picking up steam is closest in meaning to...

   a) becoming dangerous
   b) expanding quickly
   c) slowly disappearing
   d) finally changing

9. Look at the four squares [■]. They indicate where the bold sentence below could be added to paragraph 6. Select the square where you think the bold sentence could be inserted into the passage.

Mann—a leader in the temperance movement and a builder of insane asylums—was appointed secretary of Massachusetts' newly-created Board of Education, the first of its kind in America.

■ In 1837, with the public school system hitting rock bottom, Horace Mann, a social reformer and a powerful Massachusetts politician, decided enough was enough. ■ Believing that all children should learn in common schools, he set about reforming the public school system. ■ He established institutes to train teachers. ■ He increased teacher salaries, increased the school year to six months, and raised money for books and school construction.

10. In paragraph 6, pursued is closest in meaning to...

    a) perused
    b) chose
    c) reached
    d) sought

11. In paragraph 6, what does Mann argue?

    a) Mann argued that public education and a respect for private property were not related to the crime rate.
    b) Mann believed that education was a form of moral training that would result in greater equality and economic prosperity, and a reduction in criminal activity.
    c) Mann asserted that the industrial revolution was responsible for controlling the crime rate by creating more jobs for the urban poor.
    d) Mann argued that moral training should be taught in both public and private schools using standardized lessons and classroom drills.

12. In paragraph 6, why does the author mention the urban poor?

    a) to classify different levels of society in a time of educational reform
    b) to develop the topic of crime in big urban centers in big east coast cities in New England
    c) to establish a possible cause for why the public school system in early New England was steadily improving
    d) to identify the social class negatively impacted the most by the industrial revolution

13. Directions: The sentence in bold is the first sentence of a brief summary of the passage. Complete the summary by selecting three answer choices. Your choices will express the most important ideas in the passage. Some choices are not in the passage or do not express important ideas. This is a 2-point question.

The passage outlines the educational system in early New England.

-

-

-

Answer Choices

1. Founded in 1635, the Boston Latin school was the first publicly funded high school in America.

2. In early New England, circa 1600, Protestant public schools controlled the curriculum.

3. Charity schools were set up for those children who could not afford private schools.

4. Immigrants arriving in New England rejected the Protestant-controlled educational system and established their own private schools.

5. Horace Mann reformed the public education system, which he viewed as moral training.

6. Horace Mann claimed that economic equality was good for the industrial revolution.

For scoring multi-answer questions, see pg. 237.

Raw score =   / 14

Add your raw score to Test #2 box pg. 215.

Passage #2 - *Women of Influence*

1 → Jane Austen's novel *Pride and Prejudice*, voted Best British novel in a 2005 BBC poll, was originally titled *First Impressions*. Austen, born in 1775, wrote it between October 1796 and August 1797. The story centers on the Bennett family, particularly the five sisters whose mother, Mrs. Bennett—a mercurial soul always on the verge of nervous collapse—is determined to marry them off to rich husbands thus ensuring their financial futures while securing for them positions of high social status in early nineteenth-century England. Mr. Bennett, a patient and level-headed man with a modest income, puts up with his wife's machinations while displaying a particular fondness for his second oldest daughter, Elizabeth. ■ When Mr. Darcy, a rich landowner of noble birth, visits the Bennett household, Mrs. Bennett sees another marrying opportunity for her daughters. ■ Elizabeth, however, sees only the snobbish arrogance typical of Mr. Darcy's privileged class, one that is far and above the Bennett's station. ■ In time, however, Elizabeth realizes that her pride has blinded her and, as a result, prejudiced her toward Mr. Darcy, a kind man whose intellect and independence mirror Elizabeth's. ■ In short, Elizabeth and Mr. Darcy are cut from the same cloth. In this light, they are a perfect match and eventually find happiness in wedlock.

2 → *Pride and Prejudice*, a title that aptly defines the conflict Elizabeth and Mr. Darcy must face and overcome to find love, was published in 1813. The story, told from Elizabeth's point-of-view, is a window on early nineteenth-century English moral values, particularly in regard to the rights of women, or the lack thereof, a condition Jane Austen observes with no small amount of satire. To date, *Pride and Prejudice* has sold over 20 million copies, confirming Jane Austen as one of the most influential writers of the English language. In 1816, Austen fell ill and died that same year. The cause is unknown; however, recent evidence points at her contracting bovine tuberculosis from drinking unpasteurized milk.

3 → Another woman whose influence is still felt today is Dian Fossey. These days it is commonplace to see biologists on TV studying animals in the wild close up, so close it is as if the human observer were part of the animal group being studied. One of the scientists to first bridge the gap between wild animals and humans was the zoologist, Dian Fossey. Fossey, born in California in 1932, did so with the mountain gorillas of Rwanda. She studied them from 1967 up to her death in 1985. Fossey's ability to study and observe wild mountain gorillas while actually being among them revolutionized not only the study of gorillas, and wildlife in general, but also changed our view of gorillas. No longer were they King Kongs but were instead, as Fossey herself said, "dignified, highly social, gentle giants, with individual personalities, and strong family relationships." The moment Fossey was accepted into the gorillas' world occurred in 1970 when an adult male Fossey had named Peanuts, touched her hand. The moment was immortalized in a National Geographic photograph seen around the world.

4 → Fossey's reputation grew with the publication of her book *Gorillas in the Mist*. By then she'd received her PhD from Cambridge and was teaching at Cornell University. Fame brought Fossey the money she needed to support her research and to establish sanctuaries for the mountain gorillas, whose habitat was being destroyed by social unrest and whose numbers were being decimated by poachers. Fossey, determined to

stop the unlawful killing of gorillas for meat, waged war on the poachers, so much so that many believe that it was poachers who had murdered Fossey in her cabin at Karisoke, the name of her research camp in the Parc National des Volcans in Rwanda.

5 → Despite Fossey's death, her influence lives on. Thanks to the Atlanta-based Fossey Fund, directed by Sigourney Weaver, who starred as Fossey in *Gorillas in the Mist*, the mountain gorilla population has been slowly increasing from a low of 250 in the early 1980's to an estimated 480 today. Such success is attributable to Fossey's pioneering work and to ecotourism, which brings tourists to the Parc National des Volcans so that tourists too might experience mountain gorillas as Dian Fossey had.

1. In paragraph 1, the following are TRUE of the Bennett sisters EXCEPT...

   a) There are five.
   b) Their father is patient.
   c) They are nobility.
   d) Their mother is moody.

2. In paragraph 1, machinations is closest in meaning to...

   a) scheming
   b) deliberating
   c) estimations
   d) matching

3. Look at the four squares [■]. They indicate where the bold sentence below could be added to paragraph 1. Select the square where you think the bold sentence could be inserted into the passage.

   With her keen intellect and independent character, she watches with a critic's eye as her sisters find varying degrees of success while searching for husbands.

   Mr. Bennett, a patient and level-headed man with a modest income, puts up with his wife's machinations while displaying a particular fondness for his second oldest daughter, Elizabeth. ■ When Mr. Darcy, a rich landowner of noble birth, visits the Bennett household, Mrs. Bennett sees another marrying opportunity for her daughters. ■ Elizabeth, however, sees only the snobbish arrogance typical of Mr. Darcy's privileged class, one that is far and above the Bennett's station. ■ In time, however, Elizabeth realizes that her pride has blinded her and, as a result, prejudiced her toward Mr. Darcy, a kind man whose intellect and independence mirror Elizabeth's. ■ In short, Elizabeth and Mr. Darcy are cut from the same cloth.

4. In paragraph 2, aptly is closest in meaning to...

   a) unhappily
   b) perfectly
   c) approximately
   d) usually

5. In paragraph 3, what can we conclude about Dian Fossey?

   a) It took many years before the gorillas would trust her.
   b) Her method of research revolutionized the study of animals.
   c) When researching mountain gorillas, she was a biologist working for National Geographic television.
   d) She loved working with wild animals in the mountains of Africa.

6. In paragraph 3, why does the author mention National Geographic?

   a) to illustrate how a famous magazine made Dian Fossey rich and famous
   b) to describe and develop the topic of who was present when Fossey finally bridged the gap between chimpanzees and man in the mountains of Africa
   c) to illustrate how evidence of Fossey's famous encounter with Peanuts was documented and presented to the world by a famous magazine
   d) to point out that Fossey was not only a famous biologist but also a famous photographer when she had her encounter with the gorillas

7. In paragraph 3, immortalized is closest in meaning to...

   a) to make exciting
   b) to make famous
   c) to make money
   d) to make a statement

8. Which of the following sentences best restates the essential information in the highlighted sentence in paragraph 4? Incorrect choices will change the meaning and omit important information.

   a) Fossey's fame helped her stop the killing of mountain gorillas.
   b) Fossey's fame and money were stolen by corrupt politicians and hunters invading the gorillas' sanctuaries.
   c) Fame and fortune allowed Fossey to stop politicians and hunters from destroying the natural environment.
   d) Fossey used her money and influence to continue her work and protect the gorillas.

9. In paragraph 4, poachers is closest in meaning to...

   a) those who kill for food and money
   b) those who kill animals illegally
   c) those who hunt animals for food
   d) those who destroy the natural environment

10. In paragraph 5, which refers to...

    a) success
    b) work
    c) ecotourism
    d) Parc National des Volcans

11. In the passage, how does the author develop the main topic?

    a) by classifying the work of famous women
    b) by defining the work of two famous people, one from England, the other from Africa
    c) by describing the work of a famous writer and a renowned scientist
    d) by contrasting the achievements of two distinct individuals

12. <u>Directions</u>: The sentence in bold is the first sentence of a brief summary of the passage. Complete the summary by selecting three answer choices. Your choices will express the most important ideas in the passage. Some choices are not in the passage or do not express important ideas. This is a 2-point question.

    Jane Austen and Dian Fossey were women of influence.

    -
    -
    -

    ### Answer Choices

    1. Austen and Fossey changed how the world thinks.

    2. Both women are credited with advancing the cause of women's rights.

    3. Both women won lasting fame in their chosen professions.

    4. Austen was an English satirist while Fossey was an American zoologist.

    5. Austen and Fossey were dignified, highly social and had strong family relationships.

    6. Both were comparatively young when they died.

13. Directions: Complete the following table by indicating which topics go under each topic heading. This is a 4-point question.

Jane Austen	Dian Fossey
•	•
•	•
•	•
	•

1. Mr. Darcy
2. murdered
3. influential writer
4. mother was mercurial
5. PhD

6. died at 41
7. Peanuts
8. had five sisters
9. created sanctuaries

For scoring multi-answer questions, see pg. 237.

Raw Score =   / 17

Add your raw score to Test #2 box pg. 215.

Passage #3 - *Penicillin*

1 → *Penicillium chrysogenum* is a common mold, a mold being a fungus that has multi-cellular arms or filaments called hyphae. Also known as *Penicillium notatum*, *Penicillium chrysogenum* can be found living indoors on food. Its spores, units of asexual reproduction that can evolve into a new organism, are carried by the air and are a major cause of allergens in humans. In 1928, Scottish scientist Alexander Fleming discovered that *Penicillium notatum* contained a bacteria-killing antibiotic, an antibiotic Fleming named penicillin.

2 → Alexander Fleming was born in 1881 in Scotland. At the age of twenty, he entered St. Mary's Hospital in London and studied medicine, then went on to become the assistant bacteriologist to Sir Almroth Wright, a pioneer in immunology and vaccine therapy. During World War One, Fleming served as a captain in the Royal Army Medical Corps and worked on the frontlines where he witnessed firsthand soldiers dying of sepsis. Sepsis, or systematic inflammatory response (SIRS), is blood poisoning due to the presence of bacteria in the blood. To fight off the bacteria, the body enters an inflammatory state accompanied by a high fever. Fleming witnessed widespread sepsis, most of which was caused by infected wounds. Antiseptics were widely available yet Fleming believed that they killed only surface bacteria while failing to eradicate deeper bacteria. After the war, Fleming was determined to find a cure for sepsis. He discovered lysozyme, an enzyme found in tears. It was a natural anti-bacterial yet was ineffective against more powerful infections. In 1928, while researching the properties of staphylococci, a genus of gram-positive bacteria, he stumbled upon *Penicillium notatum*.

3 → By 1928, Fleming was regarded as a brilliant researcher whose laboratory was, more often than not, a mess. That same year, returning to his lab after an August holiday, Fleming discovered that his staphylococci cultures had been contaminated. Fleming was intent on throwing the cultures out when he noticed that the contaminant, an invading blue-green mold, had surrounded the staphylococci. Much to Fleming's surprise, the invading mold was a fungus that had eradicated the staphylococci, which it had surrounded whereas those colonies of staphylococci that had not been touched by the mold were still thriving. Fleming set about isolating and growing the mold which produced a substance that killed not only staphylococci, but also a number of other disease-causing bacteria, such as pneumonia, scarlet fever, meningitis and diphtheria while having no effect on typhoid fever or paratyphoid fever. Fleming called the bacteria-killing substance "mold juice." Once he'd established that the mold was in fact part of the genus penicillium, he called it penicillin.

4 → In 1929, Fleming published the results of his experiments in the *British Journal of Experimental Pathology*. Yet despite such initial promise, his work garnered little attention, for growing penicillium was difficult while extracting the antibiotic agent, the bacteria-killing penicillin itself, was even harder. These results, combined with tests proving that penicillin worked slowly, convinced Fleming that penicillin had no commercial appeal. By 1939, Fleming, having labored long and hard over penicillin, finally turned his attention to other matters. Penicillin, in his mind, had no future beyond his lab. Then, in that same year, the Australian scientist Howard Walter Florey, director of the Sir William Dunn School of Pathology at Oxford University, read Fleming's paper in which he described the anti-bacterial effects of penicillium. Florey

immediately saw the potential of penicillium and, with the help of Ernst Chain, immediately went to work.

5 → ■ With grants from the Medical Research Council in England and from the Rockefeller Foundation in the United States, Florey and Chain were able to produce one-hundred milligrams of penicillin that was only ten-percent pure. ■ Then, in one the most famous experiments in medical history, Florey injected eight mice with a lethal dose of the streptococci bacteria. ■ The four non-injected mice died. ■ Tests were then done on humans suffering from the same bacterial infections as the mice. The humans recovered at remarkable rates. However, because England was at war, there was not enough money to expand production, so Florey and Chain flew to the United States where the government became involved in large-scale production. By 1943, frontline soldiers with infections were being treated with a new wonder drug called penicillin.

1. What happened in 1928?

    a) Alexander Fleming discovered how to make *Penicillium chrysogenum*.
    b) The start of World War One in Europe.
    c) The invention of *Penicillium chrysogenum*.
    d) The discovery of a bacteria-killing antibiotic in *Penicillium notatum*.

2. In paragraph 2, everything is TRUE EXCEPT...

    a) Fleming was a captain in the Royal Army Medical Corps in World War One.
    b) Sepsis, a form of blood poisoning, was brought on by wounds.
    c) Fleming discovered a new enzyme that was also an antibiotic.
    d) Antiseptic was highly effective at killing all types of bacteria

3. In paragraph 2, eradicate is closest in meaning to...

    a) to get away with
    b) to get rid of
    c) to get off of
    d) to get into

4. In paragraph 3, contaminated is closest in meaning to...

    a) to make impure
    b) to make desirable
    c) to make contagious
    d) to make available

5. In paragraph 3, what can we conclude about the discovery of penicillin?

    a) It was the result of hard work and many years of experimenting.
    b) It happened quite by chance and much to Fleming's surprise.
    c) It was the result of mixing "mold juice" with staphylococci.
    d) It was something Fleming predicted would happen.

6. In paragraph 3, to what does which refer?

   a) cultures
   b) Fleming's surprise
   c) invading mold
   d) staphylococci

7. In paragraph 3, thriving is closest in meaning to...

   a) to develop slowly
   b) to grow vigorously
   c) to demonstrate quickly
   d) to admire greatly

8. In paragraph 4, why does the author mention the *British Journal of Experimental Pathology*?

   a) Because it was in this journal in which William Dunn read about Fleming's discovery of a bacteria-killing substance Fleming called penicillin.
   b) Because Sir William Dunn, with the help of Ernst Chain, wrote an article in this journal announcing Fleming's discovery of *Penicillium chrysogenum.*
   c) Because Howard Walter Florey learned of Fleming's work with penicillin in an article in this journal, and immediately realized penicillin's potential.
   d) Because the *British Journal of Experimental Pathology* is a respected publication, one in which Fleming wrote for during World War One.

9. Which of the following sentences best restates the essential information in the highlighted sentence in paragraph 4? Incorrect choices will change the meaning and omit important information.

   a) Fleming's work demonstrated that making penicillin was challenging.
   b) Fleming's attempt to make penicillium was promising yet difficult.
   c) Fleming's work went unnoticed since making penicillin was hard.
   d) Fleming's work promised great results but received no attention.

10. Look at the four squares [■]. They indicate where the bold sentence below could be added to paragraph 5. Select the square where you think the bold sentence could be inserted into the passage.

    He treated four of the eight mice with the penicillin.

    5 ➔ ■ With grants from the Medical Research Council in England and from the Rockefeller Foundation in the United States, Florey and Chain were able to produce one-hundred milligrams of penicillin that was only ten-percent pure. ■ Then, in one the most famous experiments in medical history, Florey injected eight mice with a lethal dose of the streptococci bacteria. ■ The four non-injected mice died. ■ Tests were then done on humans suffering from the same bacterial infections as the mice.

11. According to paragraph 5, what percentage of the one-hundred milligrams of penicillin that Florey and Chain made was unusable?

    a) ten
    b) ninety
    c) one
    d) one-hundred

12. Directions: The sentence in bold is the first sentence of a brief summary of the passage. Complete the summary by selecting three answer choices. Your choices will express the most important ideas in the passage. Some choices are not in the passage or do not express important ideas. This is a 2-point question.

    The passage describes the discovery of penicillin.

    -
    -
    -

    ### Answer Choices

    1. Alexander Fleming was born in 1891 in Scotland and graduated from St. Mary's hospital as a medical doctor.

    2. As a military doctor, Fleming witnessed firsthand many wounded soldiers suffering from staphylococci.

    3. *Penicillium notatum* proved effective in 1943 when wounded soldiers were treated with it.

    4. Alexander Fleming named the bacteria-killing substance he accidentally discovered penicillin.

    5. Fleming tried but was unable to create penicillin on a large scale.

    6. Fleming's work on penicillin was taken over by Florey and Chain, who made it into a commercially available antibiotic.

13. Directions: Complete the following table by indicating which topics go under each topic heading. This is a 4-point question.

sepsis	penicillin
•	•
•	•
•	•
	•

1. mold-juice
2. caused by infected wounds
3. type of pneumonia
4. first used in 1929
5. first used in 1943

6. Howard Walter Florey
7. bacteria in the blood
8. high fever
9. kills bacteria

For scoring multi-answer questions, see pg. 237.

Raw Score =   / 17

Add your raw score to Test #2 box pg. 215.

Test #2
Listening Section

Directions

The listening section measures your ability to answer questions specific to English conversations and lectures. The conversations and lectures are typical of the North American college and university experience.

After each conversation and lecture, you will answer questions. Answer each question based on what the speakers state or imply. Answer all questions. You will not lose points for a wrong answer.

For some questions, you will see a headset symbol: 🎧
The headset symbol means you will hear part of the conversation or lecture. After you hear part of the conversation or lecture, you will answer a question about it.

Do not look at the answers as you listen. On test day, you will not see the answers as you listen. Remember to time yourself.

> **Remember!** You have <u>60 minutes</u> to complete this section.

> **Remember!** You may take notes. Your notes will not be rated. After the test, calculate your listening score. See pg. 216.

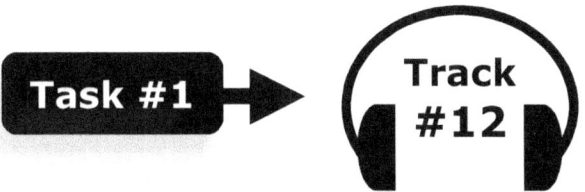

Directions: Listen as a student talks to a professor, then answer the questions on the next page.

Questions

Directions: Now get ready to answer the questions. Answer each question based on what is stated or implied in the conversation.

#1

What are the student and the professor mainly discussing?

A) the student's opinion
B) the student's essay about illegal drugs
C) the student's attendance record
D) the student's most recent grade

#2

Why does the student visit the professor?

A) to learn how to write better essays
B) to find out why she got a low grade on her essay
C) to discuss the pros and cons of the marijuana debate
D) to ask for an extension

#3

In which areas does the student's essay need revising? Select two. This is a 1-point question.

A) the developer
B) the body
C) the thesis
D) the sentence variety

#4

What does the professor think about short essays?

A) One focused page is best.
B) Short essays always get high grades.
C) A focused, short essay is best.
D) A short essay never has an opinion.

#5

Listen again to part of the conversation, then answer the question.

What does the professor imply when she says this?

A) She thinks the student hates essay writing.
B) She thinks parts of the student's essay are scratched.
C) She thinks the student's essay lacks depth.
D) She thinks the student is on the wrong track.

Raw Score =   / 5

Add your raw score to Test #2 box pg. 217.

audio script pg. 253

Task #2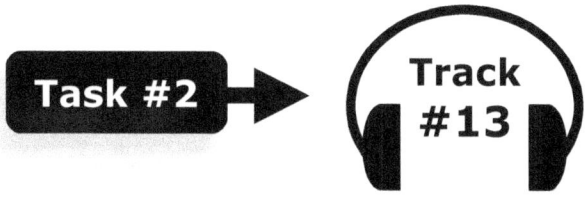

Directions: Listen to a lecture in an economics history class, then answer the questions on the next page.

Questions

Directions: Now get ready to answer the questions. Answer each question based on what is stated or implied in the lecture.

#1

What is the topic of the lecture?

A) Adam Smith and the influence of the European Enlightenment
B) Adam Smith and *The Wealth of Nations*
C) Adam Smith's life and history
D) the wisdom of Adam Smith

#2

What is the purpose of the lecture?

A) to classify Adam Smith's philosophy
B) to illustrate the important changes taking place in the mid 17th century
C) to define Adam Smith's influence
D) to illustrate how Adam Smith revolutionized economic thinking

#3

Why does the professor say this?

A) to highlight that Thomas Edison was as smart as Adam Smith
B) to illustrate that Adam Smith was greatly influenced by Thomas Edison
C) to stress that Adam Smith, like Thomas Edison, was a great thinker
D) to classify great thinkers by their achievements

#4

From the lecture, we can infer that Smith considered mercantilism to be...

A) a successful economic system
B) an economic system lacking a rational and scientific approach
C) a system that benefitted all
D) a system upon which he based his economic theories

#5

The professor describes how Adam Smith's idea of "the invisible hand" works. Put these steps in order. This is a 2-point question.

a. trade expands
b. individual needs are met
c. systematic manufacturing
d. a nation acquires wealth

1. _____
2. _____
3. _____
4. _____

#6

The professor develops three topics. Match each topic with its corresponding description. This is a 2-point question.

a. European Enlightenment	b. The Wealth of Nations	c. Mercantilism
book written by Adam Smith describing how nations acquire wealth	economic nationalism aimed at acquiring gold by any means	18th century philosophy based on science and reason

audio script pg. 255

For scoring multi-answer questions, see pg. 237.

Raw Score =   / 8

Add your raw score to Test #2 box pg. 217.

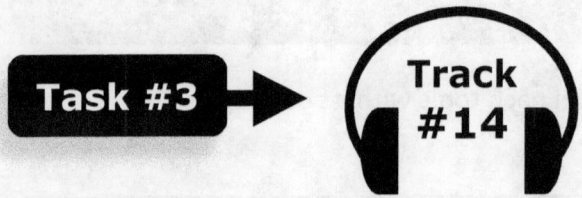

Directions: Listen as a student talks to a member of the school's IT support staff.

Questions

Directions: Now get ready to answer the questions. Answer each question based on what is stated or implied in the conversation.

#1

What are the student and the IT staffer mainly discussing?

A) the student's new iPhone
B) the student's wi-fi issue
C) the school's security system
D) the latest virus going around

#2

What is the student's problem?

A) Her new iPod has a virus.
B) She needs a new wi-fi connection.
C) She can't connect to the school's wireless network.
D) She's having problems with the network.

#3

What are the wireless security settings? Select three. This is a 2-point question.

A) WPA
B) WEP2
C) WEP
D) WPA2
E) WPA-A

#4

Why does the student say this?

A) because IT support fixed her iPod
B) because IT support was helpful
C) because IT support disconnected her
D) because IT support solved her issue

#5

Listen again to part of the conversation, then answer the question.

What does the student mean by this?

A) She needs more information.
B) She is missing the point.
C) She understands completely.
D) She is apologizing for her mistake.

Raw Score =   / 6

Add your raw score to Test #2 box pg. 217.

audio script pg. 256

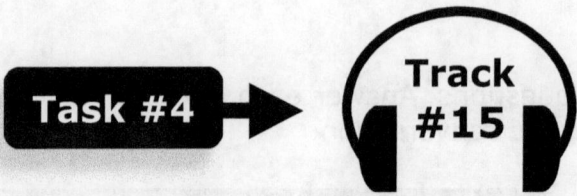

Directions: Listen to part of a discussion in an environmental class, then answer the questions on the next page.

Questions

Directions: Now get ready to answer the questions. Answer each question based on what is stated or implied in the discussion.

#1

What is the discussion mainly about?

A) the North Pacific gyre
B) how plastic is polluting the Pacific
C) the North Pacific garbage patch
D) plastic and pelagic species

#2

What is the purpose of the discussion?

A) to highlight how pollution affects ocean currents
B) to illustrate how plastic garbage is polluting the North Pacific
C) to define an environmental disaster
D) to show the relationship between a gyre and plastic water bottles

#3

Why does the professor say this?

A) to warn that plastic bottles are a growing problem
B) to stress his disbelief at the amount of plastic in daily use
C) to illustrate how much plastic he uses on a daily basis
D) to introduce the next topic

#4

Which pelagic species does the professor mention? Select two. This is a 1-point question.

A) whales
B) crabs
C) birds
D) sea turtles

#5

The professor describes how plastic becomes part of the eco-system. Put those steps in order. This is a 2-point question.

a. plastic photodegrades into particles
b. plastic ends up in the Horse Latitudes
c. plastic enters the North Pacific
d. plastic is swept along by the gyre

1. _____
2. _____
3. _____
4. _____

Turn the page for question #6

#6

In the lecture, the professor describes the Horse Latitudes. Indicate whether each of the following is a characteristic of the Horse Latitudes. This is a 3-point question.

	YES	NO
They flow clockwise.		
Worldwide there are five.		
The center is a calm area that once trapped sailing ships.		
They are home to a variety of pelagic species.		
Plastic photodecomposes on the surface into toxic particulates.		

audio script pg. 258

For scoring multi-answer questions, see pg. 237.

Raw Score =   / 9

Add your raw score to Test #2 box pg. 217.

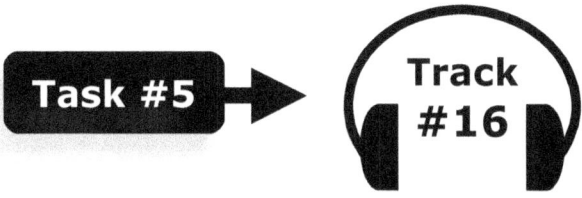

Directions: Listen to a lecture in a law class, then answer the questions on the next page.

Questions

<u>Directions</u>: Now get ready to answer the questions. Answer each question based on what is stated or implied in the lecture.

#1

What is the lecture mainly about?

A) a movie maker named Michael Moore
B) a politician named David Bossie
C) a U.S. Supreme Court ruling
D) a decision by the Elections Commission

#2

What does the professor say about *Hillary: The Movie*?

A) It won an Oscar for best documentary.
B) It is a 90-minute political attack ad.
C) It helped raise millions for Mrs. Clinton.
D) It was made by Michael Moore.

#3

Why does the professor say this?

A) to indicate that something is wrong in the U.S. Supreme Court
B) to indicate how the Supreme Court's ruling has angered Hillary Clinton
C) to draw attention to how money can buy Supreme Court decisions
D) to illustrate how the Court's ruling is already creating controversy

#4

The professor mentions Ford. Why?

A) as an example of a corporation that could influence an election
B) as an example of a famous company
C) as an example of a supporter of a political candidate
D) as a reason why the Supreme Court made the right decision

#5

Listen again to part of the lecture, then answer the question.

What does the professor mean when she says this?

A) that *Hillary: The Movie* was a big hit during the '08 presidential primary
B) that *Hillary: The Movie* had little or no influence when it was released
C) that political movies are not popular during an election
D) that *Hillary: The Movie* was as popular as Michael Moore's film *911*

#6

According to the professor, how has the Supreme Court's decision changed the political landscape? This is a 3-point answer.

	YES	NO
Corporations can now buy and sell political candidates.		
Corporations can now run for elected office.		
Candidate funding can come from foreign companies in the U.S.		
Corporations can now influence voting through candidate funding.		
A U.S. corporation is considered an individual with voting rights.		

audio script pg. 260

For scoring multi-answer questions, see pg. 237.

Raw Score =   / 8

Add your raw score to Test #2 box pg. 217.

Task #6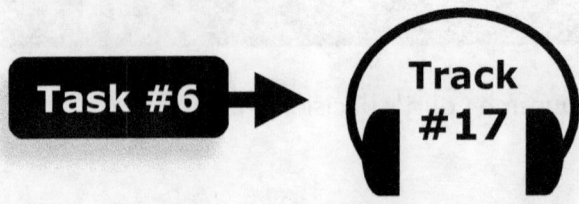

Directions: Listen to a lecture in a composition class, then answer the questions on the next page.

Questions

Directions: Now get ready to answer the questions. Answer each question based on what is stated or implied in the lecture.

#1

What is the topic of the lecture?

A) Aristotle's philosophy
B) Aristotle's writing style
C) Aristotle's ancient lesson
D) Aristotle's modes of appeal

#2

What is the purpose of the lecture?

A) to demonstrate three different types of persuasive argument
B) to illustrate how an argument can be made more persuasive
C) to highlight Aristotle's influence
D) to highlight how audiences have been persuaded

#3

According to Aristotle, which appeals make a lecture more persuasive? Select three. This is a 2-point answer.

A) ethos
B) bathos
C) pathos
D) chaos
E) logos

#4

Why does the professor say this?

A) to warn that even the best arguments can fail to persuade an audience
B) to warn that persuaded people often change their minds during elections
C) to reinforce the idea that persuasive arguments guarantee results
D) to highlight the need for arguments

#5

The professor describes President Obama's personal history. Put President Obama's personal history in the proper order. This is a 2-point question.

a. graduated from Harvard Law
b. became a U.S. Senator
c. was a community organizer
d. taught constitutional law

1. _____
2. _____
3. _____
4. _____

Turn the page for question #6

#6

In the lecture, the professor describes Aristotle's three appeals and their functions in an argument. Indicate whether each of the following is a function of Aristotle's three appeals. This is a 3-point question.

	YES	NO
Logos appeals to reason using deduction or induction		
Ethos appeals to what is morally right.		
Pathos appeals to the emotions using both words and images.		
Logos combines both ethos and pathos.		
Ethos appeals to character.		

audio script pg. 261

For scoring multi-answer questions, see pg. 237.

Raw Score =   / 10

Add your raw score to Test #2 box pg. 217.

10-minute break

Test #2
Speaking Section

Directions

For this section, you have <u>20 minutes</u> to complete six speaking tasks. The first two tasks are independent tasks. The last four tasks are integrated tasks. Begin speaking after the indicated preparation time. Remember to time yourself.

Remember! *You may take notes. Your notes will not be rated.*

Remember! *Record your responses. After the test, calculate your speaking score. See pg. 218.*

Task #1 - *Independent Speaking*

Prompt   Social networks, such as Facebook and Twitter, are a bad influence. What is your opinion? Give examples and reasons to develop and support your position.

Preparation Time – 15 seconds

Speaking Time – 45 seconds

proficiency checklist pg. 221 * rating guide pg. 222

add your rating to Test #2 box pg. 220

Task #2 - Independent Speaking

Prompt   We need zoos. Do you agree or disagree? Give examples and reasons to support and develop your argument.

Preparation Time – 15 seconds

Speaking Time – 45 seconds

proficiency checklist pg. 221   *   rating guide pg. 222

add your rating to Test #2 box pg. 220

Task #3 - *Integrated Speaking*

Directions: Read the following passage. Shelton University is introducing a new computer policy.

Reading Time - 45 seconds

Announcement

In order to reduce the school's carbon footprint, and to reduce the spiraling cost of pulp-based text books, the campus bookstore will go digital starting next semester. Students will have two e-book buying options. Using a computer terminal at the bookstore, students can purchase e-books with a credit card, then download their purchase to a storage device. Students will also be able to download e-books via the school website. The move to digital texts will result in greater savings for students when purchasing required texts. Please note: Due to the policy change, campus bookstores will no longer be offering buy-backs. If you have any questions, please contact the Dean's office.

Directions: Now listen as two students discuss the announcement.

Do not look at the reading passage as you listen to the dialogue or when you speak. After you read the passage, the passage will leave your screen and will not come back.

Track #18

_____
_____
_____
_____
_____
_____
_____

(This task continues on the next page.)

Now get ready to answer the prompt.

> Prompt   The man gives his opinion about the new policy. State his position and explain the reasons he gives for holding that opinion.

Preparation Time – 30 seconds

Speaking Time – 60 seconds

audio script pg. 263 * proficiency checklist pg. 224 * rating guide pg. 225

add your rating to Test #2 box pg. 220

Task #4 - *Integrated Speaking*

Directions: Read the following passage on animal behavior.

Reading Time – 45 seconds

Animal Behavior

Animal behavior can be classified according to the time of day an animal is active. Animals, such as horses, elephants and most birds, are said to be diurnal because they are active during the day and rest at night. Those animals active at dawn and dusk are said to be crepuscular. Beetles, skunks and rabbits fall into this category. The third group are those animals that sleep during the day and are active at night. They are called nocturnal. A good example is the bat. Bats have highly developed eyesight, hearing and smell. This helps them avoid predators and locate food. Being nocturnal also helps them avoid high temperatures during the day, especially in deserts where temperatures can reach well over one hundred degrees Fahrenheit.

Directions: Now listen to a lecture on the same topic.

Do not look at the reading passage as you listen to the dialogue or when you speak. After you read the passage, the passage will leave your screen and will not come back.

Track #19

(This task continues on the next page.)

Now get ready to answer the prompt.

> Prompt: The reading and the lecture focus on the classification of animal behavior. Describe how the reading and the lecture define and develop this idea.

Preparation Time – 30 seconds

Speaking Time – 60 seconds

audio script pg. 264 * proficiency checklist pg. 224 * rating guide pg. 225

add your rating to Test #2 box pg. 220

Task #5 - *Integrated Speaking*

Directions: Listen to a conversation between two students.

(This task continues on the next page.)

Now get ready to answer the prompt.

> Prompt   The students discuss two solutions to the man's problem. Identify the problem and the solutions, then state which solution you think is best and why.

Preparation Time – 20 seconds

Speaking Time – 60 seconds

---

audio script pg. 264 * proficiency checklist pg. 224 * rating guide pg. 225

add your rating to Test #2 box pg. 220

Task #6 - *Integrated Speaking*

Directions: Listen to a lecture in a biology class.

(This task continues on the next page.)

Now get ready to answer the prompt.

> Prompt   According to the lecture, how did Charles Darwin revolutionize agricultural science?

Preparation Time – 20 seconds

Speaking Time – 60 seconds

---

audio script pg. 265   *   proficiency checklist pg. 224   *   rating guide pg. 225

add your rating to Test #2 box pg. 220

Test #2
Writing Section

Directions

For this section, you have 53 minutes to complete two writing tasks. The first task is the integrated task. This task combines reading, listening, and writing. You will have 23 minutes to complete the integrated writing task. Next is the independent writing task. For this task, you will use your experience when writing an independent essay. You will have 30 minutes to complete this task. Remember to time yourself.

> **Remember!** *You may take notes. They will not be rated. After the test, calculate your writing score. See page 228.*

> **Remember!** *On test day, you must type your two essays.*

Task #1 - *Integrated Essay*

Directions: Read the following passage, then listen to the lecture and write an integrated essay.

Reading Time – 3 minutes

Illegally Downloading Music

Music. We all love it. In fact, I'm listening to music right now, music I downloaded off the internet without paying for it. That's right. I should've paid, but I didn't. And for that, many would call me a criminal. Well, go right ahead. As far as I'm concerned, downloading music off the internet without paying the asking price is not a crime. Why not?

Let's start with a little history. The internet was originally invented to be a source of free information benefiting all. Downloading music off the internet without paying for it is a perfect example of this democratic ideal in action. In this light, I am not criminal. I am simply exercising my democratic right to move freely in the vast new democracy called cyberspace.

Now if you're like me, you love to share music with your friends by downloading it from their computers. This is not stealing music. Hardly. My friends and I are simply sharing songs. In fact, I share music with people all over the world, people I don't know and will never meet. This process is called P2P or peer-to-peer file sharing. Now think: Is sharing something you love a crime? I don't think so.

Finally, and this point I really want to stress: What I do in the privacy of my home is nobody's business but my own. Period. I don't need the government telling me what I can or can't do with my computer. The United States is a democracy not a dictatorship.

To sum up, just because I refuse to pay for downloaded music does not make me a felon. The real criminals are those in government and business determined to deny music-loving individuals their right to freedom and privacy.

(This task continues on the next page.)

Directions: Now listen to a lecture on the same topic.

Now get ready to write your response.

> Prompt   Summarize the points made in the lecture and show how they cast doubt on the points made in the reading.

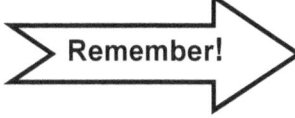 *You can look at the reading passage as you write your essay.*

Writing Time – 20 minutes

_____

audio script pg. 265   *   proficiency checklist pg. 231   *   rating guide pg. 232

add your rating to Test #2 box pg. 230

Task #2 - *Independent Essay*

Directions: Read the following prompt, then write an independent essay.

> Prompt — If you had to teach one subject, what would it be? Why? Use examples and reasons to support your argument.

Writing Time – 30 minutes

proficiency checklist pg. 234 * rating guide pg. 235

add your rating to Test #2 box pg. 230

Test 3

Test #3
Reading Section

Directions

For this section, you have 60 minutes to read three passages and answer the questions following each passage. The passages are typical of those found in North American college and university text books.

Answer each question based on what is stated or implied in the passage. You will not lose points for wrong answers. Remember to time yourself.

You may take notes. They will not be rated. After the test, calculate your reading score. See pg. 214.

Passage #1 - *Methods of Research*

1 → There are two methods of research: qualitative and quantitative. Qualitative research is based on events observed by the researcher while quantitative research is based on numerical data gathered by the researcher. A rainbow analogy exemplifies the two approaches. A researcher applying the qualitative approach would conclude, after personal observation, that a rainbow is an arc of colors with red on the outer edge of the arc and violet on the inner edge, with orange, yellow, blue and indigo in between. A researcher applying the quantitative approach would, in contrast, measure the varying intensities of color and the angle of refraction causing those colors, then compare those numbers to a broader statistical survey of rainbows. As you can see, quantitative research is scientific while qualitative research is holistic, a methodology based on observation and interpretation. Yet despite the differences, researchers use both with the intent of compiling information that is reliable and credible.

2 → To produce reliable and credible research, a researcher using the qualitative approach focuses on the why and how of decision making, specifically in regard to human behavior, such as why a child will sit in front of a computer for hours at a time or how a tribe of Amazonian Indians deals with a threat to its territory from a neighboring tribe. By observing events as they unfold—by actually being in the field—the researcher has a front row seat on trying to answer why a child is addicted to the computer or how a tribe of Amazonian Indians secures its territory from incursions. The researcher does this by focusing on language, signs, and meaning. Historically, researchers in the social sciences, such as anthropologists, sociologists and psychologists, have employed the qualitative approach, one that, by its very nature, is inductive, induction being a form of logic in which a conclusion is based on a series of observable facts. ■ To obtain information, however, the researcher must limit the focus of his or her study. ■ For example, if you are a researcher trying to answer the question why some children are addicted to the computer, it would not be possible for you to observe all the children in a particular city, state or country. ■ Yet by limiting the size of the study group, less data will be obtained which, in turn, might raise questions about the reliability of your research. ■ Also, you might come under scrutiny, for readers and other researchers might ask how neutral you were when compiling data, especially if you were observing your own children.

3 → In contrast, quantitative research focuses on the gathering of large amounts of empirical data, then feeding that data into mathematical models that, in turn, provide the researcher with statistics. From these statistics, a researcher can make conclusions based not on his own personal involvement with the subject but on what the numbers are telling him. This impersonal approach removes any researcher bias from the research process and, more importantly, increases the reliability of the research and any conclusions based on that research. Politicians often employ quantitative research. For example, the president wants to raise taxes but first he wants to know if the public is for or against the idea. To find out, he conducts a national opinion survey that asks the question: Are you in favor of raising taxes? The more people answer the survey, the more accurate the results. The more accurate the results, the more informed the president will be when finally deciding whether to raise taxes or not. This, then, is another difference between qualitative and quantitative research: quantitative research compiles data from much larger research groups while

qualitative research is limited to what the researcher can, as an individual, practically observe.

4 → Despite their differences, the two methods of research, when used in tandem, can produce reliable and credible results. For example, a researcher has concluded through observation that Hispanics make up the majority of students in a local English-as-a-second language program. By surveying other schools in her city or state—by using quantitative research—the researcher could then compile statistical data to prove if her initial hypothesis about Hispanics and English language programs is indeed accurate.

1. In paragraph 1, analogy is closest in meaning to...

   a) a describing of methods
   b) a defining of purposes
   c) a comparison of similarities
   d) an illustration of results

2. In paragraph 1, compiling is closest in meaning to...

   a) gathering and remembering
   b) collecting and analyzing
   c) classifying and concluding
   d) grouping and processing

3. In paragraph 1, why does the author use the rainbow example?

   a) to describe and classify the colors and dimensions of a typical rainbow analyzed by qualitative and quantitative scientists
   b) to define and develop what qualitative and quantitative researchers will see and experience when researching specific weather patterns
   c) to introduce and contrast how qualitative and quantitative researchers analyze the same topic but from different points of view
   d) to give the reader an idea of how qualitative and quantitative researchers draw different conclusions based on personal experience

4. In paragraph 2, unfold is closest in meaning to...

   a) evolve
   b) move
   c) conclude
   d) undo

5. In paragraph 2, to what does its refer?

   a) Amazonian
   b) child
   c) tribe
   d) researcher

6. In paragraph 2, incursions is closest in meaning to...

   a) hostile trespass
   b) endless war
   c) tribal fighting
   d) daily stealing

7. In paragraph 2, scrutiny is closest in meaning to...

   a) rejection
   b) understanding
   c) mutiny
   d) inspection

8. Look at the four squares [■]. They indicate where the bold sentence below could be added to paragraph 2. Select the square where you think the bold sentence could be inserted into the passage.

   Instead, you would establish a context or a focus group—a group of computer-using children in a neighborhood say—a group which, by its limited size, would be accessible and easily observed.

   ■ To obtain information, however, the researcher must limit the focus of his or her study. ■ For example, if you are a researcher trying to answer the question why some children are addicted to the computer, it would not be possible for you to observe all the children in a particular city, state or country. ■ Yet by limiting the size of the study group, less data will be obtained which, in turn, might raise questions about the reliability of your research. ■ Also, you might come under scrutiny, for readers and other researchers might ask how neutral you were when compiling data, especially if you were observing your own children.

9. Which of the following sentences best restates the essential information in the highlighted sentence in paragraph 3? Incorrect choices will change the meaning and omit important information.

   a) Such neutrality eliminates prejudice while creating more reliable results.
   b) Part of the research process includes conclusions based on researcher bias.
   c) By removing researcher preferences, the research process is more efficient and reliable.
   d) This method of research produces the best results while removing researcher bias.

10. In paragraph 3, what can we infer about qualitative research?

   a) Scientists are more likely to use this approach when doing field research.
   b) Scientists are more likely to use the qualitative method of research because it can cover a much wider subject area in a shorter period of time.
   c) Scientists have yet to decide which research method produces the best results, but are leaning toward the qualitative approach.
   d) Scientists cannot compile data using the qualitative approach.

11. Which of the following is NOT MENTIONED in paragraph 4?

   a) When combined, quantitative and qualitative research are effective.
   b) Qualitative research is a good way to prove a hypothesis based on research done quantitatively.
   c) A hypothesis based on qualitative research can be confirmed using quantitative research.
   d) Quantitative research can compare the results of qualitative research over a much larger surveyed area.

12. In paragraph 4, in tandem is closest in meaning to...

   a) immediately
   b) together
   c) separately
   d) regularly

13. In paragraph 4, hypothesis is closest in meaning to...

   a) decision
   b) doubt
   c) test
   d) proposition

14. What does the author conclude about qualitative and quantitative research?

   a) When combined, conclusions will be more reliable and credible because of increased research.
   b) When used in combination, they will always eliminate researcher bias thus producing honest results.
   c) When used together, researchers will be able to prove their hypotheses more quickly and with more accurate results.
   d) When used in tandem, they will give researchers the conclusions they are looking for.

15. How does the author organize the main points in the passage?

    a) using cause-and-effect and pro-con
    b) using compare-and-contrast and illustration
    c) using pro-con and compare-and-contrast
    d) using classification and illustration

16. In paragraph 4, indeed is closing in meaning to...

    a) always
    b) usually
    c) possibly
    d) truly

17. Directions: Complete the following table by indicating which topics go under each topic heading. This is a 4-point question.

quantitative research	qualitative research
•	•
•	•
•	•
	•

   1. unlimited   6. statistical
   2. measurable   7. observable
   3. political   8. why and how
   4. impersonal   9. inductive
   5. holistic

For scoring multi-answer questions, see pg. 237.

Raw Score =   / 20

Add your raw score to Test #3 box pg. 215.

Passage #2 - *Cognitive Bias*

1 → Passing judgment is human nature. Some of our judgments are accurate while others are flawed. Often a judgment is flawed because we have not taken the time to think an issue through and instead make a snap decision based on experience. A snap decision resulting in an error of judgment is called a cognitive bias. Some of the more common cognitive biases are the bandwagon effect, stereotyping, and the halo effect. Let's start with the bandwagon effect.

2 → Have you ever bought something because all your friends had bought it, or tried a new restaurant simply because all your friends had? If so, then you have demonstrated the cognitive bias called the bandwagon effect. Historically, the word bandwagon describes a wagon pulled by a horse. On the wagon, a band is playing. If you like the music, you will follow the bandwagon, maybe even jump on. Either way, you have literally joined the group. Years ago, politicians used bandwagons to spread their messages. If many voters were following a politician's bandwagon—and you concluded that so many must mean the politician deserves your vote—then you would have joined the bandwagon. How you came to that conclusion is known as an information cascade. An information cascade is an integral part of the bandwagon effect. It occurs when you conclude, without evidence, that if everybody is doing it, then they must be right and you must be wrong. Because you are wrong, you follow those who are right: the bandwagon.

3 → The bandwagon effect is not limited to politics. It also describes why some teenagers get into trouble. Not wanting to be left out of the group, a teenager will join in even if he or she knows that what they are doing is wrong. This is one way teenagers start drinking and smoking, by jumping on the bandwagon figuratively.

4 → Another example of the bandwagon effect is Black Friday. Black Friday is a national day of sales in which millions jump on the bandwagon and flock to stores looking for pre-Christmas bargains. Do these people really need to wait in front of Wal-Mart at four a.m. in order to be first in line for the best bargains, or are they all just shopaholics? If you assume that all Black Friday shoppers are shopaholics, then you would be stereotyping. Stereotyping is another common cognitive bias. When you stereotype someone, you are concluding, without evidence, that the character traits of one individual are consistent throughout the group. For example, your friend Bill eats nothing but hamburgers. ■ Because Bill is American, you conclude that all Americans eat hamburgers, which of course is not true, much like the fallacy that all Black Friday shoppers are shopaholics. ■ True, many Black Friday shoppers are shopaholics; however, many simply want to save money or are with friends or family. ■ Whatever the case, stereotyping can lead to offense, so be careful when making sweeping generalities based on experience rather than on sound evidence. ■

5 → But let's say you jump on the bandwagon anyway and join the four a.m. stampede into Wal-Mart. You want a Samsung big-screen TV so you race for the electronics department. The only problem is everybody else wanted a Samsung TV, and now they are all gone. Then a man says, "Wal-Mart TVs are just as good as Samsungs. In fact, Samsung makes Wal-Mart TVs." Is that true? You don't know. Meanwhile, the man grabs a Wal-Mart TV and everyone else jumps on the bandwagon until there is only one Wal-Mart TV left. What do you do? You grab it. Why? Because

you like Wal-Mart TVs? No. The fact is you have never heard of a Wal-Mart TV before. But you have heard of Samsung, and you know that Samsung is high quality. So what do you do? You make a snap decision based on experience: If Samsung makes Wal-Mart TVs, like the man said, then Wal-Mart TVs must be good. Only later when you get it home do you realize that your Wal-Mart TV was made by the Cheap-O TV Company. This then is an example of the halo effect. The halo effect is a cognitive bias in which you believe that the value or quality of one thing (Samsung TV) spills over and increases the value of another thing (Wal-Mart TV).

6 → Another example of the halo effect is the iPad. When it first came out, many questioned whether it would fly. Considering Apple's track record for delivering cutting-edge products, such as the wildly successful iPod, was there any doubt? No. When the iPad hit the stores, people lined up to buy it. Had they ever seen or used an iPad before? No. But that didn't stop sales from going through the roof.

1. In paragraph 1, all of the following are TRUE EXCEPT...

   a) Stereotyping, the halo effect, and the bandwagon effect are all cognitive biases.
   b) Passing judgment with cognitive biases is a flaw of human nature.
   c) An error in judgment not based on fact or forethought is called a cognitive bias.
   d) A cognitive bias is a quick conclusion based on erroneous assumptions.

2. Why does the author start paragraph 2 with a rhetorical question?

   a) to question the next topic
   b) to introduce the next topic
   c) to illustrate where biases can occur
   d) to develop a new and different topic

3. In paragraph 2, why does the author use the example of a political bandwagon?

   a) to develop and illustrate the historical meaning of the phrase cognitive bias
   b) to define and show the cause-and-effect relationship between political bandwagons and politicians during an election
   c) to develop and define the process of how everyone was influenced by large political groups many years ago when bandwagons were popular
   d) to develop and describe the process of how the bandwagon effect is comparable to, and got its name from, actual political bandwagons

4. In paragraph 2, an integral part of is closest in meaning to...

   a) a related part of
   b) an important piece of
   c) an interesting part of
   d) an noticeable element of

5. In paragraph 2, what happens as a result of an information cascade?

   a) The individual is so confused he/she does not know right from wrong.
   b) The individual passes judgment based on the facts presented.
   c) The individual concludes that more must mean right.
   d) The individual joins the bandwagon based on the right conclusions.

6. In paragraph 3, figuratively is closest in meaning to...

   a) comparatively
   b) significantly
   c) immediately
   d) metaphorically

7. In paragraph 4, which refers to...

   a) consistent throughout the group
   b) you conclude
   c) Bill is American
   d) all Americans eat hamburgers

8. Look at the four squares [■]. They indicate where the bold sentence below could be added to paragraph 4. Select the square where you think the bold sentence could be inserted into the passage.

   Just because you go shopping on Black Friday does not mean you are a shopaholic.

   ■ Because Bill is American, you conclude that all Americans eat hamburgers, which of course is not true, much like the fallacy that all Black Friday shoppers are shopaholics. ■ True, many Black Friday shoppers are shopaholics; however, many simply want to save money or are with friends or family. ■ Whatever the case, stereotyping can lead to offense, so be careful when making sweeping generalities based on experience rather than on sound evidence. ■

9. In paragraph 4, fallacy is closest in meaning to...

   a) legacy
   b) idea
   c) misconception
   d) reason

10. In paragraph 5, stampede is closest in meaning to...

    a) a group waiting patiently
    b) an orderly procession moving as one
    c) shoppers finding bargains on Black Friday
    d) a mass movement based on impulse

11. Directions: Complete the following table by indicating which topics go under each topic heading. This is a 4-point question.

bandwagon effect	stereotyping	halo effect
•	•	•
•	•	•
•		

    1. based on sound evidence
    2. idiom with historical origin
    3. Apple products
    4. more means right
    5. the value of one effects the value of another
    6. common personality flaw
    7. often offensive
    8. information cascade
    9. traits are seemingly similar

12. Directions: The sentence in bold is the first sentence of a brief summary of the passage. Complete the summary by selecting three answer choices. Your choices will express the most important ideas in the passage. Some choices are not in the passage or do not express important ideas. This is a 2-point question.

The passage describes cognitive biases.

-
-
-

Answer Choices

1. Erroneous conclusions based not on fact but on experience.

2. Started long ago when politicians used bandwagons to persuade voters to vote.

3. It is an aspect of human nature.

4. A product that sells well, like the iPad, will have an adverse effect on Apple products as a whole.

5. A cascade of information was, and still is, an integral part of the political process.

6. They can lead to poor choices, costly mistakes, and personal offense.

For scoring multi-answer questions, see pg. 237.

Raw Score =   / 16

Add your raw score to Test #3 box pg. 215.

Passage #3 - *The Railroad Boom*

1 → The verb *to gild* means to apply a layer of gold to an object. Mark Twain used the adjectival form of this verb when he coined the phrase the Gilded Age. The Gilded Age, from 1869 to 1893, represents American economic prosperity at its height. And for good reason. The Gilded Age created many firsts, such as a new class of super-rich, men like John D. Rockefeller, J. P. Morgan, Andrew Mellon, Cornelius Vanderbilt, and Andrew Carnegie. It also witnessed the birth of the first corporations, such as General Electric and Standard Oil. Yet it was the railroad companies that were the engine that drove the Gilded Age, companies like Union Pacific and the Central Pacific Railroad. In 1869, four years after the Civil War, these two railroads linked up at Promontory Summit in Utah thereby establishing the first continental railroad in North America. Instead of sailing from New York City to San Francisco south around South America—a trip that could take four weeks if the weather were good—the trip could now be made in six-days by train across the continental U.S. The impact was immediate. With the east now linked to the west, thousands seeking free land and a new future headed west. When the railroad arrived in Denver in 1870, it had a population of 5,000. Ten years later, it was 36,000.

2 → To accommodate the movement of people and material, hundreds of new railroads were built. And they needed steel. Lots of it. Yet steel making was, and still is, a capital-intensive business. It took money to build steel factories and to mine the iron ore that would be smelted in coal-fired ovens. Investment capital was needed. Banks, jumping on the bandwagon, met the demand and Wall Street came into its own. The boom in steel making created a demand not only for investment capital but for factory workers as well. Most of those workers were immigrants straight off the boat. The steel they made in east coast factories built rails and rail cars, all of it heading west to serve the ranchers and farmers who needed to ship their beef and wheat back east by rail. In this way, the railroad spawned the agricultural industry and helped to expand the telegraph industry as well, for the fastest and easiest way for telegraph companies to build telegraph lines was to follow the railroads into the newly-created towns dotting the west. This they did, and American Telephone and Telegraph (ATT) and Western Union took their place beside Union Pacific Railroad, Carnegie Steel, and Standard Oil, the most profitable companies at the time.

3 → Railroad companies are also credited with developing what today is known as the modern management system. With so much building, the railroads needed a clear chain of command to keep things running smoothly. This they did by creating clear managerial roles while establishing career goals that employees at all levels could pursue. This, combined with internal promotions, led to greater employee loyalty and productivity. Other companies soon followed suit. This gave rise to the American middle class, especially in big east coast cities.

4 → Manufacturing too benefited from the railroad boom. ■ One consumer item the railroad brought to women was the Singer Sewing machine. ■ By 1880, over three million homes had a Singer. ■ Prior to the Singer sewing machine, women had to stay home and make clothes for their families, a time-consuming task that left women with little or no free time for anything else. ■ Yet the Singer sewing machine changed all that. It not only sped up the clothes-making process, but also led to the building of textile factories where clothes, such as those for railroad workers, were mass

produced, the most famous of which was Levi's jeans. Mass-produced clothes resulted in lower prices while at home, women no longer had to hand-stitch clothes for their families. With the advent of the Singer sewing machine, women now had more free time, time they could devote to women's rights, such as the right to vote, which they won in 1920.

5 → The railroad boom, however, went bust in 1893. Like the internet bubble of 2000 and the real estate bubble of 2008, the railroad boom was a result of companies over-extending. Simply put, by 1893 there were too many railroads, too many bad loans and too much market speculation. This led to the collapse of over five-hundred banks while dozens of railroads, including the Union Pacific Railroad, declared bankruptcy. Confidence in the economy was restored when gold was found in Canada's Klondike, leading to the Klondike Gold Rush of 1897.

coined: created
boom: rapid economic expansion

1. In paragraph 1, height is closest in meaning to...

   a) nadir
   b) average
   c) zenith
   d) bottom

2. In paragraph 2, which of the following is NOT TRUE?

   a) The steel industry employed foreigners who had just arrived in the U.S.
   b) During the Gilded Age, manufacturing and finance defined the east while agriculture predominated in the west.
   c) To meet its need, the railroads depended on money raised on a new center of finance called Wall Street.
   d) The towns that dotted the west were a direct result of the railroads and telegraph companies working together to reduce costs and increase profits.

3. In paragraph 2, spawned is closest in meaning to...

   a) spanned
   b) created
   c) witnessed
   d) revolutionized

4. In paragraph 2, to what does they refer?

   a) railroads
   b) towns
   c) telegraph lines
   d) telegraph companies

5. In paragraph 3, followed suit is closest in meaning to...

   a) did the same
   b) did the opposite
   c) did what suited them
   d) did succeed

6. According to paragraph 3, what were the effects of the railroad boom on American society?

   a) The railroads, with more effective managers, created the American middle class which, in turn, worked for the railroads and shared in the profits.
   b) Increased productivity in the long term created better jobs and a happier middle class in the short term.
   c) As a direct result of more efficient managerial methods adopted by the railroad companies, the American middle class was created.
   d) The American middle class created a super-rich class of men, such as Cornelius Mellon and Andrew Vanderbilt.

7. Look at the four squares [■]. They indicate where the bold sentence below could be added to paragraph 4. Select the square where you think the bold sentence could be inserted into the passage.

   Why was this invention so revolutionary?

   4 → Manufacturing too benefited from the railroad boom. ■ One consumer item the railroad brought to women was the Singer Sewing machine. ■ By 1880, over three million homes had a Singer. ■ Prior to the Singer sewing machine, women had to stay home and make clothes for their families, a time-consuming task that left women with little or no free time for anything else. ■ Yet the Singer sewing machine changed all that.

8. In paragraph 4, what can we infer about women and the railroad boom?

   a) Without the railroad boom, women's rights, especially the right to vote, would have evolved much more slowly.
   b) With the railroad boom, women were suddenly equal to men in the new American middle class.
   c) Women, particularly in agricultural regions, were spending less time working at home and more time working at the office.
   d) The Singer sewing machine was invented by a railroad company in order to sell sewing machines to women living and working in rapidly developing new towns.

9. In paragraph 4, why does the author mention the Singer sewing machine?

    a) to compare and contrast two new technologies at the time, the train and the sewing machine
    b) to highlight the fact that the short and long term effects of the railroad boom were not limited to the railroad, the telegraph and Wall Street
    c) to define the nature of women's work prior to the boom and how it changed almost overnight
    d) to classify the various industries competing for profit during the Golden Age

10. In paragraph 4, advent is closest in meaning to...

    a) revolution of
    b) admission of
    c) invention of
    d) introduction of

11. Directions: The sentence in bold is the first sentence of a brief summary of the passage. Complete the summary by selecting three answer choices. Your choices will express the most important ideas in the passage. Some choices are not in the passage or do not express important ideas. This is a 2-point question.

    The passage describes the railroad boom in nineteenth-century America.

    -
    -
    -

Answer Choices

1. The American government played a major financial role.

2. It created a new class of super-rich and a new middle class.

3. Immigrants, fresh off the boat, found work in steel factories and in mines in the west.

4. It introduced new technologies, such as Levi's jeans, to workers in small towns.

5. It was at its height from 1869 to 1893.

6. It created social conditions that helped women win political rights.

For scoring multi-answer questions, see pg. 237.

Raw Score =   / 12

Add your raw score to Test #3 box pg. 215.

Test #3
Listening Section

Directions

The listening section measures your ability to answer questions specific to English conversations and lectures. The conversations and lectures are typical of the North American college and university experience.

After each conversation and lecture, you will answer questions. Answer each question based on what the speakers state or imply. Answer all questions. You will not lose points for a wrong answer.

For some questions, you will see a headset symbol: 🎧
The headset symbol means you will hear part of the conversation or lecture. After you hear part of the conversation or lecture, you will answer a question about it.

Do not look at the answers as you listen. On test day, you will not see the answers as you listen. Remember to time yourself.

> **Remember!** You have <u>60 minutes</u> to complete this section.

> **Remember!** *You may take notes. Your notes will not be rated. After the test, calculate your listening score. See pg. 216.*

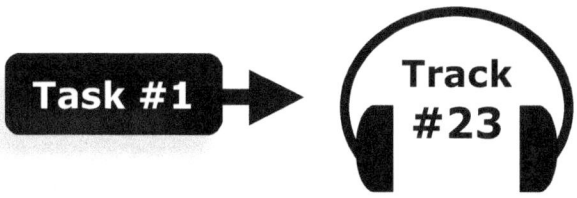

Directions: Listen as a student talks to a professor, then answer the questions on the next page.

Questions

Directions: Now get ready to answer the questions. Answer each question based on what is stated or implied in the conversation.

#1

What is the topic of the conversation?

A) the pros and cons of PowerPoint
B) a recent presentation
C) the assignment
D) the test

#2

Why does the student visit the professor?

A) to find out more about the assignment
B) to change her presentation topic
C) to pick up handouts and get advice
D) to clarify the purpose of the assignment

#3

Why does the professor say this?

A) to describe the advantages of using PowerPoint
B) to remind the student to use tools such as PowerPoint
C) to state what he strongly believes
D) to illustrate how PowerPoint is a tool often used in presentations

#4

According to the professor, what will an audience do if the presenter loses control of a presentation? Select three. This is a 2-point question.

A) start to yawn
B) start to complain
C) ask for refunds
D) check their cell phones
E) walk out

#5

Listen again to part of the conversation, then answer the question.

What does the professor imply when he says this?

A) to compare giving a presentation to walking
B) to stress the fact that the student must learn the basics first
C) to suggest that presentations move at different speeds
D) to repeat a point mentioned in the handout

Raw Score =   / 6

Add your raw score to Test #3 box pg. 217.

audio script pg. 266

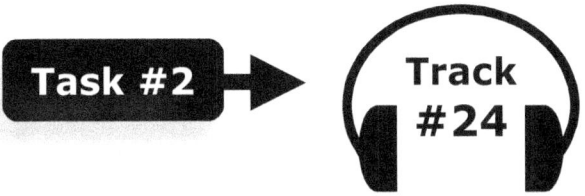

Directions: Listen to part of a lecture in a history class, then answer the questions on the next page.

Questions

Directions: Now get ready to answer the questions. Answer each question based on what is stated or implied in the lecture.

#1

What is the focus of the lecture?

A) early housing through the ages
B) housing and class structure in Europe a long time ago
C) medieval housing
D) architecture in the Middle Kingdom

#2

What is the purpose of the lecture?

A) to define and examine the evolution of medieval structures and societies
B) to describe the process of house building prior to modernization
C) to explore the lives of those who lived in ancient houses and societies
D) to classify and illustrate how housing in the middle ages reflected the prevailing social hierarchy

#3

According to the lecture, in whose house did animals do more than provide a food source?

A) the king's
B) the peasant's
C) the noble's
D) the landowner's

#4

Why does the professor say this?

A) to highlight the dangers of crowded housing built of flammable material
B) to describe how houses were built in order to prevent fires
C) to contrast how city houses were far safer than peasant structures
D) to describe the long-term effects of crowded medieval cities and towns

#5

Identify which are features of medieval housing and which are not. This is a 3-point question.

	YES	NO
In a landowner's house, the solar was above the hall.		
Thatching was used to build castle walls.		
In a city house, the kitchen was attached at the back.		
Peasant houses were smoky because they lacked chimneys.		
In a city house, the ground floor was usually a shop.		

#6

According to the lecture, a castle had two main purposes. One was military. What was the other?

A) a center of worship
B) an administrative center
C) an educational institution
D) an agricultural market

audio script pg. 267

For scoring multi-answer questions, see pg. 237.

Raw Score =   / 8

Add your raw score to Test #3 box pg. 217.

Directions: Listen to a lecture in an American literature class, then answer the questions on the next page.

Questions

Directions: Now get ready to answer the questions. Answer each question based on what is stated or implied in the lecture.

#1

What does the lecture mainly focus on?

A) a magazine called *The Black Mask*
B) the history of pulp fiction in America
C) the writers Carroll John Daly and Dashiell Hammett
D) great American detectives

#2

What is mentioned about *The Black Mask*? Select three. This is a 2-point question.

A) It was 128-pages long.
B) It started to sell in 1920.
C) It published formula writing.
D) It had no illustrations.
E) It was never popular.

#3

According to the lecture, what was Peter Collinson's real name?

A) Carroll John Daly
B) Dashiell Daly
C) Peter Hammett
D) Dashiell Hammett

#4

Why does the professor say this?

A) to identify each writer's influences
B) to illustrate that Hammett had more life experience than Daly
C) to illustrate that Hammett lived a block from Daly's house
D) to describe what Hammett and Daly were doing in 1923

#5

The professor describes the life of Carroll John Daly. Put Daly's early life in the correct order. This is a 2-point question.

a. attended art school
b. published *Three-Gun Terry*
c. ran a movie theatre in Atlantic City
d. born in Yonkers, New York

1. _____
2. _____
3. _____
4. _____

#6

The professor mentions three dates. Match each date to the corresponding event. This is a 2-point question.

a. 1889	b. 1923	c. 1894
Three Gun Terry and *Arson Plus* were published in *The Black Mask*.	Carroll John Daly was born in Yonkers, New York.	Dashiell Hammett was born on a farm in Maryland.

audio script pg. 269

For scoring multi-answer questions, see pg. 237.

Raw Score =   / 9

Add your raw score to Test #3 box pg. 217.

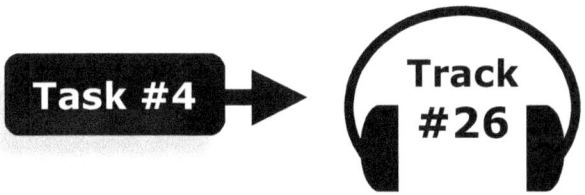

Directions: Listen to a discussion in a business class, then answer the questions on the next page.

Questions

Directions: Now get ready to answer the questions. Answer each question based on what is stated or implied in the discussion.

#1

What is the discussion mainly about?

A) counterfeit goods
B) counterfeit manufacturers
C) counterfeit currency
D) counterfeit laws

#2

What is the point of the discussion?

A) to illustrate the many ways knock-offs can enter a foreign market
B) to illustrate how consumers benefit from affordable products like fakes
C) to illustrate how counterfeit products threaten a company's bottomline
D) to illustrate unfair business practices

#3

Why does the professor say this?

A) to illustrate that the problem of knock-offs is getting bigger
B) to signal a return to the main topic
C) to indicate that the problem of knock-offs is far bigger than most realize
D) to stress that accessories are the most knocked-off products

#4

How can knock-offs hurt a company? Select three. This is a 2-point question.

A) They can diminish brand equity.
B) They can hurt consumers.
C) They can reduce market share.
D) They can dramatically decrease costs.
E) They can force companies to spend a lot of money on legal fees.

#5

From the discussion, we can infer that "touts" on Fifth Avenue are...

a) tourists buying knock-offs
b) people selling knock-offs
c) people selling designer products
d) affordable products sold in summer

#6

According to the discussion, what is true about knock-offs? This is a 3-point question.

	YES	NO
They infringe upon American trademark law.		
They pose a serious threat to consumer health.		
They are always sold on internet sites.		
They are made in the U.S. and sold abroad.		
They can adversely affect a company's financial position.		

audio script pg. 270

For scoring multi-answer questions, see pg. 237.

Raw Score =   / 9

Add your raw score to Test #3 box pg. 217.

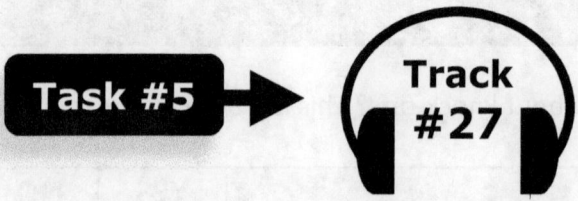

Directions: Listen as a student talks to a campus employee, then answer the questions on the next page.

Questions

Directions: Now get ready to answer the questions. Answer each question based on what was stated or implied in the conversation.

#1

What does the conversation focus on?

A) how easy e-book terminals are to use
B) problems with an e-book purchase
C) the need for secure passwords
D) fixing the kinks in the system

#2

From the conversation, we can infer that the student...

A) hates e-books
B) will never buy another e-book
C) will ask her professors for advice
D) will contact the e-book vendor

#3

What must the student's new e-book password be? Select three. This is a 2-point question.

A) at least six characters
B) at least eight characters
C) alphanumeric
D) alphabetical
E) case sensitive

#4

What can be inferred when the employee says this?

A) Problems persist with the terminals.
B) The problems have been resolved.
C) There have been many complaints.
D) The store is not part of the e-book system.

#5

Listen again to part of the conversation, then answer the question.

Why does the student say this?

A) She got the email.
B) She didn't get the email.
C) She forgot her email address.
D) She forgot to enter her email address.

Raw Score =   / 6

Add your raw score to Test #3 box pg. 217.

audio script pg. 272

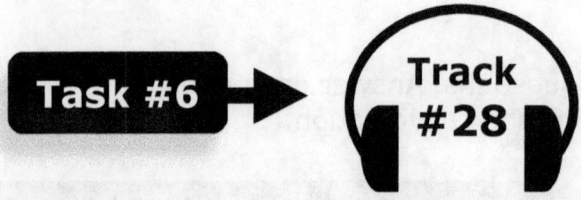

Directions: Listen to a lecture in an art history class, then answer the questions on the next page.

Questions

Directions: Now get ready to answer the questions. Answer each question based on what is stated or implied in the lecture.

#1

On what does the lecture mainly focus?

A) French and British art and artists in the nineteenth century
B) art and revolution in Europe
C) two influential nineteenth century art movements
D) how art and artists reflected social change in the eighteenth century

#2

Which three Pre-Raphaelite artists are mentioned? Select three. This is a 2-point question.

A) Charles Dickens
B) John Millais
C) Edouard Manet
D) Dante Gabriel Rossetti
E) William Holman Hunt

#3

Why does the professor say this?

A) to explain and illustrate how artists painted during that period
B) to highlight how literature influenced both art movements
C) to describe the process of painting in Britain and France
D) to contrast each movement's approach to painting

#4

What can we infer about the Impressionists and the Pre-Raphaelites?

A) At first, critics rejected their ideas.
B) Their methods were radically different.
C) They were aware of each other's work.
D) Their work eventually made them rich and famous.

#5

According to the lecture, Louis Comfort Tiffany was...

A) a leading Impressionist painter
B) a critic of early modernism
C) a part of the Art Nouveau movement
D) a Pre-Raphaelite poet

Turn the page for question #6

#6

What is true about the Impressionists and the Pre-Raphaelites? This is a 3-point question.

	YES	NO
They were radical nineteenth century art movements.		
They shared the philosophy that art was for the common man.		
The Pre-Raphaelites pre-dated the Impressionists by 20 years.		
They rejected the old in favor of the new.		
They found inspiration in Medieval themes and Mannerism.		

audio script pg. 274

For scoring multi-answer questions, see pg. 237.

Raw Score =   / 9

Add your raw score to Test #3 box pg. 217.

10-minute break

Test #3
Speaking Section

Directions

For this section, you have <u>20 minutes</u> to complete six speaking tasks. The first two tasks are independent tasks. The last four tasks are integrated tasks. Begin speaking after the indicated preparation time. Remember to time yourself.

> **Remember!** *You may take notes. Your notes will not be rated.*

> **Remember!** *Record your responses. After the test, calculate your speaking score. See pg. 218.*

Task #1 - *Independent Speaking*

> Prompt   What is your idea of a perfect neighborhood? Use examples and reasons to support and develop your argument.

Preparation Time – 15 seconds

Speaking Time – 45 seconds

___

proficiency checklist pg. 221   *   rating guide pg. 222

add your rating to Test #3 box pg. 220

Task #2 - *Independent Speaking*

> Prompt   Do you prefer to shop online or at a store? Why? Give examples and reasons to support your position.

Preparation Time – 15 seconds

Speaking Time – 45 seconds

proficiency checklist pg. 221 * rating guide pg. 222

add your rating to Test #3 box pg 220

Practice Tests for the TOEFL® iBT - 145

Task #3 - *Integrated Speaking*

Directions: Wilton University is introducing a new policy. Read about the new policy in the following announcement.

Reading Time - 45 seconds

Announcement from the Dean

Starting next semester, Wilton University will introduce a new dress code policy. This policy pertains to students, faculty and support staff. Starting next semester, the wearing of shorts will no longer be permitted inside campus buildings. Also, tank tops, and any other top that does not completely cover the mid section down to the belt, will be prohibited. Sandals and other open-toed shoes will also be prohibited, as will the wearing of hats and caps. Those individuals not in accordance with the new policy will be asked to leave the school and return properly attired. Excessive jewelry will also be prohibited. If you have any questions, please contact the Dean's office.

Directions: Now listen as two students discuss the announcement.

Do not look at the reading passage as you listen to the dialogue or when you speak. After you read the passage, the passage will leave your screen and will not come back.

Track #29

_____
_____
_____
_____
_____
_____
_____

(This task continues on the next page.)

145

Now get ready to answer the prompt.

> Prompt The woman expresses her opinion about the announcement. State her opinion and explain the reasons she gives for holding that opinion.

Preparation Time – 30 seconds

Speaking Time – 60 seconds

audio script pg. 275 * proficiency checklist pg. 224 * rating guide pg. 225

add your rating to Test #3 box pg. 220

Task #4 - *Integrated Speaking*

Directions: Read the following passage about refining.

Reading Time – 45 seconds

Refining

Refining is an industrial process whereby crude oil—raw, unprocessed oil taken directly from the ground—is refined into usable petroleum products such as gasoline, diesel fuel, asphalt, heating oil, and liquefied natural gas. This process occurs at a chemical plant called a refinery. Refineries are a mass of snaking pipes and massive metal towers connecting various parts of the refining process. Refineries are often located beside a body of water, such as a river or ocean. Such proximity expedites the off-loading of crude oil transported by ships, such as supertankers. Crude oil is black or dark brown, and consists of naturally occurring hydrocarbons and other organic compounds. It is toxic and highly flammable. It is found deep beneath the Earth's surface and is extracted by drilling wells, many of which are miles deep. With the increasing demand for oil, oil companies are now drilling offshore in areas once thought too dangerous for oil operations.

Directions: Now listen to a lecture on the same topic.

Do not look at the reading passage as you listen to the dialogue or when you speak. After you read the passage, the passage will leave your screen and will not come back.

Track #30

_____
_____
_____
_____

(This task continues on the next page.)

Now get ready to answer the prompt.

> Prompt: Refining is a complex and dangerous process. Using information from the reading and lecture, describe this process.

Preparation Time – 30 seconds

Speaking Time – 60 seconds

audio script pg. 276 * proficiency checklist pg. 224 * rating guide pg. 225

add your rating to Test #3 box pg. 220

Task #5 - *Integrated Speaking*

Directions: Listen to a conversation between two students.

(This task continues on the next page.)

Now get ready to answer the prompt.

> Prompt   The students discuss two solutions to the woman's problem. Identify the problem and the solutions, then state which solution you think is best and why.

Preparation Time – 20 seconds

Speaking Time – 60 seconds

___

audio script pg. 277   *   proficiency checklist pg. 224   *   rating guide pg. 225

add your rating to Test #3 box pg. 220

Task #6 - *Integrated Speaking*

Directions: Listen to a lecture in a sociology class.

(This task continues on the next page.)

Now get ready to answer the prompt.

> Prompt How does the lecture define and develop the concept of white-collar crime?

Preparation Time – 20 seconds

Speaking Time – 60 seconds

---

audio script pg. 277 * proficiency checklist pg. 224 * rating guide pg. 225

add your rating to Test #3 box pg. 220

Test #3 Writing Section

Directions

For this section, you have 53 minutes to complete two writing tasks. The first task is the integrated task. This task combines reading, listening, and writing. You will have 23 minutes to complete the integrated writing task. Next is the independent writing task. For this task, you will use your experience when writing an independent essay. You will have 30 minutes to complete this task. Remember to time yourself.

You may take notes. They will not be rated. After the test, calculate your writing score. See pg. 228.

On test day, you must type your two essays.

Task #1 - *Integrated Essay*

Directions: Read the following passage.

Reading Time - 3 minutes

Global Warming

Are humans responsible for global warming? This is a contentious issue. But let's be clear: The increase in CO_2 in the atmosphere is not a result of man's burning of fossil fuels. To the contrary, the increase in CO_2 specifically, and greenhouse gases generally, is a direct result of the Earth naturally warming itself. Where then, you might ask, is all that CO_2 coming from if not from man? It's coming from carbon sinks. Simply put, a carbon sink is a place where carbon dioxide is naturally stored. The largest carbon sinks are the Arctic tundra and the oceans. As the Earth warms, carbon sinks release CO_2. To state otherwise is to ignore the fact that over the past 250,000 years, periods of global warming were a direct result of large amounts of CO_2 being naturally released from carbon sinks.

In this debate, computer modeling is held up as evidence that global warming is a man-made phenomena. Let's put this issue to rest as well. Yes, computers are capable of immense calculations. However, when it comes to predicting future climate patterns, computers fail repeatedly. Case in point: Computers cannot accurately measure the global mean ocean surface temperature, or GMST. If scientists agree that measuring the GMST is the best indicator of climate change, and since we can't measure it, how can anyone state with any degree of certainty that man is responsible for global warming? Simple. They can't.

The last point I want to make concerns water vapor. Water vapor is a naturally occurring greenhouse gas. Not only that but it is also the most abundant greenhouse gas. Concentrations of water vapor are natural events caused by storms and are driven globally by the movement of ocean currents. According to one study, water vapor in the stratosphere increased the global warming rate in the 1990's by 30%. The conclusion? Why blame man when it is obvious that global warming is a natural phenomena we are just beginning to understand.

(This task continues on the next page.)

Directions: Now listen to a lecture on the same topic.

Now get ready to write your response.

Prompt   Summarize the points made in the lecture and show how they cast doubt on the points made in the reading.

 *You can look at the reading passage as you write your essay.*

Writing Time – 20 minutes

___

audio script pg. 278 * proficiency checklist pg. 231 * rating guide pg. 232

add your rating to Test #3 box pg. 230

Task #2 - *Independent Essay*

Directions: Read the following prompt, then write an independent essay.

> Prompt   We should fund a mission to Mars. What is your position? Use examples and reasons to support your argument.

Writing Time - 30 minutes

proficiency checklist pg. 234 * rating guide pg. 235

add your rating to Test #3 box pg. 230

Test 4

Test #4
Reading Section

Directions

For this section, you have 60 minutes to read three passages and answer the questions following each passage. The passages are typical of those found in North American college and university text books.

Answer each question based on what is stated or implied in the passage. You will not lose points for wrong answers. Remember to time yourself.

 *You may take notes. They will not be rated. After the test, calculate your reading score. See pg. 214.*

Passage One - *The American Bison*

1 ➔ The American bison or buffalo is the largest terrestrial animal in North America. They are endemic to the western Great Plains, a corridor of grassland stretching from the Canadian provinces of Manitoba, Saskatchewan and Alberta south through the American states of North Dakota and Montana down to Texas. Bison are herbivores with long shaggy coats. Cows are smaller than bulls, which can weigh up to 2,500 pounds. When the first white explorers came in contact with the bison, they reported herds so vast they stretched from one horizon to the next. Despite such numbers, the white man decimated the great bison herds, so much so that by the late nineteenth century, the American bison was almost extinct. The building of the railroad was a big reason for the slaughter. Hunters no longer had to ride horses to hunt buffalo. Instead, they shot buffalo by the thousands from train cars. The skins and meat were sold while the rest of the body was left to rot. Later the bones would be gathered up and sent back east for fertilizer. The killing of the buffalo opened up land for settlers flooding in from the east. A photo taken in 1870 illustrates the destruction visited upon the buffalo. In the photo, a man stands on top of a mountain of buffalo skulls rising over fifty feet.

2 ➔ The near total slaughter of the American bison had the greatest impact on the indigenous tribes of the Great Plains. For millennia, these Native Americans depended upon the bison for everything. To say that the bison was a walking supermarket is no exaggeration. Tribes such as the Sioux, the Cheyenne and the Arikara hunted buffalo for meat, which they ate raw, cooked, and preserved in a dried form called pemmican. The skin they turned into clothing and the sides of dwellings while the thick dense fur made ideal blankets for cold winter nights. The horns were used for drinking and for mixing paint, the hooves for glue, and the bones for tools and weapons. In short, the culture and survival of the plains Indian was based entirely upon the buffalo. One of the iconic figures of the American west is the Indian warrior hunting buffalo from horseback.

3 ➔ ■ However, the horse was late in arriving on the North American continent. ■ Historically, the horse arrived with Spanish explorers, circa 1500. ■ The horse they brought was the barb horse, a native of North Africa and long domesticated by Berber tribesmen. ■ The name barb is a contraction of Barbary Coast, a term Europeans gave the northern coast of Africa which, at the time, was a haven for Barbary Pirates. It was this horse, the barb horse, which the Spanish explorers brought to North America. Over time, the barb horse escaped from the Spanish and was captured and tamed by the Indians. By doing so, the plains Indian gained a new mode of transportation and an ideal platform from which to hunt the fast-moving buffalo.

4 ➔ Prior to 1500, the Indians of the Great Plains hunted buffalo on foot, a perilous endeavor that often resulted in the death of more than one hunter. The process began with the entire village heading out for the hunt. With a buffalo herd fast approaching—and here we are talking a million or more animals—the villagers would line up beside cairns, piles of rocks that had been erected by previous hunters going back to prehistoric times. The cairns acted as driving lanes that funneled the buffalo towards a cliff. The villagers lined up on both sides of the herd and, by waving blankets and skins, they would force the buffalo into a stampede.

Unable to stop, the buffalo would be forced to jump off the cliff. This form of mass hunting is called a buffalo jump. Thousands of buffalo would die. Yet they would not go to waste, for the Indians made use of everything. The largest buffalo jump in North America is Ulm Pishkun Buffalo Jump, a national park near Great Falls, Montana. The cliff there is over a mile in length with bones at the base of the cliff compacted some thirteen feet deep. That is a lot of buffalo. But remember, at that time, between 900 and 1500 CE, buffalo herds were so large, it took days for them to pass one point. Those days are long gone; however, thanks to conservation efforts, the American bison has made a strong comeback and remains to this day an enduring symbol of the American west.

1. In paragraph 1, to what does they refer?

   a) bison
   b) first white explorers
   c) herbivores
   d) cows and bulls

2. In paragraph 1, the word extinct is closest in meaning to...

   a) ancient
   b) missing
   c) endangered
   d) gone

3. In paragraph 1, why does the author mention a mountain of buffalo skulls?

   a) to describe what life was like in America in 1870
   b) to illustrate how many buffalo had been killed by 1870
   c) to support the view that buffalo hunting was popular
   d) to explain how buffalo bones were turned into fertilizer

4. In paragraph 2, the word iconic is closest in meaning to...

   a) symbolic
   b) historic
   c) ironic
   d) specific

5. In paragraph 2, what is NOT TRUE about the American bison?

   a) Indigenous tribes of the Great Plains hunted it for thousands of years.
   b) It was central to Indian culture and survival on the Great Plains.
   c) It supplied the plains Indian with almost all their needs.
   d) Cowboys are often pictured hunting it on horseback.

6. Look at the four squares [■]. They indicate where the bold sentence below could be added to paragraph 3. Select the square where you think the bold sentence could be inserted into the passage.

The horse was indeed an integral part of plains Indian culture.

■ However, the horse was late in arriving on the North American continent. ■ Historically, the horse arrived with Spanish explorers, circa 1500. ■ The horse they brought was the barb horse, a native of North Africa and long domesticated by Berber tribesmen. ■ The name barb is a contraction of Barbary Coast, a term Europeans gave the northern coast of Africa which, at the time, was a haven for Barbary Pirates.

7. In paragraph 3, the word haven is closest in meaning to...

   a) place
   b) shelter
   c) state
   d) maven

8. In paragraph 3, what can we infer about the barb horse?

   a) It was used by pirates.
   b) The Spanish sold it to the plains Indians around 1500.
   c) The Spanish had domesticated it before 1500.
   d) The barb horse was fast.

9. In paragraph 4, what does the phrase perilous endeavor mean?

   a) dangerous idea
   b) risky venture
   c) group task
   d) ancient method

10. In paragraph 4, why does the author mention the buffalo jump?

    a) to illustrate how Indians hunted buffalo in the nineteenth century
    b) to classify hunting methods prior to 1870
    c) to illustrate how the plains Indians hunted buffalo prior to the horse
    d) to develop the topic of hunting on the Great Plains

11. In paragraph 4, why does the author mention cairns?

    a) to illustrate that a buffalo jump was a dangerous form of hunting
    b) to compare how different Indians hunted on the Great Plains
    c) to demonstrate the process of building a buffalo jump circa 1500
    d) to illustrate that the same hunting site was used for thousands of years

12. Which of the following sentences best restates the essential information in the highlighted sentence in paragraph 4? Incorrect choices will change the meaning and omit important information.

    a) Rock markers lined roads on which the buffalo traveled to a cliff.
    b) Rock markers acted as guides between which the buffalo were directed toward a cliff.
    c) Piles of rock marked the edge of the cliff where the buffalo jumped.
    d) Rock piles shaped like funnels were positioned on the edge of a cliff.

13. <u>Directions</u>: The sentence in bold is the first sentence of a brief summary of the passage. Complete the summary by selecting three answer choices. Your choices will express the most important ideas in the passage. Some choices are not in the passage or do not express important ideas. This is a 2-point question.

    The passage discusses the American bison.

    -
    -
    -

Answer Choices

1. It is native to the western Great Plains of North America.
2. It was hunted to extinction.
3. It played a central role in plains Indian culture.
4. It has thick hair, weighs almost a ton, and can run very fast.
5. It was nearly wiped out by hunters in the nineteenth century.
6. The Spanish used its bones for fertilizer.

For scoring multi-answer questions, see pg. 237.

Raw Score =   / 14

Add your raw score to Test #4 box pg. 215.

Passage #2 - *Charles and Ray Eames*

1 → The motto of the husband and wife design team of Charles and Ray Eames was "the most of the best for the greatest number of people for the least." This philosophy is best represented in their form-fitting chairs.

2 → Prior to World War II, the Eames were rethinking furniture design with the aim of building furniture that was affordable, comfortable, and could be mass produced. The fruition of that idea was the Eames Lounge Chair Wood. It was made of plywood, thin layers of wood that are glued together against the grain for extra strength. The Eames molded the plywood using techniques they themselves developed. The chair won the Museum of Modern Art's Organic Furniture Competition in 1940. However, production difficulties and the start of World War II delayed production. The delay was fortuitous for the Eames for it turned their attention to making molded wooden leg splints for the military, an idea they applied to the lounge chair. The result was a stylish, simple-to-make, form-fitting chair with complex curves that formed around the back and under the knees with the seat and back joined by a flexible lumbar support making the chair one of the first with a flexible backrest. In the world of furniture and industrial design, the Eames Lounge Chair Wood was a revolution, so much so that it was called "the chair of the century." Its simplicity of design and construction stood in stark contrast to furniture of the day, which was heavy and complex to make.

3 → Today, the Eames Lounge Chair Wood is highly prized by collectors and remains an icon of modern design, as are many other Eames designs, such as the 1956 Lounge Chair and Ottoman, another example of the Eames' belief in form and function. The Eames also designed one-piece plastic chairs, fiberglass chairs, and wire-mesh chairs, as well as space-saving storage units that could be assembled quickly at home. The Eames' creations were mass produced thus in the Eames' furniture, we witness the merging of artistic design and mass production, a hallmark of post-war America consumerism. In fact, what you are sitting on now—be it a computer chair, a fiberglass seat in a McDonald's, or a metal-framed fabric chair in an airport—is a direct descendant of the Eames Lounge Chair Wood. Walk around stores like IKEA and the Pottery Barn, and you will experience firsthand the enduring influence of the Eames' pioneering furniture designs.

4 → Furniture design, however, was but one facet of the Eames' genius. They also designed textiles, buildings, toys, and made over one hundred short films on topics ranging from Franklin and Jefferson to explaining mathematical concepts, such as how computers work. ■ They are also credited with creating one of the first multi-screen films, *Glimpses of the USA*. ■ The film was commissioned by the U.S. Information agency for a 1959 exhibition in Moscow, an exhibition that showcased American progress at the height of the Cold War. ■ The film, employing seven screens, is a day-in-the-life of America with an emphasis on the power and scope of American capitalism. ■

5 → The Eames are also renowned for designing groundbreaking exhibitions, the most important of which was *Mathematica: A World of Numbers and Beyond*. In 1961, The California Museum of Science and Industry in Los Angeles opened and invited companies to present exhibitions. One company was IBM. At the time, IBM

was on the cutting edge of computer science, a science based on mathematics. IBM commissioned the Eames to design an interactive exhibition that would explain the history and the science of mathematics in a way that the layman would understand. Like all the Eames' work, the exhibition was infused with a whimsy and a playfulness that transformed the complex into something accessible to all. *Mathematica: A World of Numbers and Beyond* is considered a work of art in its own right, one that remains the model upon which all interactive science exhibitions are based.

6 → Later in life when Charles Eames was asked to explain his design philosophy, he used what he called the banana leaf parable. In southern India, the broad flat banana leaf is used as a base for food, much like a plate or dish. According to Charles Eames, the banana leaf is the foundation from which ideas grow. In other words, when designing, the Eames always imagined the banana leaf, a natural design that is simple, functional and affordable. Any ideas that developed from the banana leaf, the original basic idea, had to reflect the simplicity, the functionality, and the affordability of the banana leaf itself. The genius of Charles and Ray Eames' work is a testament to the banana leaf parable.

splint: a brace or support

1. In paragraph 1, the word motto is closest in meaning to...

   a) main topic
   b) guiding principle
   c) basic rule
   d) important message

2. In paragraph 2, fruition is closest in meaning to...

   a) realization
   b) frustration
   c) making
   d) conclusion

3. Why was the Eames Lounge Chair Wood called "the chair of the century"?

   a) because it was the best chair at the time
   b) because it was the first chair designed by a husband and wife team
   c) because it sold the most at the time
   d) because it was the most influential furniture design at the time

4. In paragraph 3, all of the following are MENTIONED EXCEPT...

   a) The Eames designed space-saving storage units.
   b) The Eames designed wire-mesh chairs.
   c) The Eames often worked alone.
   d) The Eames' influence can been seen in IKEA, McDonalds, and airports.

5. In paragraph 4, why does the author introduce the topic of the Cold War?

   a) to establish the political context in which the Eames' film *Glimpses of America* was shown to a Russian audience
   b) to remind us that America and Russia were quite different at the time
   c) to illustrate how art was not influenced by the politics of the time
   d) to describe the effects the Eames' film had on audiences

6. Look at the four squares [■]. They indicate where the bold sentence below could be added to paragraph 4. Select the square where you think the bold sentence could be inserted into the passage.

   People in Moscow, it was reported, lined up for blocks and were brought to tears by what they saw flashing by on the screens.

   They also designed textiles, buildings, toys, and made over one hundred short films with topics ranging from Franklin and Jefferson to explaining mathematical concepts, such as how computers work. ■ They are also credited with creating one the first multi-screen films, *Glimpses of the USA*. ■ The film was commissioned by the U.S. Information agency for a 1959 exhibition in Moscow, an exhibition that showcased American progress at the height of the Cold War. ■ The film, employing seven screens, is a day-in-the-life of America with an emphasis on the power and scope of American capitalism. ■

7. In paragraph 5, groundbreaking is closest in meaning to...

   a) innovative
   b) exciting
   c) breakable
   d) affordable

8. In paragraph 5, layman is closest in meaning to...

   a) audience
   b) scientists
   c) average man
   d) families

9. Which of the following sentences best restates the essential information in the highlighted sentence in paragraph 5? Incorrect choices will change the meaning and omit important information.

   a) The exhibition was easy to understand because the Eames used fantasy and humor in order to teach difficult subjects in a simple way.
   b) The exhibition combined complex science and humor to explain how to use the latest technology.
   c) The exhibition was easy to comprehend because the Eames simplified complex information so that people could play with computers.
   d) The Eames understood the importance of complex information and how to play with it.

10. In paragraph 5, which refers to...

   a) a work of art
   b) one
   c) *Mathematica: A World of Numbers and Beyond*
   d) model

11. In paragraph 6, parable is closest in meaning to...

   a) a personal philosophy
   b) a belief shared by many
   c) a story with a lesson
   d) a religious book

12. What can we infer from the passage?

   a) Everyone bought the Eames' designs.
   b) The Eames were the most important artists in post-war America.
   c) The Eames' design influence is still widely felt today.
   d) Charles and Ray Eames were happily married.

13. Directions: Complete the following table by illustrating Charles and Ray Eames' achievements in furniture design and other media. This is a 4-point question. For scoring multi-answer questions, see page 237.

furniture design	other media
•	•
•	•
•	•
•	

1. toys
2. molded plywood
3. short films
4. fiberglass
5. one-piece plastic chairs
6. computer games
7. lounge chairs
8. exhibitions
9. painting

For scoring multi-answer questions, see pg. 237.

Raw Score =   / 16

Add your raw score to Test #4 box pg. 215.

Passage #3 - *Plant Defense Mechanisms*

1 → During the Ordovician Period some four-hundred-and-fifty million years ago, land plants evolved from aquatic plants. Once on land, plants had to adapt or die. One adaptation was a protective coating to reduce the damage to tissues due to evaporation. Another was seeds that could survive dry conditions. Such defense mechanisms ensured plant survival and diversification. With such adaptation, plants were able to flourish. Yet with the proliferation of plants came a sudden increase in plant-eating insects. As a result, plants had to develop defense mechanisms against herbivory while insects, in order to survive, had to develop ways to defeat plant defense mechanisms. This process of reciprocal evolutionary change, in which life forms influence each other's development, is called co-evolution. Co-evolution is generally regarded as having led to the creation of much of the Earth's biomass.

2 → The defense mechanisms plants employ against herbivores and other potential threats, such as fungus and bacteria, are either constitutive or induced. Constitutive defense mechanisms are those defenses which a plant has developed over time. For example, to prevent deer from eating it, the raspberry plant has long stems which are covered with sharp thorns while fruit trees produce gummosis, a sticky, sap-like material that traps insects. One plant, the voodoo lily, protects itself by smelling like rotting flesh. This unusual defense mechanism keeps herbivores away while attracting carrion-eating insects that pollinate the lily thus ensuring its survival.

3 → Another form of constitutive defense occurs at the molecular level. These are toxins which the plant produces. If ingested, the results can be fatal. One of the more famous examples is the Greek philosopher Socrates. Accused of corrupting the youth of Athens, Socrates was condemned to death by drinking poison hemlock. Its cousin, water hemlock, is considered the most toxic plant in North America. Many common vegetables and fruits are also poisonous. The potato, for example, is a member of the deadly nightshade family. The stems and leaves of the potato plant contain a glycoalkaloid poison, a toxin that manifests itself as a green color in old potatoes or potatoes exposed to prolonged periods of light.

4 → In contrast, induced defense mechanisms are those which a plant develops and sends to the part of it which has been injured. Such mechanisms occur at the molecular level and are produced by the plant only when needed. For example, in an article by T. R. Green and C. A. Ryan, when a potato plant is attacked by the Colorado potato beetle, the action will induce in the potato plant the production of a proteinase inhibitor which targets those parts of the potato plant that are exposed to air due to wounding. Proteinase inhibitors are enzymes that break down protein left behind at the wound by the potato beetle thus preventing infection. Another induced defense mechanism occurs when an herbivore eats part of a plant. ■ This, in turn, induces the release and activation of a cyanogenic glycoside, a poison common in the leaves of many popular fruit and nut trees, such as the cherry, the almond, the peach, and the apple. ■ In an herbivore, these can cause extreme salivation, gastroenteritis, and diarrhea. ■ An herbivore, having been afflicted this way, will think twice the next time it approaches a tree or plant with such a defense mechanism. ■

5 ➔ Plants can also defend themselves from herbivores by changing shape. This induced mechanism is called thigmonasty. Mimos pudica, commonly known as the shy plant, is a salient example of such behavior. When touched or shaken, the leaves of the shy plant fold inward and the plant itself droops. Scientists speculate that this induced movement can shake off harmful insects or frighten away other herbivores. Another explanation is that by folding up and drooping, the shy plant is pretending to be dead thus presenting itself as unappetizing.

reciprocal: mutual exchange

1. In paragraph 1, flourish is closest in meaning to...

    a) thrive
    b) reproduce
    c) flounder
    d) vanish

2. In paragraph 1, what does herbivory mean?

    a) feeding on seeds
    b) feeding on biomass
    c) feeding on insects
    d) feeding on plants

3. What constitutive defense mechanisms does the author compare and contrast in paragraph 2?

    a) raspberry gummosis, fruit tree thorns, voodoo lily smell
    b) raspberry stems, fruit tree fungus, voodoo lily bacteria
    c) voodoo lily smell, raspberry thorns, fruit tree traps
    d) raspberry thorns, fruit tree gummosis, voodoo lily smell

4. In paragraph 3, why does the author use the example of Socrates?

    a) to show how the early Greeks used plant medicine
    b) to illustrate the effects of poison hemlock
    c) to add to the classification of dangerous plants
    d) to warn that hemlock can be fatal if ingested

5. In paragraph 3, manifests is closest in meaning to...

    a) manipulates
    b) multiplies
    c) reveals
    d) reviles

6. In paragraph 4, to what does which refer?

   a) potato plant
   b) proteinase inhibitor
   c) production
   d) Colorado potato beetle

7. In paragraph 4, all of the following are TRUE EXCEPT...

   a) proteinase inhibitors are enzymes
   b) the potato plant uses proteinase inhibitors as a defense mechanism
   c) proteinase inhibitors target exposed areas resulting from herbivory
   d) proteinase inhibitors are constitutive defense mechanisms

8. Look at the four squares [■]. They indicate where the bold sentence below could be added to paragraph 4. Select the square where you think the bold sentence could be inserted into the passage.

   By chewing a leaf, for example, enzymes in the herbivore's saliva break down the cell membranes.

   Another induced defense mechanism occurs when an herbivore eats part of a plant. ■ This, in turn, releases and induces the activation of cyanogenic glycosides, a poison common in the leaves of many popular fruit and nut trees, such as the cherry, the almond, the peach, and the apple. ■ In the herbivore, these can cause extreme salivation, gastroenteritis, and diarrhea. ■ An herbivore, having been afflicted this way, will think twice next time it approaches a tree or plant with such a defense mechanism. ■

9. In paragraph 4, afflicted is closest in meaning to...

   a) harmed
   b) depicted
   c) warned
   d) killed

10. In paragraph 4, why does the author mention gastroenteritis?

    a) to give an example of an effect resulting from consuming leaves containing cyanogenic glycoside
    b) to give an example of an effect resulting from consuming leaves containing proteinase inhibitors
    c) to provide another a reason for supporting the argument that cyanogenic glycosides are the most effective form of induced plant defense mechanism
    d) to illustrate an effect resulting from consuming leaves containing toxins

11. From the passage, it can be inferred that...

    a) Through co-evolution, plants have developed many ways to defend themselves against herbivory.
    b) Scientists have been able to identify how plants defend themselves from environmental factors.
    c) By successfully defending against herbivory, plants one day will no longer be threatened by herbivores, such as deer and insects.
    d) The evolutionary process of plants is little understood by scientists.

12. Which of the following sentences best restates the essential information in the highlighted sentence in paragraph 5? Incorrect choices will change the meaning and omit important information.

    a) The shy plant protects itself by convincing herbivores that it is not alive thus probably wouldn't taste very good.
    b) By drooping over and folding up, the shy plant dies thus herbivores will have no appetite for it.
    c) Herbivores are less interested in eating dead plants than living plants.
    d) The reason why the shy plant pretends to be dead is because it cannot protect itself from herbivores.

13. Directions: The sentence in bold is the first sentence of a brief summary of the passage. Complete the summary by selecting three answer choices. Your choices will express the most important ideas in the passage. Some choices are not in the passage or do not express important ideas. This is a 2-point question.

    The passage discusses plant defenses.

    -
    -
    -

    ### Answer Choices

    1. Plant defenses are a result of co-evolution.
    2. Plant defenses are either constitutive or induced.
    3. Thigmonasty is an induced plant defense characteristic of the potato plant.
    4. Toxic defense mechanisms in plants are always fatal.
    5. Herbivory is the science of plant defense mechanisms.
    6. Plant defense mechanisms evolved when land plants evolved from water plants.

14. <u>Directions</u>: Complete the following table by indicating which plant defense mechanisms are induced and which are constitutive. This is a 4-point question. For scoring multi-answer questions, see page 237.

Induced	Constitutive
•	•
•	•
•	•
	•

1. cyanogenic glycoside
2. gummosis
3. glycoalkaloid poison
4. thigmonasty
5. foul odor

6. thorns
7. nightshade
8. proteinase inhibitors
9. glucose enzymes

For scoring multi-answer questions, see pg. 237.

Raw Score =   / 18

Add your raw score to Test #4 box pg. 215.

Test #4
Listening Section

Directions

The listening section measures your ability to answer questions specific to English conversations and lectures. The conversations and lectures are typical of the North American college and university experience.

After each conversation and lecture, you will answer questions. Answer each question based on what the speakers state or imply. Answer all questions. You will not lose points for a wrong answer.

For some questions, you will see a headset symbol: 🎧
The headset symbol means you will hear part of the conversation or lecture. After you hear part of the conversation or lecture, you will answer a question about it.

Do not look at the answers as you listen. On test day, you will not see the answers as you listen. Remember to time yourself.

> **Remember!** You have <u>60 minutes</u> to complete this section.

> **Remember!** You may take notes. Your notes will not be rated. After the test, calculate your listening score. See pg. 216.

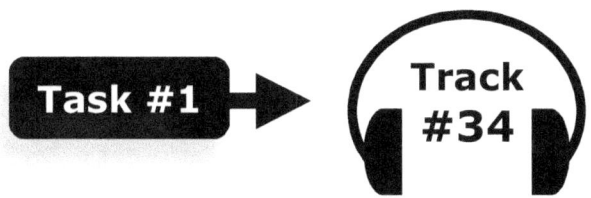

Directions: Listen to part of a discussion in a computer class, then answer the questions on the next page.

Questions

Directions: Now get ready to answer the questions. Answer each question based on what is stated or implied in the discussion.

#1

What is the discussion mainly about?

A) malicious computers
B) Trojan horses
C) viruses
D) malware

#2

What is the purpose of the discussion?

A) to highlight various internet dangers
B) to identify types of malicious software and their effects
C) to describe the history of the internet in America
D) to classify methods of virus protection

#3

Why does the student say this?

A) to compare the fate of the Trojans to users infected with Trojan horses
B) to illustrate where the name Trojan comes from
C) to develop the history of malware
D) to stress that Trojan horses are the most dangerous malware

#4

The student describes the history of computer viruses. Put that history in order. This is a 2-point question.

a. The Elk Clone virus attacks Apple computers.
b. The Brain appears to defend against software pirating.
c. The Creeper virus appears on ARPANET.
d. Computer scientists started writing about computer viruses.

1. _____
2. _____
3. _____
4. _____

#5

In the discussion, the student describes Trojan horses and computer viruses. Identify the characteristics of each. This is a 3-point question.

	Trojan horse	virus
Designed to disrupt or crash a host computer.		
Designed to secretly download a host computer's files.		
Spreads via portable media, such as flash drives.		
Often shows up as a legitimate link in an email message.		
First appeared on ARPANET as an innocuous experiment.		

#6

Listen to part of the discussion, then answer the question.

Why does the student say this?

A) to express empathy
B) to express shock
C) to express disgust
D) to express anger

audio script pg. 279

For scoring multi-answer questions, see pg. 237.

Raw Score =   / 9

Add your raw score to Test #4 box pg. 217.

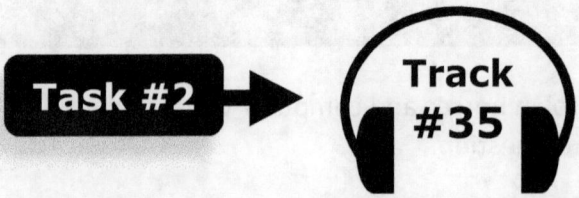

Directions: Listen to part of a lecture in a history class, then answer the questions on the next page.

Questions

Directions: Now get ready to answer the questions. Answer each question based on what is stated or implied in the lecture.

#1

What is the topic of the lecture?

A) the American Canal
B) the Panama Canal Company
C) Ferdinand de Lesseps
D) the Panama Canal

#2

Why does the professor say this?

A) to establish what people thought about the Panama Canal
B) to provide historical context
C) to point out when construction on the canal actually started
D) to compare and contrast two oceans connected by a canal

#3

What do we know about the Panama Canal? Select three. This is a 2-point question.

A) built by Ferdinand de Lesseps
B) finished in 1914
C) completed by the United States
D) completed in 1904
E) all electronic controls

#4

Listen again to part of the lecture, then answer the question.

What does the professor mean when she says this?

A) World events overshadowed the opening of the Panama Canal.
B) The Panama Canal, once opened, was important militarily.
C) Europeans and Americans fought over the canal during World War One.
D) Canal construction continued despite the start of World War One.

#5

The professor mentions three dates. Match each date to the corresponding event. This is a 2-point question.

a. 1904	b. 1869	c. 1888
Suez Canal was opened.	U.S. bought the Panama Canal from the French.	French started to build the Panama Canal.

#6

After the Panama Canal was built, the time a ship had to travel from New York City to San Francisco was cut by how much?

A) a third
B) a quarter
C) a half
D) two-thirds

audio script pg. 280

For scoring multi-answer questions, see pg. 237.

Raw Score =   / 8

Add your raw score to Test #4 box pg. 217.

Task #3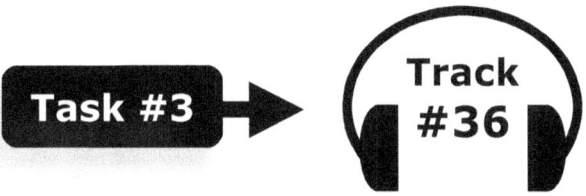

Directions: Listen to part of a lecture in an anthropology class, then answer the questions on the next page.

Questions

<u>Directions</u>: Now get ready to answer the questions. Answer each question based on what is stated or implied in the lecture.

#1

What is the lecture about?

A) the Indians of the American west and northwest
B) the Indians of northern Canada
C) indigenous cultures of the Pacific northwest
D) Pacific northwest arts and culture

#2

What is mentioned about totem poles? Select three. This is a 2-point question.

A) made of cedar
B) few remain
C) carved on an angle
D) attached to plank houses
E) held no religious importance

#3

Why does the professor say this?

A) to describe how most houses die
B) to illustrate how natural houses are eventually destroyed
C) to imply that native houses and nature have an ancient relationship
D) to describe how plank houses have vanished over time

#4

According to the lecture, which idiom originated with the totem pole?

A) The low man in the social hierarchy.
B) A totem is worth two in the bush.
C) Don't judge a totem by its cover.
D) The low man on the totem pole.

#5

What are the unique features of a plank house? Select three. This is a 2-point question

A) attached to totem poles
B) angled roof
C) made of animal skins
D) carved symbols on exterior walls
E) large interior space

#6

Why does the most famous shame totem pole remind the world of Lee Raymond?

A) He gave much money to the tribes.
B) He forgot to pay for his mistakes.
C) He is worshipped as a god.
D) He failed to clean up an oil spill.

audio script pg. 282

Raw Score = _____ **/ 8**   *Add your raw score to Test #4 box pg. 217.*

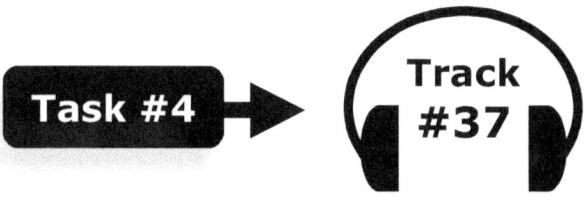

Directions: Listen as a student talks to a professor, then answer the questions on the next page.

Questions

Directions: Now get ready to answer the questions. Answer each question based on what is stated or implied in the conversation.

#1

What is the topic of the conversation?

A) daily English usage
B) slang, jargon and idioms
C) slang and jargon
D) types of codes

#2

Why does the student visit the professor?

A) to see if she can redo the test
B) to ask about her notes
C) to get advice for her presentation
D) to clarify points she missed in class

#3

Why does the student say this?

A) to highlight the exclusive nature of codes
B) to clarify the meaning of the code
C) to draw a conclusion on what the professor just said
D) to prove a point with an illustration

#4

The professor mentions three sociolects. What are they? Select three. This is a 2-point question.

A) police jargon
B) rapper slang
C) internet slang
D) cell phone slang
E) mechanic jargon

#5

Listen again to part of the conversation, then answer the question.

What does the professor mean when he says this?

A) Excellent.
B) Indeed.
C) On the contrary.
D) Of course.

Raw Score =   / 6

Add your raw score to Test #4 box pg. 217.

audio script pg. 284

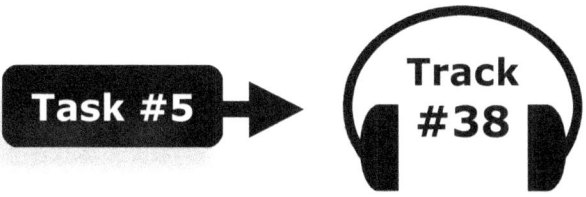

Directions: Listen as a student talks to a campus employee, then answer the questions on the next page.

Questions

Directions: Now get ready to answer the questions. Answer each question based on what is stated or implied in the conversation.

#1

What is the topic of the conversation?

A) applying for an internship
B) finding out about internships
C) deciding which offer is best
D) researching possible employers

#2

What can we infer about the student?

A) She has a clear idea as to what she will do after she graduates.
B) She is confused about interning.
C) She wants to get paid while interning.
D) Her future is still up in the air.

#3

Why does the admin say this?

A) to emphasize GE's reputation as a leader in corporate tax planning
B) to warn the student that GE is a tough place to work
C) to highlight GE's main business
D) to suggest that not all applicants are accepted as GE employees

#4

The admin mentions three internships. What are they? Select three. This is a 2-point question.

A) Bobby's Discount Nut Shop
B) General Electric
C) Donny's Discount Donuts
D) Apple
E) Microsoft

#5

Listen again to part of the conversation, then answer the question.

Why does the admin say this?

A) to encourage the student to apply for a more high-profile position
B) to the warn the student that if she waits, she might be out of luck
B) to remind the student that time is running out
D) to warn the student that the careers office will be closing soon

Raw Score =   / 6

Add your raw score to Test #4 box pg. 217.

audio script pg. 285

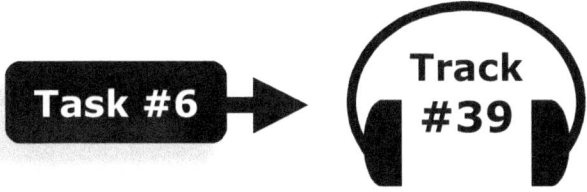

Directions: Listen to part of a lecture in a history class, then answer the questions on the next page.

Questions

Directions: Now get ready to answer the questions. Answer each question based on what is stated or implied in the lecture.

#1

What is the lecture mainly about?

A) the rise and fall of the Roman empire
B) European empires at war
C) the Early Middle Ages
D) great kings of early Europe

#2

What vanished with the fall of Rome? Select three. This is a 2-point question.

A) knights
B) the merchant class
C) pottery making
D) silk and spices
E) vassals

#3

What does the lecture tell us about Martel? Select three. This is a 2-point question.

A) started the feudal system
B) defeated the Muslims at Rome
C) Charlemagne was his grandson
D) created the Holy Roman Empire
E) born in 686

#4

Why does the professor say this?

A) to develop the topic of Rome and its European empires
B) to compare two different cultures
C) to illustrate the changes happening at the end of the Roman empire
D) to highlight the effect of Rome's absence in Europe

#5

What can we infer about Martel?

A) He was crowned the Holy Roman Emperor by Pope Leo III.
B) He wanted to be emperor of Rome.
C) He was not influenced by Roman traditions.
D) He had many grandsons.

#6

The professor mentions three dates. Match each date to its corresponding topic. This is a 2-point question.

a. AD 476	b. AD 732	c. AD 814

death of Charlemagne	Battle of Tours	fall of Rome

audio script pg. 287

For scoring multi-answer questions, see pg. 237.

Raw Score =   / 9

Add your raw score to Test #4 box pg. 217.

10-minute break

Test #4
Speaking Section

Directions

For this section, you have <u>20 minutes</u> to complete six speaking tasks. The first two tasks are independent tasks. The last four tasks are integrated tasks. Begin speaking after the indicated preparation time. Remember to time yourself.

Remember! → *You may take notes. Your notes will not be rated.*

Remember! → *Record your responses. After the test, calculate your speaking score. See pg. 218.*

Task #1 - *Independent Speaking*

> Prompt   What is your idea of happiness? Use examples and reasons to support and develop your argument.

Preparation Time – 15 seconds

Speaking Time – 45 seconds

proficiency checklist pg. 221 * rating guide pg. 222

add your rating to Test #4 box pg. 220

Task #2 - *Independent Speaking*

> Prompt   Which has influenced you the most, art or science? Why? Give examples and reasons to support your argument.

Preparation Time – 15 seconds

Speaking Time – 45 seconds

proficiency checklist pg. 221 * rating guide pg. 222

add your rating to Test #4 box pg. 220

Task #3 - Integrated Speaking

Directions: Read the following announcement from the student government at Greenwich College.

Reading Time – 45 seconds

Announcement from the Student Government

Recently the student body submitted ideas for a new mascot. Your ideas were then voted on. The final two choices for the new school mascot are a bear and a chicken. When voting, please keep in mind that a mascot should symbolize the strengths and traditions of our three-hundred-year-old institution. Please remember as well that the mascot's image will appear on a variety of media, including school uniforms, the school website, school stationery, and school clothing. Voting will occur next Monday in the Student Government office, room 310. Each student will get one vote. The results are final. If you have any questions, please contact the Mascot Committee, room 310. Don't forget to vote!

Directions: Now listen as two students discuss the announcement.

Do not look at the reading passage as you listen to the dialogue or when you speak. On test day, after you read the passage, it will leave your screen and will not come back.

Track #40

(This task continues on the next page.)

Now get ready to answer the prompt.

> Prompt   The woman expresses her opinion about the announcement. State her opinion and explain the reasons she gives for holding that opinion.

Preparation Time – 30 seconds

Speaking Time – 60 seconds

___

audio script pg. 288 * proficiency checklist pg. 224 * rating guide pg. 225

add your rating to Test #4 box pg. 220

Task #4 - *Integrated Speaking*

Directions: Read the following passage on brown-headed cowbirds.

Reading Time – 45 seconds

The Brown-Headed Cowbird

Brown-headed cowbirds are native to North America. Size wise, they are about eight inches long from the tip of the beak to the end of the tail. The cowbird is a brood-parasitic icterid. Icterids are small to medium-sized passerine birds, passerine meaning to perch. Before European settlers arrived in North America, the cowbird followed the buffalo across the Great Plains, eating the insects stirred up by the passing herds. In this way, cowbirds were nomadic, always on the move in search of food, much like the buffalo. However, with the clearing of land and the introduction of grazing animals, cowbirds found a ready food source: the insects stirred up by domesticated animals, such as cows and sheep. As a result, the cowbird became a permanent resident in agricultural areas. Today, cowbirds are a common sight at backyard birdfeeders, arriving in early spring and staying till late September when they head south for winter.

Directions: Now listen to a lecture on the same topic.

Do not look at the reading passage as you listen to the dialogue or when you speak. On test day, after you read the passage, it will leave your screen and will not come back.

Track #41

_____
_____
_____
_____

(This task continues on the next page.)

Now get ready to answer the prompt.

> Prompt The brown-headed cowbird is a brood parasite. How do the reading and lecture define and develop this classification?

Preparation Time – 30 seconds

Speaking Time – 60 seconds

audio script pg. 289 * proficiency checklist pg. 224 * rating guide pg. 225

add your rating to Test #4 box pg. 220

Task #5 - *Integrated Speaking*

Directions: Listen to a conversation between two students.

(This task continues on the next page.)

Now get ready to answer the prompt.

> Prompt The students discuss two solutions to the woman's problem. Identify the problem and the solutions, then state which solution you think is best and why.

Preparation Time – 20 seconds

Speaking Time – 60 seconds

_____
_____
_____
_____
_____
_____
_____
_____
_____
_____
_____
_____
_____
_____
_____
_____
_____
_____
_____
_____

audio script pg. 289 * proficiency checklist pg. 224 * rating guide pg. 225

add your rating to Test #4 box pg. 220

Task #6 - *Integrated Speaking*

Directions: Listen to part of a lecture in a science class.

(This task continues on the next page.)

Now get ready to answer the prompt.

> Prompt   How does the lecture define and develop the concept of homeostasis?

Preparation Time – 20 seconds

Speaking Time – 60 seconds

audio script pg. 290 * proficiency checklist pg. 224 * rating guide pg. 225

add your rating to Test #4 box pg. 220

Test #4
Writing Section

Directions

For this section, you have 53 minutes to complete two writing tasks. The first task is the integrated task. This task combines reading, listening, and writing. You will have 23 minutes to complete the integrated writing task. Next is the independent writing task. For this task, you will use your experience when writing an independent essay. You will have 30 minutes to complete this task. Remember to time yourself.

Remember! *You may take notes. They will not be rated. After the test, calculate your writing score. See pg. 228.*

Remember! *On test day, you must type your two essays.*

Task #1 - *Integrated Essay*

Directions: Read the following passage.

Reading Time – 3 minutes

Standardized Testing

A hot-button issue in education these days continues to be standardized testing. Simply put, a standardized test measures the general knowledge of a particular student group. The SAT, taken nation-wide by graduating high school seniors, is perhaps the most well-known standardized test in the U.S. Standardized tests, such as the SAT, do indeed have their detractors; however, as an experienced educator, I support standardized testing for both high school and middle school students.

One of the greatest benefits of standardized testing is the statistics afforded to administrators. These statistics provide invaluable insight into a school's academic performance. Administrators can then compare their school's performance to other schools within the same district and within the same state. The end result is that administrators can accurately assess the efficacy of the educational system at the local, state, and national level. By doing so, administrators know which schools are performing below average and can take the appropriate action to improve those scores.

Teachers also benefit from standardized testing. For example, if students in a particular middle school are scoring consistently low in math, their teachers can spend more class time on math. By targeting low-scoring subjects, teachers can make better use of class time. In short, standardized testing helps teachers plan their curriculum with a particular focus on maximizing standardized test scores.

Finally, standardized testing not only measures student performance but teacher performance as well. High school students who score consistently high on the SAT, for example, obviously have results-driven teachers. Conversely, if high school students score consistently low on the SAT, a teacher review is warranted. More often than not, low standardized test scores are directly traceable to a lack of teacher performance. Armed with the information, administrators can replace teachers as needed.

(This task continues on the next page.)

Directions: Now listen to a lecture on the same topic.

Now get ready to write your response.

Prompt   Summarize the points made in the lecture and show how they cast doubt on the points made in the reading.

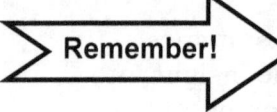   *You can look at the reading passage as you write your essay.*

Writing Time – 20 minutes

___

audio script pg. 291   *   proficiency checklist pg. 231   *   rating guide pg. 232

add your rating to Test #4 box pg. 230

Task #2 - *Independent Essay*

Directions: Read the following prompt, then write an independent essay.

> Prompt   How has learning a new language changed you? Use examples and reasons to support your argument.

Writing Time – 30 minutes

proficiency checklist pg. 234 * rating guide pg. 235

add your rating to Test #4 box pg. 230

Answer Key

PG.	TEST ONE	TRK	QUESTION	ANSWER
12	**READING SECTION**			
13	#1 - *Tulip Bubble*		1	B
			2	A
			3	C
			4	D
			5	4
			6	C
			7	B
			8	C
			9	A
			10	A
			11	A
			12	D
			13	2 4 5
17	#2 - *Women of Liberia...*		1	C
			2	B
			3	A
			4	B
			5	A
			6	A
			7	1
			8	D
			9	C
			10	C
			11	A
			12	1 4 5
			13	Taylor: 3 4 9
				Gbowee: 2 6 7 8
21	#3 - *Crypsis*		1	1
			2	C
			3	C
			4	B
			5	B
			6	A

PG.	TEST ONE	TRK	QUESTION	ANSWER
21	#3 - Crypsis (cont'd)		7	D
			8	B
			9	B
			10	A
			11	A
			12	1 4 6
			13	frogmouth: 3 5 9
				lo moth: 4 6 8
				octopus: 2
26	**LISTENING SECTION**			
27	#1 - Alzheimer's...	1	1	C
			2	B
			3	A
			4	B C
			5	B A D C
			6	Y N N Y Y
30	#2 - Bio Classification	2	1	B
			2	A C D
			3	A
			4	A C D
			5	B
			6	B A C
33	#3 - Wernher Von Braun	3	1	A
			2	A D E
			3	A
			4	A
			5	D C A B
			6	N Y Y Y N
36	#4 - Flooding	4	1	B
			2	B
			3	D
			4	B
			5	B C A D
			6	C A B

PG.	TEST ONE	TRK	QUESTION	ANSWER
39	#5 - *Vivisection*	5	1	C
			2	D
			3	B
			4	B
			5	A
41	#6 - *Art Exhibition*	6	1	D
			2	B
			3	D
			4	C
			5	B
44	**SPEAKING SECTION**	7-10		For scoring, see pg. 218
55	**WRITING SECTION**	11		For scoring, see pg. 228
59	**TEST TWO**	**TRK**	**QUESTION**	**ANSWER**
60	**READING SECTION**			
61	#1 - *Public Education*		1	A
			2	B
			3	A
			4	D
			5	D
			6	B
			7	C
			8	B
			9	2
			10	D
			11	B
			12	D
			13	2 3 5
66	#2 - *Women of Influence*		1	C
			2	A
			3	1
			4	B
			5	A
			6	C
			7	B

PG.	TEST TWO	TRK	QUESTION	ANSWER
66	#2 - Women... (cont'd)		8	D
			9	B
			10	C
			11	C
			12	3 4 6
			13	Austen: 1 3 6
				Fossey: 2 5 7 9
71	#3 - Penicillin		1	D
			2	D
			3	B
			4	A
			5	B
			6	D
			7	B
			8	C
			9	B
			10	3
			11	B
			12	4 5 6
			13	sepsis: 2 7 8
				penicillin: 1 5 6 9
76	**LISTENING SECTION**			
77	#1 - Low Essay Grade	12	1	D
			2	B
			3	B C
			4	C
			5	C
79	#2 - Adam Smith	13	1	B
			2	D
			3	C
			4	B
			5	C B A D
			6	B C A

PG.	TEST TWO	TRK	QUESTION	ANSWER
82	#3 - Wi-fi Problem	14	1	B
			2	C
			3	A C D
			4	D
			5	B
84	#4 - Garbage Patch	15	1	C
			2	B
			3	B
			4	A C
			5	C D B A
			6	N N Y Y
87	#5 - Supreme Court Case	16	1	C
			2	B
			3	D
			4	A
			5	B
			6	N N Y Y
90	#6 - Aristotle's Appeals	17	1	D
			2	B
			3	A C E
			4	A
			5	C A D B
			6	Y N Y N Y
94	**SPEAKING SECTION**	18-21		For scoring, see pg. 218
105	**WRITING SECTION**	22		For scoring, see pg. 228
109	**TEST THREE**	**TRK**	**QUESTION**	**ANSWER**
110	**READING SECTION**			
111	#1 - Research Methods		1	C
			2	B
			3	C
			4	A
			5	C
			6	A

PG.	TEST THREE	TRK	QUESTION	ANSWER
111	#1 - Research... (cont'd)		7	D
			8	3
			9	A
			10	A
			11	B
			12	B
			13	D
			14	A
			15	B
			16	D
			17	quantitative: 2 4 6
				qualitative: 5 7 8 9
116	#2 - Cognitive Bias		1	B
			2	B
			3	D
			4	B
			5	C
			6	D
			7	D
			8	2
			9	C
			10	D
			11	bandwagon: 2 4 8
				stereotyping: 7 9
				halo effect: 3 5
			12	1 3 6
120	#3 - Railroad Boom		1	C
			2	D
			3	B
			4	D
			5	A
			6	C
			7	3
			8	A
			9	B
			10	D
			11	2 5 6

PG.	TEST THREE	TRK	QUESTION	ANSWER
124	**LISTENING SECTION**			
125	#1 - *PowerPoint*	23	1	C
			2	D
			3	C
			4	A D E
			5	B
127	#2 - *Housing Middle Ages*	24	1	C
			2	D
			3	B
			4	A
			5	Y N N Y Y
			6	B
130	#3 - *Black Mask*	25	1	C
			2	A B C
			3	D
			4	B
			5	D A C B
			6	B A C
133	#4 - *Knock-offs*	26	1	A
			2	C
			3	C
			4	A C E
			5	B
			6	Y Y N N Y
136	#5 - *eBooks*	27	1	B
			2	D
			3	B C E
			4	A
			5	B
138	#6 - *Impressionists...*	28	1	C
			2	B D E
			3	D
			4	C
			5	C
			6	Y N Y Y N

PG.	TEST THREE	TRK	QUESTION	ANSWER
142	**SPEAKING SECTION**	29-32		For scoring, see pg. 218
153	**WRITING SECTION**	33		For scoring, see pg. 228

PG.	TEST FOUR	TRK	QUESTION	ANSWER
157				
158	**READING SECTION**			
159	#1 - *American Bison*		1	B
			2	D
			3	B
			4	A
			5	D
			6	1
			7	B
			8	C
			9	B
			10	C
			11	D
			12	B
			13	1 3 5
163	#2 - *Eames*		1	B
			2	A
			3	D
			4	C
			5	A
			6	4
			7	A
			8	C
			9	A
			10	D
			11	C
			12	C
			13	furniture: 2 4 5 7
				other: 1 3 8
167	#3 - *Plant Defenses...*		1	A
			2	D
			3	D
			4	B

PG.	TEST FOUR	TRK	QUESTION	ANSWER
167	#3 - Plants... (cont'd)		5	C
			6	B
			7	D
			8	1
			9	A
			10	A
			11	A
			12	A
			13	1 2 6
			14	induced: 1 4 8
				constitutive: 2 3 5 6
172	**LISTENING SECTION**			
173	#1 - Malware	34	1	D
			2	B
			3	A
			4	D C A B
			5	V, TH, V, TH, V
			6	A
176	#2 - Panama Canal	35	1	D
			2	B
			3	B C E
			4	A
			5	B A C
			6	C
179	#3 - Pacific NW Tribes	36	1	C
			2	A B E
			3	D
			4	D
			5	B D E
			6	D
181	#4 - Slang vs. Jargon	37	1	C
			2	D
			3	C
			4	B C E
			5	B

PG.	TEST FOUR	TRK	QUESTION	ANSWER
183	#5 - Internship	38	1	B
			2	D
			3	A
			4	B C D
			5	B
185	#6 - Early Middle Ages	39	1	C
			2	B C D
			3	A B E
			4	D
			5	C
			6	C B A
189	**SPEAKING SECTION**	40-43		For scoring, see pg. 218
200	**WRITING SECTION**	44		For scoring, see pg. 228

Reading: Calculating Scores

To calculate reading section scores, follow these steps.

1) Total the number of correct answers for each task (see box below). Total the three task scores for a raw score.

TEST #1 – PAGE 12

Task #1	=	10 / 14
Task #2	=	15 / 17
Task #3	=	15 / 17
Raw Score	**=**	**40 / 48**

2) Convert your raw score to a speaking section score (see chart on next page).

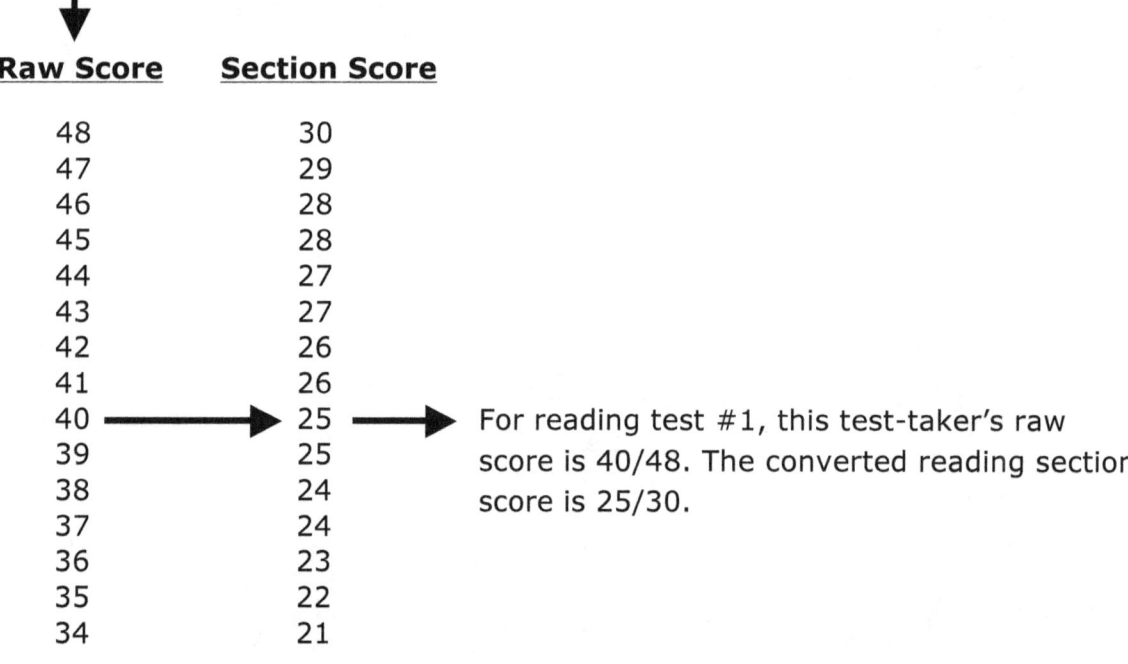

Raw Score	Section Score
48	30
47	29
46	28
45	28
44	27
43	27
42	26
41	26
40	25
39	25
38	24
37	24
36	23
35	22
34	21

For reading test #1, this test-taker's raw score is 40/48. The converted reading section score is 25/30.

3) Repeat these steps for each reading section. Record your raw scores on the next page. Use the conversion chart to find your reading section scores.

4) Add your reading section scores to the applicable test box on page 238.

Reading Sections: *Raw Scores*

TEST #1 – PAGE 12	
Task #1 =	/ 14
Task #2 =	/ 17
Task #3 =	/ 17
Raw Score =	/ 48

TEST #2 – PAGE 60	
Task #1 =	/ 14
Task #2 =	/ 17
Task #3 =	/ 17
Raw Score =	/ 48

TEST #3 – PAGE 110	
Task #1 =	/ 20
Task #2 =	/ 16
Task #3 =	/ 12
Raw Score =	/ 48

TEST #4 – PAGE 158	
Task #1 =	/ 14
Task #2 =	/ 16
Task #3 =	/ 18
Raw Score =	/ 48

Reading Section Conversion Chart

Raw Score	Section Score	Raw Score	Section Score
48	30	33	21
47	29	32	20
46	28	31	20
45	28	30	19
44	27	29	19
43	27	28	18
42	26	27	17
41	26	26	17
40	25	25	16
39	25	24	15
38	24	23	14
37	24	22	14
36	23	21	13
35	22	20	12
34	21		

Listening: Calculating Scores

To calculate each listening section score, follow these steps.

1) Total the number of correct answers for each task (see box below). Total the six task scores for a raw score.

Test #1 – Page 26		
Task #1	=	9 / 9
Task #2	=	9 / 9
Task #3	=	6 / 10
Task #4	=	8 / 8
Task #5	=	4 / 5
Task #6	=	4 / 5
Raw Score	=	**40 / 46**

2) Convert your raw score to a listening section score (see chart on next page).

Raw Score	Section Score
44	29
43	28
42	28
41	27
40	27
39	26
38	25
37	25
36	24

For test #1, this test-taker's raw score is 40/46. The converted listening section score is 27/30.

3) Repeat these steps for each listening section. Record your raw scores on the next page. Use the conversion chart to find your listening section scores.

4) Add your listening section scores to the applicable test box on page 238.

Listening Sections: *Raw Scores*

TEST #1 – PAGE 26	
Task #1 =	/ 9
Task #2 =	/ 9
Task #3 =	/ 10
Task #4 =	/ 8
Task #5 =	/ 5
Task #6 =	/ 5
Raw Score =	/ 46

TEST #2 – PAGE 76	
Task #1 =	/ 5
Task #2 =	/ 8
Task #3 =	/ 6
Task #4 =	/ 9
Task #5 =	/ 8
Task #6 =	/ 10
Raw Score =	/ 46

TEST #3 – PAGE 124	
Task #1 =	/ 6
Task #2 =	/ 8
Task #3 =	/ 9
Task #4 =	/ 9
Task #5 =	/ 6
Task #6 =	/ 9
Raw Score =	/ 47

TEST #4 – PAGE 172	
Task #1 =	/ 9
Task #2 =	/ 8
Task #3 =	/ 8
Task #4 =	/ 6
Task #5 =	/ 6
Task #6 =	/ 9
Raw Score =	/ 46

Listening Section Conversion Chart

Raw Score	Section Score	Raw Score	Section Score
47	30	32	22
46	30	31	22
45	29	30	20
44	29	29	19
43	28	28	19
42	28	27	18
41	27	26	17
40	27	25	17
39	26	24	16
38	25	23	15
37	25	22	15
36	24	21	14
35	24	20	14
34	23	19	13
33	23	18	13

Speaking: Calculating Scores

According to Educational Testing Service, each spoken response will be rated by "3 to 6 certified raters." Their ratings will be averaged, then converted into an official speaking section score out of 30 total points. If you can find "3 to 6 certified raters," great. If not, calculate your speaking scores by following these steps.

1) Record your responses using an audio recording device.

2) Check tasks #1 and #2 for proficiency using the *Independent Speaking Proficiency Checklist* on page 221. Using the checklist, rate tasks #1 and #2 using the *Independent Speaking Rating Guide* on page 222. For example, you rated 2.5-3.0/4.0 for tasks #1 and #2. Add these ratings to the test #1 ratings box (see box A below). Note: See page 220 for speaking section rating boxes.

3) Check each integrated task (tasks #3, #4, #5, #6) for proficiency using the *Integrated Speaking Proficiency Checklist* on page 224. Rate each response using the *Integrated Speaking Rating Guide* on page 225. Add your ratings to the test #1 ratings box (see box B below).

A

TEST #1 – PAGE 44		
Task #1 =	**2.5-3.0**	**/ 4.0**
Task #2 =	**2.5-3.0**	**/ 4.0**
Task #3 =		/ 4.0
Task #4 =		/ 4.0
Task #5 =		/ 4.0
Task #6 =		/ 4.0
Rating =		/ 24.0

B

TEST #1 – PAGE 44		
Task #1 =	2.5-3.0	/ 4.0
Task #2 =	2.5-3.0	/ 4.0
Task #3 =	**2.5-3.0**	**/ 4.0**
Task #4 =	**2.5-3.0**	**/ 4.0**
Task #5 =	**2.5-3.0**	**/ 4.0**
Task #6 =	**2.5-3.0**	**/ 4.0**
Rating =		/ 24.0

4) Total your six task ratings for a rating out of 24.0 total points.

TEST #1 – PAGE 44

Task #1	=	2.5-3.0	/ 4.0
Task #2	=	2.5-3.0	/ 4.0
Task #3	=	2.5-3.0	/ 4.0
Task #4	=	2.5-3.0	/ 4.0
Task #5	=	2.5-3.0	/ 4.0
Task #6	=	2.5-3.0	/ 4.0

Rating = 15.0-18.0 / 24.0

5) Divide your rating (15.0-18.0) by 6 (six tasks) = 2.5-3.0 / 4.0

6) Convert your average rating (2.5-3.0) to a speaking section score.

Rating	Section Score
4.0	30
3.75	28
3.5	27
3.25	25
3.0	23
2.75	21
2.5	19
2.25	17
2.0	15
1.75	14
1.5	12
1.25	10
1.0	8

For test #1, this test-taker's rating is 2.5-3.0. On test day, this test-taker will score in the 19-23 range with a mid-point speaking section score of 21/30.

7) Repeat these steps for each speaking section. Record your ratings on the next page. Use the conversion chart to find your speaking section scores.

8) Add your mid-point speaking section scores to the applicable test box on page 238.

Speaking Sections: *Ratings*

TEST #1 – PAGE 44	
Task #1 =	/ 4
Task #2 =	/ 4
Task #3 =	/ 4
Task #4 =	/ 4
Task #5 =	/ 4
Task #6 =	/ 4
Rating =	/ 24

TEST #2 – PAGE 94	
Task #1 =	/ 4
Task #2 =	/ 4
Task #3 =	/ 4
Task #4 =	/ 4
Task #5 =	/ 4
Task #6 =	/ 4
Rating =	/ 24

TEST #3 – PAGE 142	
Task #1 =	/ 4
Task #2 =	/ 4
Task #3 =	/ 4
Task #4 =	/ 4
Task #5 =	/ 4
Task #6 =	/ 4
Rating =	/ 24

TEST #4 – PAGE 189	
Task #1 =	/ 4
Task #2 =	/ 4
Task #3 =	/ 4
Task #4 =	/ 4
Task #5 =	/ 4
Task #6 =	/ 4
Rating =	/ 24

Speaking Section Conversion Chart

Rating	Section Score	Rating	Section Score
4.0	30	2.25	17
3.75	28	2.0	15
3.5	27	1.75	14
3.25	25	1.5	12
3.0	23	1.25	10
2.75	21	1.0	8
2.5	19		

Independent Speaking Proficiency Checklist

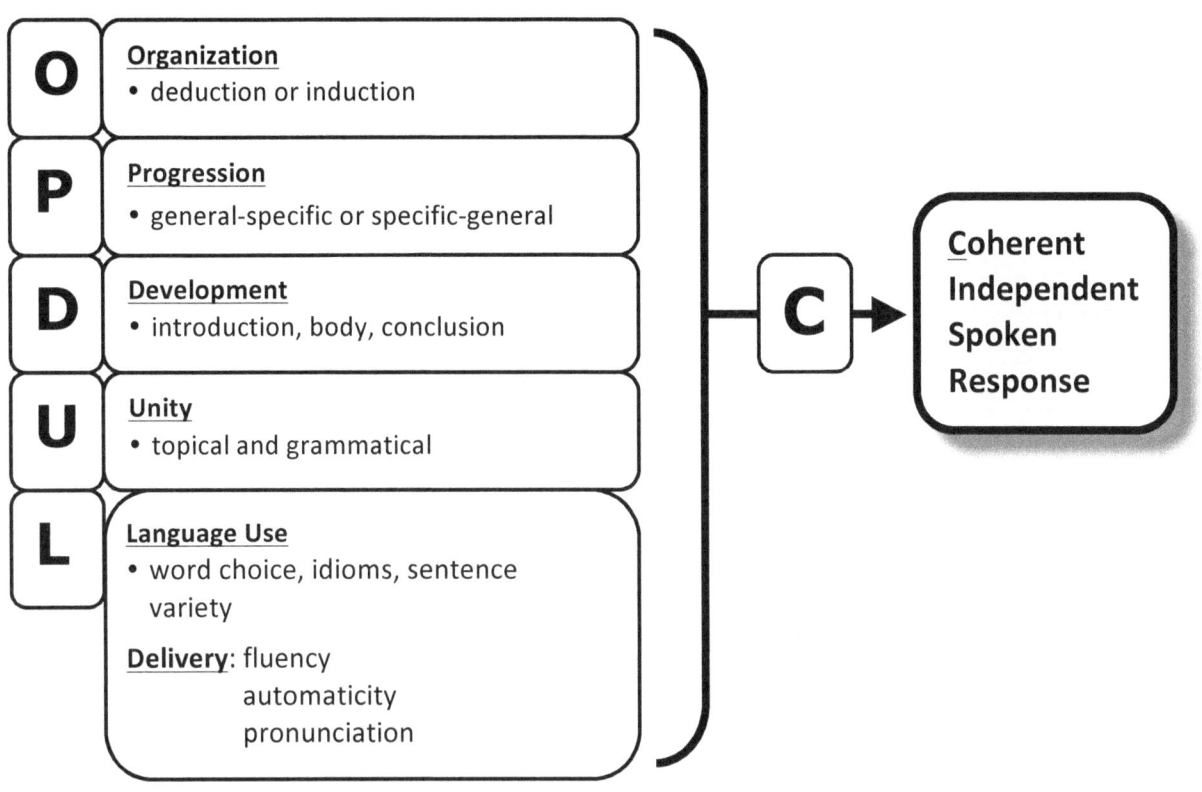

Checklist

1. Does my response demonstrate organization?

   - Deduction   Yes ___ No ___
   - Induction   Yes ___ No ___

2. Does my response demonstrate progression?

   - General-specific   Yes ___ No ___
   - Specific-general   Yes ___ No ___

3. Does my response demonstrate development?

   - Introduction   Yes ___ No ___
   - Body   Yes ___ No ___
   - Conclusion   Yes ___ No ___

4. Does my response demonstrate unity?

   - Topical   Yes ___ No ___
   - Grammatical   Yes ___ No ___

5. Does my response demonstrate proficient language use?

   - Word Choice   Yes ___ No ___
   - Idioms   Yes ___ No ___
   - Sentence variety   Yes ___ No ___

   Is my delivery proficient?

   - Fluency   Yes ___ No ___
   - Automaticity   Yes ___ No ___
   - Pronunciation   Yes ___ No ___

6. Does my response demonstrate coherence?

   Yes ___ No ___

Independent Speaking Rating Guide

Task Rating: 3.5 - 4.0

A response in this range is <u>C</u>oherent because it generally demonstrates proficiency in **all** of the following areas.

<u>O</u> The response demonstrates a clear and consistent method of organization.

<u>P</u> The response demonstrates a clear and consistent progression of ideas.

<u>D</u> The response demonstrates development of the introduction, body and conclusion; the supporting illustrations are clear and well-developed; minor omissions do not effect meaning or coherence.

<u>U</u> The response demonstrates topical and grammatical unity; the relationship between ideas is clear and accurate both topically and grammatically.

<u>L</u> The response demonstrates clear and accurate language use; minor errors in word choice and/or idiom usage and/or syntax do not affect meaning or coherence.

The delivery demonstrates consistent and accurate fluency, pronunciation and automaticity; minor difficulties in each area do not affect meaning and/or coherence, or require listener effort to understand.

Task Rating: 2.5 - 3.0

A response in this range demonstrates proficiency in at least **two** of the following areas.

<u>O</u> The response demonstrates organization.

<u>P</u> The response demonstrates a progression of ideas.

<u>D</u> The response demonstrates limited development; the introduction, body and/or conclusion might lack development, particularly in the body.

<u>U</u> The response demonstrates topical and grammatical unity; however, the relationship between ideas might not always be clear or accurate.

L The response demonstrates a limited range of word choice and/or idiom usage, and/or sentence variety; inaccurate word choice and/or idiom usage, and/or syntax errors might make the meaning of some words and sentences unclear.

The delivery demonstrates fluency, pronunciation and automaticity; however, difficulties in one or more areas requires listener effort to understand.

Task Rating: 1.5 – 2.0

A response in this range demonstrates a lack of proficiency in at least **two** of the following areas.

O The response demonstrates a serious lack of organization.

P The response demonstrates a serious lack of progression.

D The response demonstrates limited development; the examples lack details and repeat.

U The response demonstrates a lack of topical and grammatical unity; the connection of ideas is not clear or accurate.

L The response demonstrates a limited range of word choice and/or idiom usage and/or sentence variety; however, inaccurate word choice and/or idiom usage, and/or syntax errors makes the meaning of words and sentences unclear. The delivery demonstrates difficulties in fluency and/or pronunciation, and/or automaticity; these difficulties make the meaning of words and sentences unclear and require listener effort to understand.

Task Rating: 0.0 - 1.0

A response in this range demonstrates a serious lack of proficiency in at least **two** of the following areas.

O The response demonstrates a serious lack of organization.

P The response demonstrates a serious lack of progression.

D The response demonstrates a serious lack of development in all areas.

U The response demonstrates a serious lack of topical and grammatical unity.

L The response demonstrates a serious lack of language use in all areas.

Integrated Speaking Proficiency Checklist

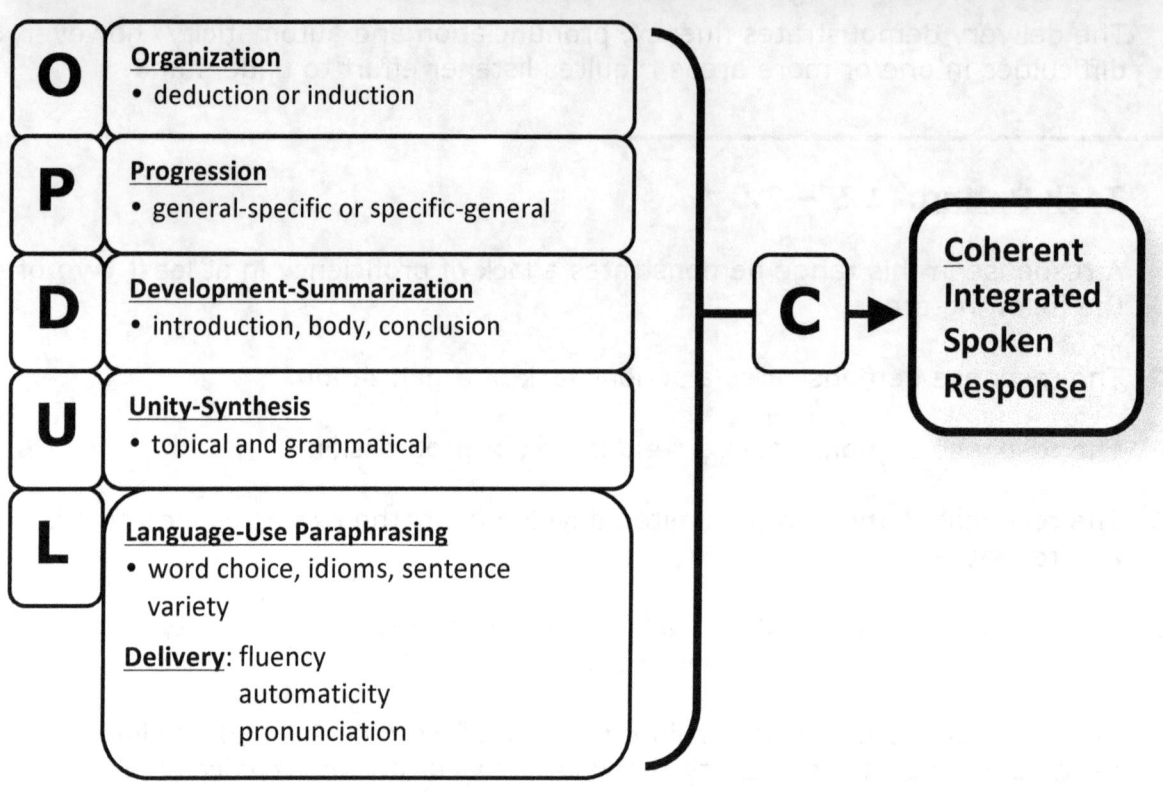

Checklist

1. <u>Does my response demonstrate organization?</u>

    • Deduction   Yes ___ No ___
    • Induction   Yes ___ No ___

2. <u>Does my response demonstrate progression?</u>

    • General-specific   Yes ___ No ___
    • Specific-general   Yes ___ No ___

3. <u>Does my response demonstrate development-summarization?</u>

    • Introduction   Yes ___ No ___
    • Body   Yes ___ No ___
    • Conclusion   Yes ___ No ___

4. <u>Does my response demonstrate unity-synthesis?</u>

    • Topical   Yes ___ No ___
    • Grammatical   Yes ___ No ___

5. <u>Does my response demonstrate proficient language-use paraphrasing?</u>

    • Word choice   Yes ___ No ___
    • Idioms   Yes ___ No ___
    • Sentence variety   Yes ___ No ___

    <u>Is my delivery proficient?</u>

    • Fluency   Yes ___ No ___
    • Automaticity   Yes ___ No ___
    • Pronunciation   Yes ___ No ___

6. <u>Does my response demonstrate coherence?</u>

    Yes ___ No ___

Integrated Speaking Rating Guide

Task Rating: 3.5 - 4.0

A response in this range is <u>C</u>oherent because it generally demonstrates proficiency in **all** of the following areas.

<u>O</u> The response demonstrates a clear and consistent method of organization.

<u>P</u> The response demonstrates a clear and consistent progression of ideas.

<u>D</u> The response demonstrates development-summarization of the introduction, body and conclusion; the main idea and supporting illustrations are well developed; minor omissions do not affect meaning or coherence.

<u>U</u> The response demonstrates unity-synthesis; the relationship between ideas is clear and accurate both topically and grammatically.

<u>L</u> The response demonstrates clear and accurate language-use paraphrasing; minor errors in word choice and/or idiom usage, and/or syntax do not affect meaning or coherence.

The delivery demonstrates consistent and accurate fluency, pronunciation and automaticity; minor difficulties in each area do not affect meaning and/or coherence.

Task Rating: 2.5 - 3.0

A response in this range demonstrates proficiency in at least **two** of the following areas.

<u>O</u> The response demonstrates organization.

<u>P</u> The response demonstrates a progression of ideas; however, it might not always be accurate or clear.

<u>D</u> The response demonstrates development-summarization; however, the introduction, body and/or conclusion might be incomplete due to a lack of details and/or a point not being sufficiently explained.

<u>U</u> The response demonstrates unity-synthesis; however, the relationship between ideas might not always be clear, accurate or consistent due to a lack of topical and/or grammatical unity.

L The response demonstrates limited language-use paraphrasing; word choice and/or idiom usage, and/or syntax might be inaccurate or incomplete making the meaning of words and sentences unclear.

Minor difficulties in fluency and/or pronunciation and/or automaticity require listener effort to understand.

Task Rating: 1.5 - 2.0

A response in this range demonstrates a serious lack of proficiency in at least **two** of the following areas.

O The response demonstrates a serious lack of organization.

P The response demonstrates a serious lack of progression.

D The response demonstrates limited and incomplete development-summarization.

U The response demonstrates a lack of unity-synthesis; the connection of ideas is
not clear, accurate or consistent; the response is often off topic because the test-taker does not understand the requirements of the task.

L The response demonstrates limited language use with little or no paraphrasing; inaccurate word choice and/or syntax errors makes the meaning of words and sentences consistently unclear.

The delivery demonstrates frequent difficulties in fluency and/or pronunciation and/or automaticity; these difficulties make the meaning of words and sentences unclear and require listener effort to understand.

Task Rating: 0.0 - 1.0

A response in this range demonstrates a serious lack of proficiency in **two or more** of the following areas.

O The response demonstrates a serious lack of organization.

P The response demonstrates a serious lack of progression.

D The response demonstrates a serious lack of development-summarization in all areas.

U The response demonstrates a serious lack of unity-synthesis in all areas.

L The response demonstrates a serious lack of language-use paraphrasing in all areas.

Notes

Writing: Calculating Scores

According to ETS, each written response will be rated by "2 to 4 certified raters." Their ratings will be averaged, then converted into an official writing section score out of 30 total points. If you can find "2 to 4 certified raters," great. If not, calculate your practice writing responses by following these steps.

1) Check your integrated essay for proficiency using the *Integrated Essay Proficiency Checklist* on page 231, then rate it using the *Integrated Essay Rating Guide* on page 232. For example, you checked, then rated your integrated essay. You rated 4.0-5.0/5.0 Enter this score (see box A below). <u>Note</u>: See page 230 for writing section rating boxes.

2) Check your independent essay for proficiency using the *Independent Essay Proficiency Checklist* on page 234, then rate it using the *Independent Essay Rating Guide* on page 235. For example, you checked, then rated your independent essay. You rated 4.0-5.0/5.0 Enter this score (see box B below).

A

TEST #1 – PAGE 55		
Task #1 =	**4.0-5.0**	**/ 5.0**
Task #2 =		/ 5.0
Rating =		/ 10.0

B

TEST #1 – PAGE 55		
Task #1 =	4.0-5.0	/ 5.0
Task #2 =	**4.0-5.0**	**/ 5.0**
Rating =		/ 10.0

3) Total your two task scores for a rating out of 10.0.

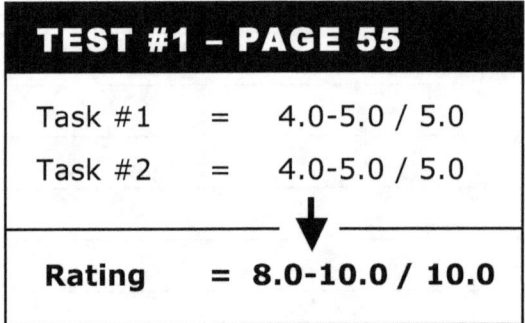

4) Divide your rating (8.0-10.0/10.0) by 2 (two tasks) = 4.0-5.0 / 5.0

5) Convert your rating (4.0-5.0/5.0) to a writing section score.

Rating	Section Score
5.0	30
4.75	29
4.5	**28**
4.25	27
4.0	25
3.75	24
3.5	22
3.25	21
3.0	20
2.75	18
2.5	17
2.25	15
2.0	14
1.75	12

For test #1, this test taker's rating is 4.0-5.0. On test day, this test-taker will score in the 25-30 range with a mid-point writing section score of 28/30.

6) Repeat these steps for each writing section. Record your ratings on the next page. Use the conversion chart to find your writing section scores.

7) Add your mid-point writing section scores to the applicable test box on page 238.

Writing Sections: *Ratings*

TEST #1 – PAGE 55	
Task #1 =	/ 5.0
Task #2 =	/ 5.0
Rating =	/ 10.0

TEST #2 – PAGE 105	
Task #1 =	/ 5.0
Task #2 =	/ 5.0
Rating =	/ 10.0

TEST #3 – PAGE 153	
Task #1 =	/ 5.0
Task #2 =	/ 5.0
Rating =	/ 10.0

TEST #4 – PAGE 200	
Task #1 =	/ 5.0
Task #2 =	/ 5.0
Rating =	/ 10.0

Writing Section Conversion Chart

Rating	Section Score	Rating	Section Score
5.0	30	3.25	21
4.75	29	3.0	20
4.5	28	2.75	18
4.25	27	2.5	17
4.0	25	2.25	15
3.75	24	2.0	14
3.5	22	1.75	12

Integrated Essay Proficiency Checklist

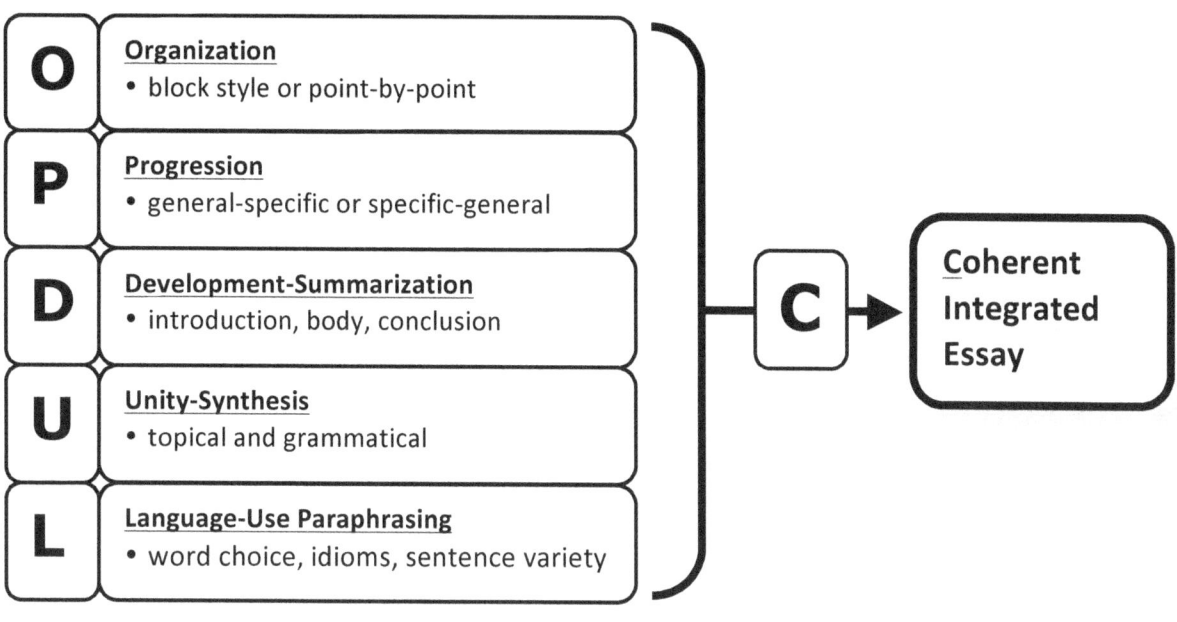

Checklist

1. Does my essay demonstrate organization?

   - Block style   Yes ___ No ___
   - Point-by-point   Yes ___ No ___

2. Does my essay demonstrate progression?

   - General-specific   Yes ___ No ___
   - Specific-general   Yes ___ No ___

3. Does my essay demonstrate development-summarization?

   - Introduction   Yes ___ No ___
   - Body   Yes ___ No ___
   - Conclusion   Yes ___ No ___

4. Does my essay demonstrate unity-synthesis?

   - Topical   Yes ___ No ___
   - Grammatical   Yes ___ No ___

5. Does my essay demonstrate proficient language-use paraphrasing?

   - Word choice   Yes ___ No ___
   - Idioms   Yes ___ No ___
   - Sentence variety   Yes ___ No ___

6. Does my essay demonstrate coherence?

   Yes ___ No ___

Integrated Essay Rating Guide

Task Rating: 4.0 - 5.0

An essay in this range is <u>C</u>oherent because it generally demonstrates proficiency in **all** of the following areas.

<u>O</u> The essay demonstrates a clear and consistent method of organization that accurately shows how the main points in the lecture relate to the main points in the reading.

<u>P</u> The essay demonstrates a clear and consistent progression of ideas.

<u>D</u> The essay demonstrates development-summarization of the introduction, body and conclusion of both the lecture and the reading; the main points are clear and well-developed; some points might lack development and/or a lecture point might not be completely explained.

<u>U</u> The essay demonstrates unity-synthesis; some topical and/or grammatical connections between the lecture and the reading might not be clear or accurate. These errors are minor and do not affect meaning or coherence.

<u>L</u> The essay demonstrates consistent and accurate language-use paraphrasing; some word choice and/or idiom usage might not be accurate or clear, and/or there might be syntax errors. These errors are minor and do not affect meaning or the connection of the main points.

Task Rating: 2.5 - 3.5

An essay in this range demonstrates a lack of proficiency in **one or more** of the following areas.

<u>O</u> The essay demonstrates organization; however, the connection between the main points in the lecture and the main points in the reading is not always clear or consistent.

<u>P</u> The essay demonstrates a progression of ideas; however, it might not always be clear or consistent.

<u>D</u> The essay demonstrates development-summarization; however, the main points in the introduction, body and/or conclusion of the lecture and/or the reading might lack development, and/or a main point in the lecture might be missing.

U The essay demonstrates topical and grammatical unity; however, the connection between the main lecture and reading points is not always clear or accurate.

L The essay demonstrates basic language-use paraphrasing with limited sentence variety; frequent and inaccurate word choice and/or idiom usage, and/or errors in syntax make the meaning of some sentences and connections unclear.

Task Rating: 1.0 - 2.0

An essay in this range demonstrates a serious lack of proficiency in **one or more** of the following areas.

O The essay demonstrates a serious lack of organization; the connection between the main points in the lecture and the main points in the reading is not clear or accurate.

P The essay demonstrates a serious lack of progression.

D The essay demonstrates a serious lack of development-summarization in the introduction, body and conclusion of the lecture and the reading; some points have been summarized; however, most lecture points are missing, and/or the summarization of the lecture and/or the reading is not clear or accurate.

U The essay demonstrates a serious lack of topical and grammatical unity; the main points in the lecture and the reading are not topically related and/or the connections between points is not accurate or clear.

L The essay demonstrates a serious lack of language-use paraphrasing; frequent errors in basic word choice and/or syntax make the meaning of sentences unclear.

Independent Essay Proficiency Checklist

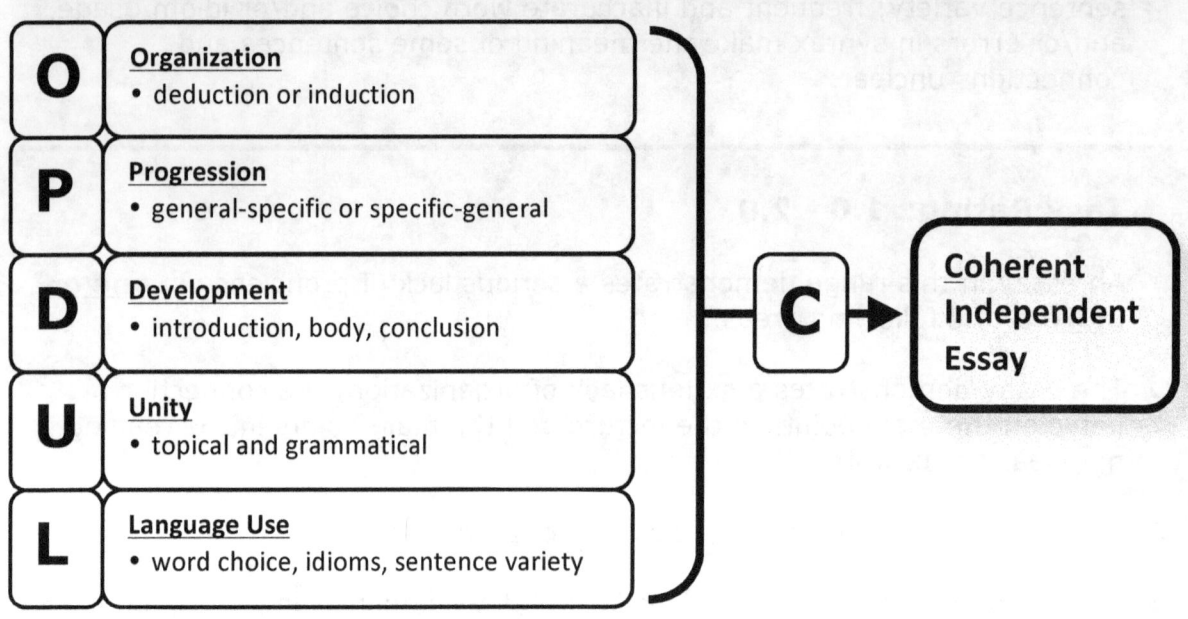

Checklist

1. <u>Does my essay demonstrate organization?</u>

   - Deduction   Yes ___ No ___
   - Induction   Yes ___ No ___

2. <u>Does my essay demonstrate progression?</u>

   - General-specific   Yes ___ No ___
   - Specific-general   Yes ___ No ___

3. <u>Does my essay demonstrate development?</u>

   - Introduction   Yes ___ No ___
   - Body   Yes ___ No ___
   - Conclusion   Yes ___ No ___

4. <u>Does my essay demonstrate unity?</u>

   - Topical   Yes ___ No ___
   - Grammatical   Yes ___ No ___

5. <u>Does my essay demonstrate proficient language use?</u>

   - Word choice   Yes ___ No ___
   - Idioms   Yes ___ No ___
   - Sentence variety   Yes ___ No ___

6. <u>Does my essay demonstrate coherence?</u>

                        Yes ___ No ___

Independent Essay Rating Guide

Task Rating: 4.0 - 5.0

An essay in this range is <u>C</u>oherent because it generally demonstrates proficiency in **all** of the following areas.

<u>O</u> The essay demonstrates a clear and consistent method of organization.

<u>P</u> The essay demonstrates a clear and consistent progression of ideas.

<u>D</u> The essay demonstrates development of the introduction, body and conclusion; the supporting illustrations are clear and well developed; some areas might lack development and/or an idea might not be completely explained.

<u>U</u> The essay demonstrates topical and grammatical unity; some topical and/or grammatical connections might not be clear or accurate. These errors are minor and do not affect meaning or coherence.

<u>L</u> The essay demonstrates consistent language use; some word choice and/or idiom usage might not be clear or accurate, and/or there might be syntax errors. These errors are minor and do not affect meaning or coherence.

Task Rating: 2.5 - 3.5

An essay in this range demonstrates a lack of proficiency in **one or more** of the following areas.

<u>O</u> The essay demonstrates organization; however, it might not always be clear or consistent.

<u>P</u> The essay demonstrates a progression of ideas; however, it might not always be clear or consistent.

<u>D</u> The essay demonstrates development; however, the introduction, body and/or conclusion might lack development, and/or might not provide enough supporting examples or be sufficiently explained.

<u>U</u> The essay demonstrates topical and grammatical unity; however, there might be topical digressions and/or connections that are not always clear or accurate.

L The essay demonstrates basic but accurate language use with limited sentence variety; inaccurate word choice and/or idiom usage, and/or syntax errors might make the meaning of some sentences unclear.

Task Rating: 1.0 - 2.0

An essay in this range demonstrates a serious lack of proficiency in **one or more** areas:

O The essay demonstrates a serious lack of organization.

P The essay demonstrates a serious lack of progression.

D The essay demonstrates a serious lack of development in all areas.

U The essay demonstrates a serious lack of topical and grammatical unity.

L The essay demonstrates a serious lack of language use in all areas.

Notes

Scoring Multi-Answer Questions

Use this guide when scoring all multi-answer reading and listening questions.

1-point question =	2 ✓ =	1 point
	1 ✓ =	0 points
2-point question =	3 ✓ =	2 points
	2 ✓ =	1 point
	1 ✓ =	0 points
2-point question =	4 ✓ =	2 points
	3 ✓ =	1 point
	2 ✓ =	0 points
	1 ✓ =	0 points
3-point question =	5 ✓ =	3 points
	4 ✓ =	2 points
	3 ✓ =	1 point
	2 ✓ =	0 points
	1 ✓ =	0 points
4-point question =	7 ✓ =	4 points
	6 ✓ =	3 points
	5 ✓ =	2 points
	4 ✓ =	1 points
	3 ✓ =	0 point
	2 ✓ =	0 points
	1 ✓ =	0 points

Test Scores

To calculate each test score, first enter each section score, then total the four section scores for a test score out of 120 total points. Next, calculate your TOEFL iBT range score on the next page.

TEST #1 – PAGE 11

Reading	=	/ 30
Listening	=	/ 30
Speaking	=	/ 30
Writing	=	/ 30
Score	=	/ 120

TEST #2 – PAGE 59

Reading	=	/ 30
Listening	=	/ 30
Speaking	=	/ 30
Writing	=	/ 30
Score	=	/ 120

TEST #3 – PAGE 109

Reading	=	/ 30
Listening	=	/ 30
Speaking	=	/ 30
Writing	=	/ 30
Score	=	/ 120

TEST #4 – PAGE 157

Reading	=	/ 30
Listening	=	/ 30
Speaking	=	/ 30
Writing	=	/ 30
Score	=	/ 120

Range Scores

When doing practice tests, it is not possible to replicate official test conditions thus it is not possible to determine a single-number TOEFL iBT score. However, you can calculate your range score. To calculate your range score, follow these steps.

1) Total your section scores for a test score out of 120 total points (see pg. 238).

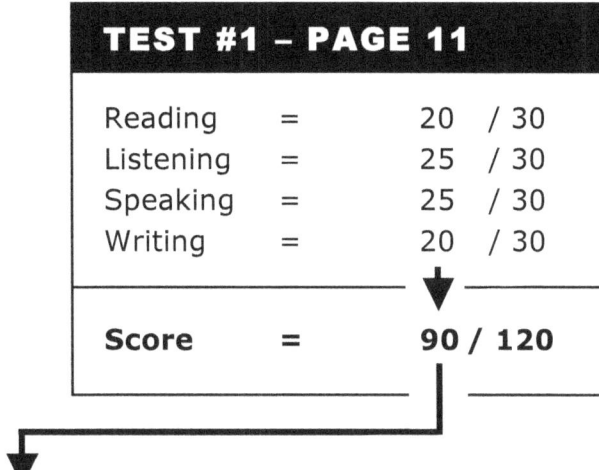

2) Convert your <u>score</u> into an eleven-point range score with the test score (in this example 90) the mid-point of the range.

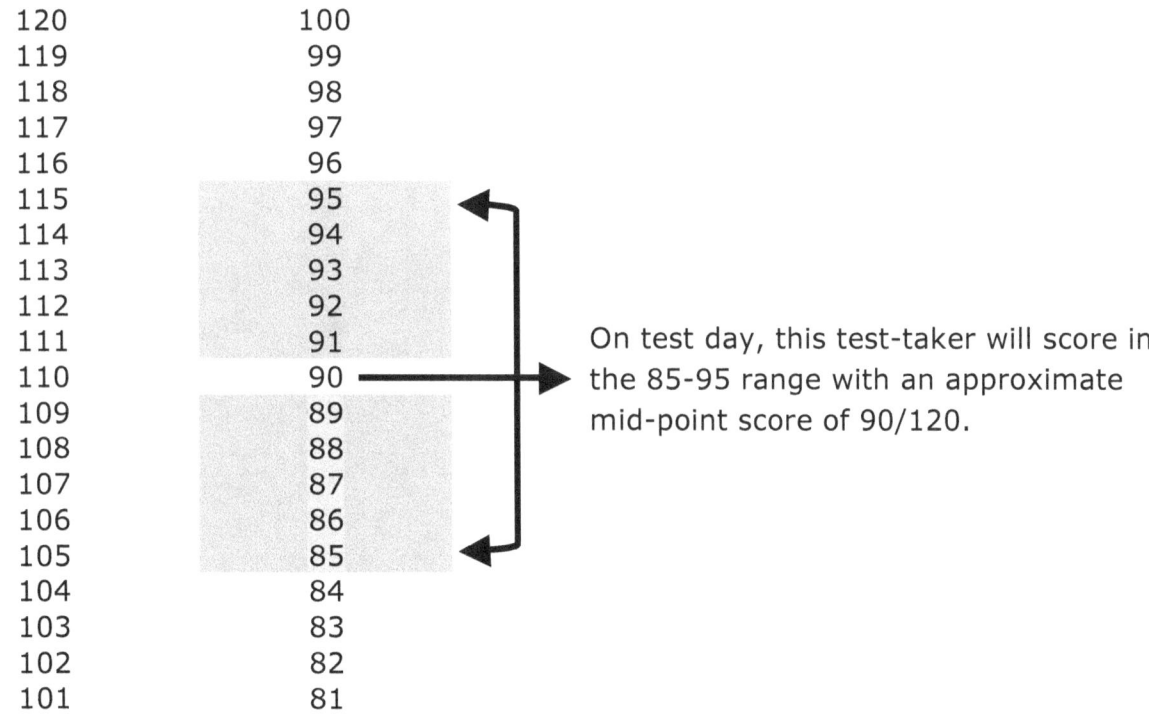

On test day, this test-taker will score in the 85-95 range with an approximate mid-point score of 90/120.

Range Score Conversion Chart

120	100	80	60
119	99	79	59
118	98	78	58
117	97	77	57
116	96	76	56
115	95	75	55
114	94	74	54
113	93	73	53
112	92	72	52
111	91	71	51
110	90	70	50
109	89	69	49
108	88	68	48
107	87	67	47
106	86	66	46
105	85	65	45
104	84	64	44
103	83	63	43
102	82	62	42
101	81	61	41

 In 2010, the average worldwide TOEFL iBT score was 80/120.*
In 2009... 79/120.*
In 2008... 79/120.*

* Data courtesy of Educational Testing Service (ETS)

Audio Scripts

Test 1 - Listening - Page 26

Task 1 - *Alzheimer's Disease* - Track 1 - Page 27

Narrator: Task one. Directions. Listen to a discussion in a geriatrics class, then answer the questions on the next page.

Prof: Good morning, everyone. We're going to continue our survey of geriatric diseases and disorders. So far we've covered Parkinson's Disease and osteoporosis. Today, we're going to begin our look at Alzheimer's Disease. From the reading, what can you tell me about AD? Betty?

Betty: AD is a degenerative disease. It's the most common form of dementia, dementia being a progressive deterioration of mental functions. The disease bears the name of Alois Alzheimer, a German neuropathologist and psychiatrist born in 1864 in Bavaria. Early in his career, Alzheimer wrote extensively on depression and schizophrenia with a focus on the cerebral cortex.

Prof: And what is that, the cerebral cortex? Steve?

Steve: The cerebral cortex is a thin layer of neural tissue that covers the cerebrum. Basically, it's a thin gray layer that covers what we call the brain. It's responsible for higher-order functions, such as thinking and understanding language, hearing and vision, all of which contribute to memory and reasoning.

Prof: Good. Anything else?

Steve: In 1901, Alzheimer noticed that an older female patient could not recognize family members and was getting lost in her own home. When the woman died, Alzheimer autopsied her brain and discovered a dramatically reduced number of cells in the cerebral cortex and something he called "tangles."

Prof: Betty, what are tangles? In other words, what had Alzheimer stumbled upon?

Betty: First of all, we need to understand that between brain cells there are microscopic fibers that carry information between cells. These fibers consist primarily of a protein called tau.

Prof: Why is that significant?

Betty: Why? Because Alzheimer discovered abnormal amounts of tau on the cell fibers in the woman's cerebral cortex. This build up—as we now know—causes the nerve cells to become "tangled" or bunched together. A by-product of the tangles is plaque, a protein build up between brain cells. Together, the gradual accumulation of tangles and plaque cuts off the electrical impulses transmitted between nerve cells in the cerebral cortex. The result is neuronal dysfunction and cell death. This leads to the cerebral cortex atrophying, which, in turn, leads to a deterioration in cognitive skills and death. That is what Alzheimer discovered.

Prof: Do we know why tau and plaque combine to cause AD? Steve?

Steve: Unfortunately, no. AD is one of the most widely researched diseases with over 500 clinical trials since 2008, yet we're no closer to understanding its cause or why it progresses. We can only treat it. We can't stop it or reverse its effects.

Prof: Betty, can you describe the types of AD?

Betty: Sure. There's early-onset AD, late-onset AD, and Familial AD. Familial AD is inherited and accounts for only one percent of cases. Early-onset, which is also rare, occurs in ten percent of AD patients before the age of 65. Late-onset AD,

Prof: the most common form of AD, accounts for ninety percent of cases after 65 and affects almost half of those over the age of eighty-five.

Prof: And what are the four stages of AD? Steve?

Steve: It starts with pre-dementia, which is often mistaken for aging or stress. Signs of pre-dementia are problems with daily activities. Memory loss is also an indication of pre-dementia. The patient demonstrates difficulty remembering learned facts and has difficulty acquiring new information.

Prof: Good. The next stage? Betty?

Betty: That would be early AD. Impaired learning and short-term memory loss are more pronounced at this stage. A patient can communicate basic ideas but a loss of vocabulary and a decreasing fluency severely impair oral and written communication. It is during this stage that patients need help or supervision with daily activities. The next stage is moderate AD. With moderate AD, a patient is unable to perform basic activities. Speech is difficult due to a loss or inability to recall words while reading and writing skills are also severely reduced. Subjects also experience anosognosia.

Prof: Could you define that for us?

Steve: Sure. Anosognosia in AD patients is the inability to recognize that they have a disease. Also, patients tend to wander and are irritable. This, in turn, causes great stress for caregivers. It's during this stage that the patient is put into a long-term care facility.

Prof: And the final stage?

Betty: Advanced AD. In this stage, the patient is unable to perform basic activities and is thus completely dependent on caregivers. The ability to speak is reduced to words and phrases, or lost completely. Keep in mind that AD, while a terminal disease, does not cause death. Death in Advanced AD patients results from pneumonia or pressure ulcers.

Prof: Very good. Let me just add that approximately five million Americans have AD and that the incidence of the disease doubles every five years beyond sixty-five. With baby boomers entering retirement age, those numbers will continue to grow exponentially.

Narrator: Now get ready to answer the questions. Answer each question based on what is stated or implied in the discussion.

1. What is the discussion mainly about?
2. What is the point of the discussion?

3. Why does the professor say this?

Prof: With baby boomers entering retirement age, those numbers will continue to grow exponentially.

4. According to the discussion, what don't we know about Alzheimer's Disease? Select two. This is a 1-point question.
5. According to the discussion, Alzheimer's Disease has four stages. Put the stages in order. This is a 2-point question.
6. Complete the chart based on information from the discussion. This is a 3-point question.

Task 2 - *Bio Classification* - Track 2 - Page 30

Narrator: Task two. Directions. Listen to a lecture in a biology class, then answer the questions on the next page.

Prof: 1 → In biological classification, the eight major classifications are ranked hierarchically starting with Life and ending with the Common name. Life is the label given to those objects that have self-sustaining biological processes. Objects that do not signal a self-sustaining biological process are either inanimate, such as rocks, or dead. For an organism to be a self-sustaining biological process, it must have a metabolism, a metabolism being a series of integrated chemical processes that enable the organism to maintain an input-output balance called homeostasis. Homeostasis, in turn, allows a living organism to maintain its structure, to grow, and to reproduce. All living organisms on Earth, including humans, are carbon and water-based cellular structures.

2 → In order to understand the vast complexities of Life, scientists have divided it into Domains. According to the three-Domain system developed by Carl Woese in 1990, Life is comprised of three Domains: Archaea, Bacteria, and Eukarya. Archaea are a large group of prokaryotes, prokaryotes being single-celled microorganisms with no nucleus. Woese discovered and named Archaea in the late 1970's. Archaea live in extreme environments, such as hot springs and deep petroleum deposits. Bacteria are also prokaryotes, yet they are genetically and biochemically distinct from Archaea. At over five nonillion, bacteria form much of the Earth's biomass. Finally, there are Eukarya. Cells within this group are called eukaryotes. These cells have a wall or membrane inside of which there is a nucleus that contains genetic material. Humans cells are eukaryotic.

3 → Following Life and Domain is Kingdom. In 1735, Carl Linnaeus, a Swedish botanist and zoologist credited with establishing binomial nomenclature, the naming of species, believed that there were two kingdoms: Vegetabilia and Animalia. Today that list has grown to six: Bacteria (prokaryotes), Protozoa (eukaryotes), Chromista (a eukaryotic super group), Fungi (eukaryotic organisms, such as yeasts molds and mushrooms), Plantae (trees, herbs, bushes, grasses), and Animalia (multicellular eukaryotic organisms). The Kingdom Plantae is subdivided into three divisions or Phylum: Magnoliopsida, Pinophyta, Bryophyta while the Kingdom Animalia is divided into two Phylum: Chordata (vertebrates, such as humans) and Arthropoda (invertebrates, such as insects). Each Phylum is further divided into a Class. For example, Chordata is divided into two Classes: Amphibia and Mammalia. Amphibians, such as frogs and salamanders, are ectothermic or cold-blooded. However, not all Amphibia are the same thus they are divided into Orders based on the similarities they share. The same holds true for homeothermic Mammalians. One Order of Mammalians is Primates.

4 → Primates are mammals that have large brains, walk on two or four limbs and rely on stereoscopic vision. In Order Primates, there are two distinct classifications called Families: Hominidae (hominids) and Cercopithecidae. Cercopithecidae are Old World monkeys native to Asia and Africa, monkeys such as baboons and macaques while Family Hominidae represents the great apes (gorillas, chimpanzees, orangutans) and humans. One criterion for classifying humans and apes in the same Family is that humans and apes share 97% of the same DNA.

5 → Next, Family Hominidae is divided by genus. Genus is Latin meaning type. The genus Homo includes extinct early humans species. Species, the lowest order of classification, describes a group of organisms that can be classified based on similar physical characteristics and, more importantly, the ability to reproduce their kind. Early human species are Homo neanderthalis, who lived between 130,000 to 30,000 years ago, and Homo habilis, who lived approximately 2.5 million years ago. These early species of the genus Homo had large brains, lived in social groups, and walked upright. The only living species of the Homo genus is the species Homo sapiens, the Common name for which is humans.

6 → Working backwards, human is the Common name for the species Homo sapiens. Homo Sapiens, in turn, belong to the Genus Homo which belongs to the Hominidae Family in the Order Primates, Primates being a part of the Class Mammalia, which is one of the two sub groups in the Phylum Chordata belonging to the Kingdom Animalia, which, along with Kingdom Plantae, comprises Life as we know it.

Narrator: Now get ready to answer the questions. Answer each question based on what is stated or implied in the lecture.

1. What is the topic of the lecture?
2. According to the lecture, Primates have what? Select three. This is a 2-point question.

3. Why does the professor say this?

Prof: However, not all Amphibia are the same thus they are divided into Orders based on the similarities they share.

4. According to Carl Woese, Life is divided into three Domains. What are they? Select three. This is a 2-point question.
5. From the lecture, what can we infer about humans and apes?
6. The professor mentions three topics. Match each topic to its corresponding description. This is a 2-point question.

Task 3 - *Wernher Von Braun* - Track 3 - Page 33

Narrator: Task three. Directions. Listen to a lecture in a history class, then answer the questions on the next page.

Prof: 1 → Everyone knows that America put the first man on the moon. What most don't realize, however, is that the Saturn V, the launch rocket that sent Apollo 11 astronauts Neil Armstrong, Buzz Aldrin and Michael Collins to the moon, was designed by Germans, in particular the rocket scientist and space architect Wernher Von Braun. In 1975, Von Braun was awarded America's highest science award, the National Medal of Science. Many consider Von Braun to be the preeminent rocket scientist of the twentieth century. Others believe that Von Braun was a war criminal.

2 → Wernher Von Braun was born into an aristocratic family on March 23, 1912 in Wirsitz, Germany, now present-day Poland. As a boy, Von Braun did not do well in school. Mathematics and physics gave him particular trouble. Then he read *The Rocket into Interplanetary Space* by rocket pioneer Hermann Oberth. It was a turning point. Inspired by Oberth's book, Von Braun put his nose to the grindstone and

finished at the top of his class. Von Braun, envisioning one day that man would fly to the moon, went on to receive various technical degrees and became a member of the German Society for Space Travel, where he worked with Oberth on liquid-fueled rocket engines. However, the Nationalist Socialist German Workers Party, which took power in 1932, banned all work on rockets that was not government related. Von Braun, not wanting to give up his dream of putting man in space, found work with the German army, designing and testing rockets. By 1934, one of his rockets had flown to a height of 3.5 kilometers. With the German army on the move, rocket development became a top priority of the German military. As a result, a large rocket facility was built at Peenemünde. There Von Braun became the leader of "the rocket team" and was instrumental in developing the V-2, a liquid-propelled, 46-foot long ballistic missile that could hit London five-hundred miles away. The V-2, built by slave labor in underground factories, represents the birth of the rocket age, a lineage that extends through both the American and Russian post-war missile and space programs to this day.

3 → In the spring of 1945, with World War Two rapidly drawing to a close, Von Braun orchestrated the surrender of himself and five hundred of his top scientists to the rapidly advancing American army. By then, the Americans were well aware of Von Braun, so much so that he had topped America's black list, a secret list of German scientists and engineers the Americans were intent on capturing for the knowledge they possessed. Under a plan called Operation Paperclip, Von Braun and many of his colleagues secretly went to work for the American government at Fort Bliss, Texas. There, they continued to design and build rockets, their association with the Nazi party secretly expunged from their public record. Throughout the 1950's, Von Braun and his Peenemünde team represented the cutting edge of rocket technology. They built the Jupiter missile, the first missile to carry a nuclear warhead. Soon after, Von Braun and his team built the Jupiter-C, which carried the first American satellite into Earth orbit, thus signaling the start of the space race.

4 → In 1955, Von Braun became a naturalized American citizen. Meanwhile, he continued to champion the idea of building rockets that would explore space. As early as 1952, his plans for space exploration included space stations and trips to Mars. He even wrote a science fiction novel exploring the possibilities. The American government, however, was more interested in containing the Russian threat than in exploring space. In 1958, the American government formed NASA, the National Aeronautic and Space Program. Two years later, NASA opened the Marshall Space Flight Center and Von Braun was chosen to be the director. Von Braun agreed but on one condition: that he could develop the Saturn rocket, the launch rocket that would send Apollo 11 to the moon. The American government relented. And the rest is history. On July 16, 1969, Von Braun's boyhood dream of sending a man to the moon was realized when Apollo 11 commander Neil Armstrong was the first man to walk on the moon.

5 → Despite Von Braun's achievements, many continue to question his past affiliation with the Nazi party and to what extent he condoned slave labor to build Nazi Germany's rocket program. However history judges Wernher Von Braun, one thing cannot be denied: He put America on the moon.

Narrator: Now get ready to answer the questions. Answer each question based on what is stated or implied in the lecture.

1. On what does the lecture mainly focus?
2. Which three astronauts flew to the moon on Apollo 11? Select three. This is a 2-point question.

3. Why does the professor say this?

Prof: Despite Von Braun's achievements, many continue to question his past affiliation with the Nazi party and to what extent he condoned slave labor to build Nazi Germany's rocket program.

4. From the lecture, what can we infer about Wernher Von Braun?
5. The professor describes the rockets and missiles Wernher Von Braun designed. Put them in historical order. This is a 2-point question.
6. What is true about Wernher Von Braun? This is a 3-point question.

Task 4 - *Flooding* - Track 4 - Page 36

Narrator: Task four. Directions. Listen to a lecture in a science class, then answer the questions on the next page.

Prof: 1 → Water. We take it for granted. Yet without it, life, as we know it, would perish. We use water in myriad ways. We use it for cooking, for cleaning, for generating electricity, and for relaxation. We use it in religious ceremonies, in agriculture, and for transportation. Suffice it to say, water's value is inestimable. And there is a lot of it. Seventy percent of the Earth is covered in water while three-quarters of the human body is water. Some theorize that human blood tastes salty because eons ago, our ancestors lived in the oceans, the salty taste of human blood evidence proving that our ancestors did indeed have aquatic origins. Whatever the case may be, water is the source of life, not only for humans but for all organisms on Earth.

2 → However, much like the Roman god Janus, water has two faces. One is of life while the other is of death. Water's dual nature as savior and destroyer is evidenced in the natural phenomenon known as flooding. In a nutshell, flooding occurs when a body of water escapes its natural boundaries and temporarily submerges the surrounding landscape. Historically, flooding has caused untold human misery and destruction. Witness the Central China floods of 1931, the greatest natural disaster ever recorded. Three great rivers—the Yellow, the Yangtze, and Huai—flooded and left over three million people dead. Yet without flooding, we might not be where we are today.

3 → As a naturally occurring phenomenon, flooding has been, since the dawn of time, an integral part of human evolution. A prime example is the Nile River in Egypt. For ancient Egyptians, the flooding of the Nile was an auspicious event. The Egyptians believed that the flooding was caused by the tears of the goddess Isis as she cried for her dead husband, Osiris. However, a more mundane reason can be found, one that occurred then and today, two thousand miles south of Egypt in equatorial Africa. There, in the hills and mountains of present-day Rwanda, Tanzania and Ethiopia, torrential rains fall from June to September. The rain fills the lakes and rivers that feed the Nile, forcing the Nile to flood its banks as it races north to Egypt and the Mediterranean. For the ancient Egyptians, the annual Nile flood symbolized rebirth. The flooding waters recharged the depleted groundwater while leaving behind a layer of silt in the fields. The silt added much needed nutrients to the heavily farmed soil. This, in turn, fertilized crops, such as flax and wheat, a valuable food source the Egyptians exported. By doing so, the early Egyptians developed wealth and became a major power in the Middle East. In short, without the annual flooding of the Nile, Egyptian civilization, as we now know it, would not exist. The same holds true for Mesopotamia, the land between the Tigris and Euphrates Rivers flowing south through Iraq and into the Persian Gulf. Flood

waters caused by rain and snow melt in Syria and Turkey forced the Tigris and Euphrates to flood their banks and replenish crop fields with much needed silt. This cycle of rebirth through flooding is as old as the Earth itself, for even if man does not stand to benefit, endemic biomass does. The flooding of the Amazon River is a good example of how flood water has sustained the endemic biomass for millennia, in this case the flora and fauna that comprise the immense area called the Amazon Basin.

4 → Yet flooding is indeed a double-edged sword, the aforementioned China floods of 1931 one of the more salient examples of the destructive power of flood water. Another, more recent example, was the 2010 Pakistan flood. Unusually heavy monsoon rains, the worst in almost a century, caused flash flooding, particularly along the Indus River. At one point, one-fifth of Pakistan—an area the size of England—was under water. All told, some twenty million people were affected while over two thousand died. Worse, Pakistan's infrastructure was severely disrupted with the total economic cost estimated at forty billion dollars. And there's a new threat on the horizon. With Arctic and Antarctica ice melting at precipitous rates, scientists predict that before the end of the century, Manhattan will be under water.

Narrator: Now get ready to answer the questions. Answer each question based on what is stated or implied in the lecture.

1. What is the lecture mainly about?
2. What percentage of the Earth is covered in water?
3. Besides agriculture, what else throughout time has benefitted from flooding?

 4. Why does the professor say this?

Prof: In short, without the annual flooding of the Nile, Egyptian civilization, as we now know it, would not exist.

5. The professor describes the flooding of the Nile during the time of ancient Egypt. Put those steps in order. This is a 2-point question.
6. The professor mentions three rivers that flood. Match each river to its country. This is a 2-point question.

Task 5 - *Vivisection* - Track 5 - Page 39

Narrator: Task five. Directions. Listen as a student talks to a professor, then answer the questions on the next page.

Student: Professor Dirk? Is this a good time?
Prof: Cindy. It's always a good time. Come in. Come in.
Student: I've been reviewing my notes and what you said last time we met.
Prof: Good. Good. And? What's wrong? Cold feet?
Student: Frozen, actually. I know that it's all part of the scientific process, but I'm not sure if I can go through with it, you know, vivisection. I know all the arguments—that it's for science, and it's how progress is made, and to fight disease we have no other choice—but I just can't do it. I can't hurt a living animal.
Prof: Keep in mind, Cindy, that we breed these mice especially for this purpose. They are not pets; they have no names, have very little human contact. They are simply objects of investigation, an essential link—a critical link—in medical research. Did you know that in the twentieth century almost every medical achievement was based on animal testing? Even today, right now, schools and

	labs all over the country are doing the same thing: using animals to advance the cause of mankind.
Student:	Right. Is it possible to do it digitally?
Prof:	Vivisection? I'm afraid not. True, we have some pretty amazing software, but a computer can't extract DNA. And that's what this assignment is all about: cells extracted to process DNA. One day I'm sure it'll all be done virtually, but that is then and this is now. Like it or not, vivisection is the only way to get the target DNA—and to complete the assignment.
Student:	Would it be all right if I just watched?
Prof:	I'm afraid not. This is a hands-on assignment. It constitutes 40% of your final grade. I really need to see the extraction process from start to finish. That said, class starts in ten minutes. So, what've you decided?
Student	I've decided that I'm not cut out for this.
Prof:	But you want to be a vet, yes?
Student:	I did. I'm great at chemistry and biology. I am. I even thought I could work with animals in a lab, but obviously I can't. The thing is I never would have known that if I hadn't taken this course. The thought of experimenting on a living animal no matter what the reason is...Well, I think you know where I stand.
Prof:	Then you're dropping the course. Is that what I'm hearing?
Student:	I am. That's why I came by. I wanted to thank you for all your help, and for listening to me, strange as it must seem.
Prof:	It's not strange at all. Life is full of crossroads. What about your other courses?
Student:	I'll finish them and take a break for awhile. Maybe work for a year of two. I need to rethink just what it is I want to do. Being a vet obviously isn't in the cards.
Narrator:	Now get ready to answer the questions. Answer each question based on what is stated or implied in the conversation.

1. What is the main topic of the conversation?
2. What percentage of the assignment is the student's final grade?

3. Why does the student say this?

Student: Being a vet obviously isn't in the cards.

4. What does the student's decision imply?

5. Listen again to part of the talk, then answer the question.

Student: I'm great at chemistry and biology. I am. I even thought I could work with animals in a lab, but obviously I can't. The thing is I never would have known that if I hadn't taken this course. The thought of experimenting on a living animal no matter what the reason is...Well, I think you know where I stand.

Narrator: What does the student mean when she says this?

Student: Well, I think you know where I stand.

Task 6 - *Art Exhibition* - Track 6 - Page 41

Narrator: Task six. Directions. Listen as a student talks to a campus employee, then answer the questions.

Student: Hello?
Admin: Yes? Oh, come in. Can I help you?
Student: Are you Bill Jenkins? The gallery manager?
Admin: I am.
Student: Professor Gainsborough said I should talk to you about having a show here in the gallery.
Admin: Oh, right. You must Sylvia. So nice to meet you. Professor Gainsborough speaks very highly of you.
Student: Really?
Admin: He does. So tell me. What did you have in mind?
Student: I'd like to exhibit my graduate portfolio.
Admin: Great. What medium?
Student: I'm not sure how to classify it. Lately, I've been combining photographs and old computer parts.
Admin: Oh, really?
Student: I found them, actually. The computer parts. In a dumpster. In fact, I find all my material. I can't remember the last time I bought something.
Admin: Found art. I see. Sounds intriguing. Do you have anything I can look at?
Student: Yes. I brought some examples. It's not exactly mainstream. Most of the time I'm pushing the envelope.
Admin: Oh, I like this. Does it have a title?
Student: No. I just number them.
Admin: Why's that?
Student: Well, I can never think of a good title. They all sound, you know, lame. So how is the schedule? You must be really booked.
Admin: Let me check. Ah, next month...Let's see. Gloria Samuels will show for the first two weeks. She works in oil. Landscapes. Very traditional. Ah, after Gloria, for the last two weeks of the month, it's David Hopkins.
Student: Really? David Hopkins the sculptor?
Admin: The one and only. Straight from a show in London. Have you heard?
Student: No. What?
Admin: The Queen bought one of his pieces. Ah, will you price your work?
Student: You mean sell it?
Admin: That's right. How about next Monday? Emily Lopez was slated to show, but she had to cancel. She called just before you walked in. Mind you, it would only be for a week. That's the best I can do, I'm afraid. It's short notice, I know but...
Student: No. No. Next Monday would be great. What should I do?
Admin: Well, today's Thursday. I suggest we meet here tomorrow morning. Let's say, ah, nine? Bring whatever work you want to show and we'll go from there. The current show, Joseph Sands—have you seen it?
Student: Yes. I'm not a big fan of expressionism. Not that it's bad. It's just not my cup of tea.
Admin: To each his own. Anyway, Joseph will be out of here Saturday night. That gives us all day Sunday to get your show up and running.
Student: What about pricing? I'd really like to try and sell a few pieces.
Admin: Pricing is up to you. That said, I wouldn't go crazy. For example, this piece here...
Student: Number nine?
Admin: Easily five hundred.
Student: Five hundred?

Admin: Maybe more. You know, I think I'll call Karen Goldblatt. She's the editor of Art House Magazine. She really should see these. She'll know how to price them.

Narrator: Now get ready to answer the questions. Answer each question based on what is stated or implied in the conversation.

1. To whom is the student speaking?
2. From the conversation, we can infer that the student...
3. How long will the student's exhibition last?
4. Who is Karen Goldblatt?

 5. Listen again to part of the conversation, then answer the question.

Admin: Pricing is up to you. That said, I wouldn't go crazy. For example, this piece here...

Narrator: Why does the employee say this?

Admin: That said, I wouldn't go crazy.

Test 1 - Speaking - Page 44

Task 3 - *No Computers in Class* - Track 7 - Page 47

Narrator: Task three. Directions. Now listen as two students discuss the announcement.

Woman: You've got to be kidding. No laptops in class? Where did you hear this?
Man: I read it on the school website. Starting Monday, you can't use a laptop in class. If you do, you'll be asked to leave or turn it off. Actually, I think it's a good idea. In my psychology class, everybody's taking notes on their laptops. That's forty people all typing away. You can't believe the noise.
Woman: But my laptop is my life. I always take notes with it. And now they expect me to use a pen? Forget it. Writing by hand is too slow. Not only that but I'll have to rewrite my notes when I get home. Talk about a waste of time. This new policy is definitely going to make a lot of people angry.
Man: I don't think so. The school is just trying to improve classroom conditions. Imagine trying to teach when everybody is looking at their computers and not at you. Laptops are definitely coming between the teacher and the students.
Woman: What angers me is the school said I had to buy a laptop. It was a requirement. So I bought one even though I couldn't afford it. And now the school is telling me not to use the laptop they told me I had to buy? Ridiculous. If I can't use my laptop in class, then the school should refund the cost of buying it. It's only fair.

Narrator: Now get ready to answer the prompt. The woman expresses her opinion about the new policy. State her opinion and explain the reasons she gives for maintaining that position. You have 30 seconds to develop your response and 60 seconds to speak.

Task 4 - *The Green Revolution* - Track 8 - Page 49

Narrator: Task four. Directions. Now listen to a lecture on the same topic.

Prof: 1 ➔ The benefits of the Green Revolution cannot be denied. Yet, as with all revolutions, it takes time to measure the full impact of change both in the short and the long term.

2 ➔ During the Green Revolution, only a select few crops were grown. Those crops, such as wheat, were grown on a massive scale. As a result, soil quality decreased dramatically as the wheat drained nutrients from the soil. Instead of letting the land regenerate by letting it go fallow, or rest, for a year—as was the traditional practice—farmers instead added synthetic fertilizers to boost crop yields. The result was the complete exhaustion of soil quality, so much so that today many large expanses of land are simply dead.

3 ➔ At the same time that a wheat crop was being fed a diet of synthetic fertilizer, it was also being protected against insects with pesticides, such as DDT. DDT, along with many other synthetic pesticides, has since proven to be carcinogenic. DDT was so dangerous, in fact, it was banned because it was wiping out the American bald eagle. And where did all that fertilizer and pesticide end up? In the water system. This caused an explosion of water plants such as algae that thrives on nitrogen-rich fertilizers. This, in turn, reduced the oxygen level to the point where today many once-healthy bodies of water are now dead zones.

Narrator: Now get ready to answer the prompt. What is the Green Revolution and what are its short and long term effects? You have 30 seconds to develop your response and 60 seconds to speak.

Task 5 - *Harvard Law* - Track 9 - Page 51

Narrator: Task five. Directions. Listen to a conversation between two students.

Man: Hi, Betty. What's wrong?
Woman: Well, there's good news and bad.
Man: Okay, so what's the good news?
Woman: I got accepted into Harvard Law.
Man: Congratulations! That's fantastic.
Woman: Thanks. Now for the bad news. Harvard is not cheap. I nearly died when I saw the tuition.
Man: Yeah, but it's Harvard. Ivy League.
Woman: I know. I want to go, but I can't afford it. I already have four years worth of undergrad loans at this school. If I do three years of Harvard Law, I'll be even more in debt. I'm not sure what to do.
Man: What about applying for a scholarship? How are your grades?
Woman: I'm at the top of my class.
Man: There you go. You'd have a really good chance of getting a scholarship. Some scholarships pay all your tuition. If you don't get a full scholarship, you should at least get something for books. I got a scholarship here, and boy did I save a bundle.
Woman: Applying for a scholarship is definitely an option. I'll have to check it out.
Man: You could also take time off and work for a year or two, you know,

	postpone admittance. That way you could save money for tuition. You might not be able to pay off the full cost, but you could at least pay off some of it. That way you'd owe less in the long run.
Woman:	Yeah. Obviously, I have a decision to make.
Narrator:	Now get ready to answer the prompt. The students discuss two solutions to the woman's problem. Identify the problem and the solutions, then state which solution you think is best and why. You have 20 seconds to develop your response and 60 seconds to speak.

Task 6 - *HRT* - Track 10 - Page 53

Narrator: Task six. Directions. Listen to a lecture in a women's studies class.

Prof: 1 ➔ In women, estrogen regulates the development of female sexual characteristics and reproduction. As a woman reaches middle age, around age 45, the estrogen level decreases. Indications of decreased estrogen are hot flashes, mood swings, and weak or broken bones due to a loss of bone mass. It wasn't until the early 1960's that author Robert Wilson in his book *Feminine Forever* recommended that women could stop the aging process by taking estrogen pills. Suddenly, women started taking estrogen and were feeling much better for it. However, in the early 1970's, a rise in uterine cancer was connected to an increase in estrogen usage, so women stopped taking estrogen almost overnight. In the late 1970's, doctors did an about face and said that it was okay to take estrogen combined with another hormone, progestin. By the 1990's, doctors were so enthusiastic about the estrogen-progestin combination that they were telling women that hormone replacement therapy—HRT for short—was the solution to stopping heart attacks. In short, HRT was a life-saver. By 2000, almost six million women in the United States were taking some form of HRT. That, then, is a brief history of estrogen use in America. But is the news all good? No.

2 ➔ A lot of research has been done on estrogen, the most striking of which was a report by the Women's Health Initiative. Of the 16,000 women they were studying, HRT had increased the risk of heart attack by 29%, breast cancer by 24%, blood clots by 100%, and stroke by 41%. The evidence was clear: hormone-replacement therapy was life-threatening.

Narrator: Now get ready to answer the prompt. The lecture talks about hormone replacement therapy (HRT). Summarize the recent history of HRT usage in the United States and its impact on women's health. You have 20 seconds to develop your response and 60 seconds to speak.

Test 1 - Writing - Page 55

Task 1 - *Cell Phones* - Track 11 - Page 56

Narrator: Task one. Directions. Now listen to a lecture on the same topic.

Prof: 1 ➔ According to the article you read for homework, cell phones are a silent killer threatening us all. If you believe that, then you also believe in the tooth fairy. Let me set the record straight. Cell phones do not cause cancer. Period. Why not? Because cell phone radiation is non ionizing. What does that mean? It means that cell phone radiation has too few electrons thus cannot cause cancer unlike ionizing radiation produced by X-rays. Moreover, cell phone RF levels are tested and retested by the manufacturers to ensure that radiation levels meet the strict standards set by the Federal Communications Commissions. That said, put to rest any notion that you might be harming yourself whenever you make a call.

2 → And, yes, cell phones can be a distraction, but they are not the only distraction on the roads today. Drive along any interstate and you'll be distracted by any number of things, from billboards to speeding transport trucks to construction crews, not to mention little Jilly and Billy screaming for attention in the back seat. Suffice it to say, the world is full of distractions.

3 → As for colony collapse disorder, cell-phone usage is only one of many factors that must be taken into account. Other factors include the bacterial infection called foulbrood, and the varroa mite, an infectious insect that preys on bee larvae. Climate change too is suspected. Global warming has brought new and invasive species. One such species, the Asian hornet, has spread across Europe and into Britain. The Asian hornet raids hives for bee larvae and the bees are powerless to stop this invader. To say that the cell phone threatens honey bees with extinction is like saying hamburgers are responsible for childhood obesity without considering chocolate and high-fructose breakfast cereals.

Narrator: Now get ready to write your response. Summarize the points made in the lecture and show how they cast doubt on the points made in the reading. You have 20 minutes to complete the task.

Test 2 - Listening - Page 76

Task 1 - *Low Essay Grade* - Track 12 - Page 77

Narrator: Task one. Directions. Listen as a student talks to a professor, then answer the questions on the next page.

Student: Professor Morgan? Hi. Do you have a minute?
Prof: Sure, Sue. Come in. What's up?
Student: I have a question about my essay you just gave back. Where should I start? I worked really hard on it and...Well, I thought I'd get a better grade. But...Yeah. Talk about a shock. Anyway, can you tell me why I got such a low grade?
Prof: Sure. Do you have the essay with you?
Student: Yes. Right here. It's on the question of legalizing marijuana. You asked us to pick a side and argue in favor of it. I took the pro side.
Prof: Yes. Now I remember. Let me take a look at it. Right. Right.
Student: Is it too short? Is that why I didn't get an A?
Prof: No. Length is really not an issue. Let me rephrase that. There's no connection between length and quality. Some might disagree, but frankly, some of the best essays I've graded have been short. Not one-page short, mind you, but, you know, a couple of really focused pages that address the subject with no extra verbiage. Some of the worst essays I've seen have been...Well, let's just leave it at that, shall we?
Student: Well, if length isn't a problem, then what is?
Prof: Well, it all starts with your opinion. Show me which sentence is your opinion?
Student: It's this one right...here.
Prof: Sorry, but that's not an opinion. You're simply telling me what you'll write about. Remember, your opinion must be arguable. Since you're arguing the pro

	side of the marijuana issue, you really need to state what you believe in no uncertain terms. By doing do so, your audience will know from the start where you stand.
Student:	That's exactly what I was having trouble with. My opinion.
Prof:	Try this. Simply say, *Personally, I believe that...*, and then add what you believe. For example, *I believe that Americans should have the right to choose* or *I believe that marijuana should be legalized for medical purposes.* Got it?
Student:	Yeah. Okay. I see.
Prof:	Also, your opinion must be supportable. When I say supportable, I mean each sentence—sorry, I meant each body paragraph—must have one specific topic, then you must develop that topic in detail. Look at body paragraph one. You start off by saying *legalizing marijuana would be good for the economy* in the first sentence, then you suddenly switch to *it has many medical benefits* in the next sentence. This signals a clear lack of development of both topics.
Student:	But that's what I believe.
Prof:	Yes. But now we're talking the mechanics of developing and supporting your opinion. Do so by giving each supporting topic its own body paragraph. In this case, *legalizing marijuana would be good for the economy* is the topic of your first body paragraph, and the medical benefits is the topic of your second body paragraph.
Student:	You mean, do what I did in paragraph three?
Prof:	Exactly. In body paragraph three, you focus on how legalizing marijuana will decrease the crime rate. However, you still need to develop this topic in detail. Give an example. One with statistics. You know what I mean. Do the same for body paragraphs one and two. Remember: The more you develop your supporting examples, the more persuasive your argument will be. Right now, you're just scratching the surface. To be honest, this reads more like a first draft.
Student:	I see what you mean. Can I rewrite it for a higher grade?
Prof:	Sure. Can you have it on my desk by nine tomorrow morning?
Student:	By nine? I'll try.
Narrator:	Now get ready to answer the questions. Answer each question based on what is stated or implied in the conversation.

    1. What are the student and the professor mainly discussing?
    2. Why does the student visit the professor?
    3. In which areas does the student's essay need revising? Select two. This is a 1-point question.
    4. What does the professor think about short essays?
    5. Listen again to part of the conversation, then answer the question.

Prof:	Remember: The more you develop your supporting examples, the more persuasive your argument will be. Right now, you're just scratching the surface. To be honest, this reads more like a first draft.
Narrator:	What does the professor imply when she says this?
Prof:	Right now, you're just scratching the surface.

Task 2 - *Adam Smith* - Track 13 - Page 79

Narrator: Task two. Directions. Listen to a lecture in an economics history class, then answer the questions on the next page.

Prof: 1 → Adam Smith was born in Scotland in 1723. As a young man, he studied moral philosophy at the University of Glasgow and at Oxford. He eventually went on to tutor a nobleman's son. The position freed Smith from his daily work while affording him the opportunity to tutor while traveling throughout Europe. In France, Smith met Rousseau and Voltaire, leading proponents of the European Enlightenment. At its core, the European Enlightenment, guided by reason and science, questioned customs, morals, and traditional institutions, namely monarchies.

2 → Returning to Scotland, Smith set about writing his seminal *An Inquiry into the Nature and Causes of the Wealth of Nations*. In it, Smith argues that building national economic wealth begins with a division of labor. Smith supports his argument by using a pin factory. In a typical pin factory of the day, each worker was responsible for making pins from start to finish. A worker would start by cutting the pin to size from a piece of wire, then straighten it, then sharpen the end, affix a head, polish it, then package it. In short, one man was responsible for each step of the pin-making process. Smith argued that such an approach was not only counter-productive but also time consuming inasmuch as once a worker finished one part of the task—say polishing a pin—he would pause before moving onto the next task. Such an approach, Smith argued, was inefficient, for workers were likely to "saunter" or pause between steps, which wasted time and substantially reduced productivity. Smith argued that the most efficient way to make pins was through a division of labor. Instead of ten men each separately making a pin from start to finish, each would be assigned one task, for example, one man would sharpen pins all day, another would polish them while a third would package them, and so on. By dividing labor this way, Smith theorized that the production of pins would dramatically increase. As a result, there would be more pins to sell and thus more money to be made. Smith's scientific approach to rationalizing the manufacturing process for greater productivity was indeed the product of Enlightenment thought.

3 → A division of labor, however, was but one part of Smith's argument for creating wealth. An integral part of the wealth-making process, Smith claims, is the pin worker himself. He is performing a task not for society's benefit nor for the benefit of the company, but for his own personal gain and security. The same follows with the owner of the pin factory. He too is out for personal gain, the health and wealth of the nation the least of his, and his workers', worries. Yet by pursuing individual gain, Smith argues that the worker and the factory owner are, in fact, directly adding to the wealth of the nation by utilizing a more efficient manufacturing process, one which stimulates trade, the buying and selling of goods, locally, nationally, and internationally. Smith coined this process "the invisible hand."

4 → *The Wealth of Nations* is very much a reaction to the predominating economic theory of the day, that of Mercantilism. Mercantilists posited that the wealth of a nation depended on developing and maintaining national power thus it was a form of economic nationalism. Spain, at the time of Columbus, is a prime example of just such a nation. A nation like Spain preserved national power by accumulating as much gold as possible through strong exports, the limitation of imports, and a large population of poorly paid workers. To develop

exports, companies were subsidized by the government, which also wrote laws to limit imports. By limiting imports, the gold used to pay for imports would stay in the country and create a greater money supply and more credit. Nations, such as Spain, England and Holland were geared toward acquiring and maintaining gold at all costs, including warring with each other. Witness England and Holland battling for control of today's Manhattan in the early 1600's. Adam Smith, however, argued that free trade benefitted all nations and that gold was not equal to wealth. Gold, Smith said, was like any other commodity, such as wheat or wool, and that it deserved no special treatment. More importantly, Smith says that the wealth of a nation is not based on the hoarding of gold, but on the free flow of goods manufactured in a systematic way, a way that serves the needs of the individual and, ultimately, the nation as a whole. With that, Adam Smith gave birth to what we now call economic theory. As Thomas Edison is to the light bulb, Adam Smith is to the science of economics.

Narrator: Now get ready to answer the questions. Answer each question based on what is stated or implied in the lecture.

1. What is the topic of the lecture?
2. What is the purpose of the lecture?

3. Why does the professor say this?

Prof: As Thomas Edison is to the light bulb, Adam Smith is to the science of economics.

4. From the lecture, we can infer that Smith considered mercantilism to be...
5. The professor describes how Adam Smith's idea of "the invisible hand" works. Put these steps in order. This is a 2-point question.
6. The professor develops three topics. Match each topic with its corresponding description. This is a 2-point question.

Task 3 - *Wi-fi Problem* - Track 14 - Page 82

Narrator: Task three. Directions. Listen as a student talks to a member of the school's IT support staff.

Student: Hi. Is this IT support?
Support: Yes, it is. How can I help you? Let me guess. Your computer got hit by the email virus going round and you want to know how to restore your corrupted files, right?
Student: Actually, my computer didn't get hit.
Support: Oh, one of the lucky ones. So, what's up?
Student: I just bought an iPod Touch.
Support: Sweet. How much?
Student: A lot. Look, the reason I'm calling is because I can't connect my iPod to the internet.
Support: You mean the school's wireless network?
Student: Right.
Support: What exactly is the problem?
Student: When I open my email, a dialogue box asks me to log on to the school's wireless network. I log on with my school ID and my password, just like with my laptop, then another dialogue box pops up and says, "No wireless network." How can there be no wireless network when everybody around me is connected? I'm

Support: like totally confused. This never happens with my laptop. What am I doing wrong? It's something really simple, right?
Support: Probably security. What kind of encryption are you using?
Student: Excuse me?
Support: Encryption. The school's wireless network is encrypted.
Student: I'm sorry. I don't follow.
Support: Encryption basically means the wireless signal floating around the school here—well, not so much floating but, you know, covering—has been scrambled into a secret code that can only be opened by the right security setting on the device you're using. The old kind of wireless encryption is called WEP. That's short for wired-equivalent privacy. The school stopped using it two years ago because it had serious security issues. We now use WPA. That's short for wi-fi protected access. Your iPod is probably set for WEP.
Student: Ahhh...Right. Can you just tell me how to set it up? I'm kind of in a hurry here.
Support: Sure. Boot up your iPod. Go to your home screen. Open settings, then go to network. See it?
Student: Network...Network...Right.
Support: Open network, then open wi-fi.
Student: Okay. It's open.
Support: At the top of the screen, you should see security. Open it.
Student: Open security. Got it.
Support: You should see a menu that gives you a choice of encryption settings starting with WEP. See it?
Student: Got it. There's WEP followed by WPA and WPA2. Those are wireless security settings?
Support: Bingo. The school uses WPA, so select it and you should be good to go.
Student: Oh, my God. You're a genius!
Support: Sweet. Anything else I can help you with?
Student: Nope. That's it.
Support: Hey, would you mind filling out a survey? It's about how well I solved your problem. It would only take a sec.
Student: Sure. No, problem.

Narrator: Now get ready to answer the questions. Answer each question based on what is stated or implied in the conversation.

1. What are the student and the IT staffer mainly discussing?
2. What is the student's problem?
3. What are the wireless security settings? Select 3. This is a 2-point question.

4. Why does the student say this?

Student: Oh, my God. You're a genius!

5. Listen again to part of the conversation, then answer the question.

Support: What exactly is the problem?
Student: When I open my email, a dialogue box asks me to log on to the school's wireless network. I log on with my school ID and my password, just like with my laptop, then another dialogue box pops up and says, "No wireless network." How can there be no wireless network when everybody around me is connected? I'm like totally confused. This never happens with my laptop. What am I doing wrong? It's something really simple, right?
Support: Probably security. What kind of encryption are you using?

Student: Excuse me?
Support: Encryption. The school's wireless network is encrypted.
Student: I'm sorry. I don't follow.

Narrator: What does the student mean by this?

Student: I'm sorry. I don't follow.

Task 4 - *Garbage Patch* - Track 15 - Page 84

Narrator: Task four. Directions. Listen to part of a discussion in an environmental class, then answer the questions on the next page.

Prof: Today, we're going to discuss a man-made problem that's impacting oceans worldwide, a problem with no solution in sight. That problem is right in front you. When you're finished with them, hopefully—as concerned and responsible citizens—you'll recycle so they won't end up on a Pacific island or a Cape Cod beach. Of course, you all know what I'm talking about: the ubiquitous polyethylene terephthalate. That said, let me begin by giving you a few eye-popping stats. Every year, Americans buy over 50 billion—yes, billion—bottles of water. That equates to 1,500 bottles consumed every second—every second. That number beggars the imagination. Of that number, eight out of ten end up in a landfill with the remaining twenty-percent recycled. And those numbers are only in America. What about the rest of the world? What about countries that can't afford to build expensive recycling plants? And what about all those bottles that are not recycled or dumped in landfills, in America and worldwide? Where does all that polyethylene terephthalate end up? Carol?

Carol: In the oceans.
Prof: Exactly. Can you elaborate on the homework?
Carol: Sure. According to the reading, there's this huge floating patch of garbage in the North Pacific. It's made up mostly of plastic bottles, but you can also find fish nets and micro pellets used for abrasive cleaning, plus all the stuff tossed off freighters and cruise ships. All this garbage is being swept along on what's called the North Pacific gyre.
Prof: Sorry, what exactly is that? A gyre?
Carol: It's the prevailing ocean current. In the North Pacific, the gyre moves west along the equator, then up past Japan to Alaska, then down the west coast of North America to the equator again. It's kind of like water spinning in a toilet bowl.
Prof: Good. So what's the connection between the North Pacific gyre and pelagic plastic?
Ann: Sorry, professor, what does pelagic mean again?
Prof: It means living or occurring at sea. The albatross, for example, is a pelagic bird. Carol?
Carol: Right, so where was I? Okay, so the stuff, I mean, you know, all the pelagic plastic, is swept along clockwise by the gyre. Eventually all that plastic junk finds its way into the center of the gyre and becomes stationary, you know, just sits there in an area called the Horse Latitudes, this area of calm in the center of the gyre. Years ago sailors would get trapped there due to a lack of wind and current. Today, it's basically one big, continuously-fed garbage dump in which pelagic plastic is the prevailing contaminant.
Prof: And it isn't going anywhere. In fact, it's spreading due to the decomposing nature of the contaminants themselves. Ann, can you jump in here and talk about the photodegradation process?
Ann: So when all this floating plastic is exposed to the sun, it begins to photodegrade until it reaches the molecular level. For example, take this book. Let's say it's

	floating in the center of the gyre, okay? The first thing to go are the covers, then the pages decompose freeing all the words. Next, the words break apart into letters. Finally, the ink in the letters photodecomposes into molecules. All that ends up in the gyre forming this thick, soupy liquid full of floating plastic particles that look like confetti.
Prof:	A sea of confetti. That's a good way to put it. Beautiful, I'm sure, what with all that colored plastic floating around, but deadly. Very. All that particulate matter? It doesn't sink. Instead, it stays in the upper water column where it poses a significant threat to endemic wildlife. Pelagic birds, for example, consume the particulate matter mistaking it for food. They, in turn, feed it to their young who die of starvation or are poisoned by the toxic nature of polyethylene terephthalate. Other contaminants identified in the patch are PCB, DDT and PAH. When ingested, some of these toxins imitate estradiol which, as you know, is a naturally occurring estrogenic hormone secreted mainly by the ovaries. You can imagine the effect these toxins have on the reproduction systems of endemic species, such as whales. Fish too ingest the decomposed plastic and become contaminated.
Carol:	Professor, is it possible to clean it up?
Prof:	So far? No. The particulate matter is so small, you need extremely fine nets—micronets basically—to scoop it up. But even if we had such nets, remember, the North Pacific is vast. It would take an armada constantly going back and forth to even put a dent in all that plastic while at the same time, new plastic—tons of it—is entering the gyre every day. How many bottles of water do Americans drink every year?
Carol:	Fifty billion.
Prof:	Precisely. And that statistic is already out of date.
Ann:	That's a lot of garbage.
Prof:	It is. And the thing is, we don't even know how big the patch is. Satellites can't pick up the particulate matter because it's too small. Not only that but when you're parked in the middle of it on a boat or a ship, you can't see it. The particulate matter is that small. So, how big is the great North Pacific garbage patch? Well, some say it's the size of Texas. Others claim it's twice the size of the U.S. Big no matter how you cut it. Okay, so that's the North Pacific. Worldwide how many gyres are there?
Carol:	Five.
Prof:	So if the center of the North Pacific gyre is one huge, floating garbage dump, what does that tell us about the other four gyres?
Narrator:	Now get ready to answer the questions. Answer each question based on what is stated or implied in the discussion.

1. What is the discussion mainly about?
2. What is the purpose of the discussion?

 3. Why does the professor say this?

Prof: That number beggars the imagination.

4. Which pelagic species does the professor mention? Select two. This is a 1-point question.
5. The professor describes how plastic becomes part of the eco-system. Put those steps in order. This is a 2-point question.
6. In the lecture, the professor describes the Horse Latitudes. Indicate whether each of the following is a characteristic of the Horse Latitudes. This is a 3-point question.

Task 5 - *Supreme Court* - Track 16 - Page 87

Narrator: Task five. Directions. Listen to a lecture in a law class, then answer the questions on the next page.

Prof: 1 → In January, 2010, the Supreme Court of the United States ruled on the case the U.S. Supreme Court vs. the Federal Elections Commission. In this landmark ruling, the bitterly-divided Court ruled 5-4 that corporations enjoy the same First Amendment rights as do individuals. In other words, a corporation, no matter what the size, is considered a citizen. Microsoft, General Electric, Exxon, in the eyes of the Supreme Court, they are all citizens—individuals—thus legally entitled to protection under the Constitution. That protection includes the right to free speech. Suffice it to say, the ruling set off a firestorm of protest. But before we get to that, let's map out how this landmark ruling came about.

2 → In 2004, Oscar-winning documentary filmmaker Michael Moore released *Fahrenheit 911*, a scathing indictment of how then Republican President George W. Bush failed to act during the 9/11 crisis. In Moore's film, Bush comes off looking like a man entirely unsuited to be president. In short, Moore argues that President Bush failed in a time of national crisis. The Republicans were furious. Not to be outdone, David Bossie, a veteran Republican strategist, made a film attacking Democrat Hillary Clinton, who was then starting her run for president. But the movie, titled *Hillary: The Movie*, barely appeared on the radar during the 2008 presidential primary season. Why? Because the Federal Elections Commission restricted Bossie's film from being shown. The decision to restrict the film was based on the fact that the film was made not by David Bossie himself, as an individual, but by a corporation. That corporation was Citizens United. A lower court ruled that *Hillary: The Movie* wasn't a movie at all, but instead a 90-minute attack ad telling voters not to vote for Hillary Clinton. In that light, the lower court ruled that under the current campaign rules established by the Federal Elections Commission, Citizens United—being a legal corporate entity—was prohibited from financing political commercials. Basically, the Federal Elections Commission said corporate money has no place in American politics. What did David Bossie do? He turned around and sued the Federal Elections Commission, the argument being that Citizens United was being denied the right to free speech. In January, 2010, the Supreme Court agreed with Bossie's argument and overruled the lower court's decision. In delivering its ruling, the Supreme Court said, and I quote, *"Political spending is a form of protected speech under the First Amendment, and the government may not keep corporations or unions from spending money to support or denounce individual candidates in elections."* It doesn't get much clearer than that.

3 → Now, you may wonder, why is this such a big deal? Why has this decision sent shock waves through the American political system? Think of it this way: the Supreme Court says that if the Ford Motor Company wants to donate a billion dollars to help elect a candidate—a candidate who will help Ford move its factories overseas—then Ford, as an individual, has every right to do so. Those opposed to the decision say that this is patently unfair. Corporate money, they argue, will go directly into political advertising which, in turn, will give an unfair advantage to corporate-sponsored candidates. For example, imagine you are a school teacher and you decide to run for Congress and your opponent is funded by IBM, or Google even. In short, those who oppose corporate political funding fear that the American political system is no longer based on the one person, one vote proposition. Instead, elections will simply be bought by the

candidate who has the most money, namely, corporate money. And smoke is already on the horizon.

4 → Recently it has been revealed that the American Chamber of Commerce—the largest association of businesses in America, representing every type of business from Microsoft down to your local gas station owner—has been soliciting money from foreign corporations with U.S. operations, money which is finding its way into the American political system regardless of what members of the Chamber of Commerce might think. Let's examine the evidence.

Narrator: Now get ready to answer the questions. Answer each question based on what is stated or implied in the lecture.

1. What is the lecture mainly about?
2. What does the professor say about *Hillary: The Movie*?

3. Why does the professor say this?

Prof: And smoke is already on the horizon.

4. The professor mentions Ford. Why?

5. Listen again to part of the lecture, then answer the question.

Prof: The Republicans were furious. Not to be outdone, David Bossie, a veteran Republican strategist, made a film attacking Democrat Hillary Clinton, who was then starting her run for president. But the movie, titled *Hillary: The Movie*, barely appeared on the radar during the 2008 presidential primary season.

Narrator: What does the professor mean when she says this?

Prof: But the movie, titled *Hillary: The Movie*, barely appeared on the radar during the 2008 presidential primary season.

6. According to the professor, how has the Supreme Court's decision changed the political landscape? This is a 3-point answer.

Task 6 - *Aristotle* - Track 17 - Page 90

Narrator: Task six. Directions. Listen to a lecture in a composition class, then answer the questions on the next page.

Prof: 1 → According to Aristotle, an argument can be made more persuasive by using three appeals: logos, pathos, and ethos.

2 → Let's start with logos. Logos, or logic, appeals to reason. One way to appeal to reason is by using deduction. Deduction—and we'll come back to this later on—is a form of reasoning in which you make a conclusion based on a series of related facts or premises. Let's work through an example. First, you start with a major premise, such as...Oh, I don't know—*All English teachers are poor*. This general statement is followed by a specific statement or minor premise, in this case *Bob is an English teacher*. From these two premises, a conclusion logically follows: *Bob is poor*. Put it all together and it reads like this: *All English teachers are poor. Bob is an English teacher. Bob is poor.* As you can see, deduction can be

pretty persuasive. Its closed or formal structure leaves no doubt as to Bob's financial situation relative to his profession. Induction is another form of logic that appeals to reason. When inducing, you combine a series of related facts, such as *Joan loves apples, Joan loves blueberries, Joan loves mangos*. From these facts, we can make a conclusion, in this case *Joan loves fruit*. Does she love all fruit? We don't know. She might abhor apricots. As you can see, induction is not as closed or conclusive as deduction. Still, add numbers to an inductive mix and the logic behind an argument whether to invest in a company can be quite appealing. For example, *ABC Company made a $20 billion profit last year; ABC made a $40 billion profit this year; ABC will make a $60 billion profit next year*. Conclusion? You do the math.

3 → Pathos, in contrast, is an appeal to the emotions. By appealing to the emotions, the arguer can evoke sympathy from an audience. Sympathy, in turn, makes an argument more persuasive. Movies regularly employ pathos. Did you cry when E.T. finally went home? Were you terrified when *Titanic* sank or when Jaws rose out of the water, teeth flashing? If so, then the director persuaded you that two-dimensional images on a movie screen are so real, so life-like, you reacted to them emotionally. Pathos can also support logos. For example, photographs often support news stories. What better way to evoke audience anger at an oil company than to place a photo of an oil-covered pelican next to an article about an oil spill.

4 → Next we have ethos. Ethos is an appeal to character. For example, from whom would you buy a computer, a man in a business suit or a man in a T-shirt? Ethically, some might eschew the man in the T-shirt, a T-shirt being the antithesis of business attire therefore unethical, not trustworthy. However, such ethical conclusions have been turned on their heads, especially in America. Case in point: Whenever Apple introduces a new product, CEO Steve Jobs introduces the product wearing jeans and a T-Shirt. Does Jobs' choice of clothes diminish the quality of the product? No. If anything, Jobs' casual look enhances Apple's cool factor. As you can see, what was once ethically unacceptable—wearing jeans to work—is now perfectly acceptable.

5 → Those, then, are Aristotle's three appeals. It's important to remember that a successful argument—a persuasive argument—combines all three appeals. Look at President Obama. As an argument for president, his life story was quite compelling. Why? Because it was defined by the three appeals. As a youth, he was a community organizer (ethos and pathos). He then studied law at Harvard (logos and ethos). After he graduated, he taught constitutional law at the University of Chicago (logos and ethos). He then became a U.S. senator (logos, pathos and ethos). Combined, these three appeals made Barack Obama a persuasive argument to be president of the United States.

6 → That said, keep in mind, however, that even when supported by all three appeals, there is no guarantee that a politician seeking office—or any other argument—will persuade an audience, for if any of the three appeals come under fire, the audience will fail to be persuaded.

Narrator: Now get ready to answer the questions. Answer each based on what is stated or implied in the lecture.

1. What is the topic of the lecture?
2. What is the purpose of the lecture?

3. According to Aristotle, which appeals make a lecture more persuasive? Select three. This is a 2-point question.

 4. Why does the professor say this?

Prof: That said, keep in mind, however, that even when supported by all three appeals, there is no guarantee that a politician seeking office—or any other argument—will persuade an audience, for if any of the three appeals come under the fire, the audience will fail to be persuaded.

5. The professor describes President Obama's personal history. Put President Obama's personal history in the proper order. This is a 2-point question.
6. In the lecture, the professor describes Aristotle's three appeals and their functions in an argument. Indicate whether each of the following is a function of Aristotle's three appeals. This is a 3-point question.

Test 2 - Speaking - Page 94

Task 3 - *Digital Book Store* - Track 18 - Page 97

Narrator: Task three. Directions. Now listen as two students discuss the announcement.

Woman: Hey, Steve. Have you heard about the campus bookstore going digital? What a great idea. Digital texts are definitely the wave of the future. Now, instead of lining up to buy texts, we can just download them at home.

Man: I don't know. Whenever I read a computer screen for a long time, I get wicked headaches. I prefer paper, really. With a regular book, I can study for hours and not feel like my brain is melting. Believe me, I'm not looking forward to studying organic chemistry off a computer screen.

Woman: You should upgrade. Get a computer with a better screen, like my iPad. It's amazing. The screen resolution is so good, I no longer buy regular books. Upgrade, definitely. Your brain will thank you for it.

Man: I'm sorry but upgrading my computer is a luxury I can't afford, what with my car and rent. But with this new policy, I'll have to buy one. Obviously, the school thinks students are made of money.

Woman: Think of it this way: going digital is good for the environment. Think of all the trees you'll be saving. Mother Nature will thank you for it.

Man: What I don't like is there's longer a buy-back. It was great, the book store buying back all our old texts at the end of the semester. But now, with this new policy, I'm out a couple hundred bucks easy. With that money, I could've bought a new computer.

Woman: Try selling your old texts on eBay.
Man: You just read my mind.

Narrator: Now get ready to answer the prompt. The man gives his opinion about the new policy. State his position and explain the reasons he gives for holding that opinion. You have 30 seconds to develop your response and 60 seconds to speak.

Task 4 - *Animal Behavior* - Track 19 - Page 99

Narrator: Task four. Directions. Now listen to a lecture on the same topic.

Prof: 1 → Good afternoon. In this lecture, we'll focus on a common nocturnal animal, the bat. There are two types of bat: micro bats, or true bats, and mega bats, also called fruit bats. Let's start with mega bats.

2 → Size wise, mega bats are from two to sixteen inches in length. Mega bats have extremely sensitive sight and smell. This helps them locate the flowers and fruit upon which they feed. It is while eating that mega bats play an important role in the distribution of plants. Like bees, mega bats serve as pollinators. When they lick nectar or eat flowers, their bodies become covered in pollen which they, in turn, carry to other trees and plants thereby acting as pollinators. In fact, many of the fruits and vegetables on our tables, such as bananas and peaches, would not be there if mega bats did not pollinate plants and trees.

3 → Next are micro bats. As the name implies, micro bats are quite small, about the size of a mouse. To find food, micro bats use echolocation, high frequency sounds they bounce off insects. The most common micro bat is the vesper or evening bat. Like mega bats, micro bats play an important role in the environment. The average vesper bat, for example, can eat one thousand mosquitoes in one night. By doing so, they control the mosquito population.

Narrator: Now get ready to answer the prompt. The reading and the lecture focus on the classification of animal behavior. Describe how the reading and the lecture define and develop this idea. You have 30 seconds to develop your response and 60 seconds to speak.

Task 5 - *Euthanasia Debate* - Track 20 - Page 101

Narrator: Task five. Directions. Listen to a conversation between two students.

Man: Hey, Sue. You got a minute?
Woman: Sure, Brian. What's up?
Man: I'm taking Political Science. Part of my course requirement is to debate some hot-button issue, you know, like amnesty for illegals or gay marriage.
Woman: So what's the problem? Why so wound up?
Man: The topic is euthanasia. I'm supposed to argue against it, but I'm pro euthanasia. I believe people have the right to die whenever and however they please. Call it freedom of choice. Call it whatever. No way am I arguing against a person's right to choose.
Woman: Know what I think? I think you're blowing this thing way out of proportion. I also think Professor Smith gave you the con side as a way of teaching you.
Man: Teaching me? Teaching me what?
Woman: Think about it. By arguing the opposite of what you believe, maybe Professor Smith wants you to see both sides of the argument. Maybe this is really an exercise in understanding. In that case, I think you should do it. I mean, life is not always about getting your own way, you know.
Man: True.
Woman: Another option is to tell Professor Smith you refuse to debate on moral grounds. You'd be true to your beliefs, and I'm sure he'd understand. But he might also fail you, so you're definitely taking a risk if you back out. Look. There's Professor Smith now. So, what're you going to do?
Man: I don't know. I'm still debating.

Narrator: Now get ready to answer the prompt. The students discuss two solutions to the man's problem. Identify the problem and the solutions, then state which solution you think is best and why. You have 20 seconds to develop your response and 60 seconds to speak.

Task 6 - *Darwin* - Track 21 - Page 103

Narrator: Task six. Directions. Listen to a lecture in a biology class.

Prof: 1 → In Darwin's lifetime, *On the Origin of Species* sold well; however, it did not sell as well as another popular Darwin book. That book, published in 1881, is titled *The Formation of Vegetable Mould Through the Action of Worms, With Observations on Their Habits.* With the publication of this book, Darwin revolutionized soil and agricultural science. Let's take a look at how he did it.

2 → While most people saw earthworms as an ugly, useless nuisance, Darwin realized their value through a series of experiments. However, his research was overtaken by the writing of *On the Origin of Species.* Later in life, Darwin returned to his study of earthworms and proved that earthworms were not useless pests but in fact played a crucial role in maintaining healthy soil. Darwin observed that earthworms were busy at work turning over the soil by eating it and excreting it. The turning of soil allowed water to penetrate more deeply and allowed more oxygen to enter the ground while the fertilizing added nutrients.

3 → Darwin proved the earthworm's value by doing a simple experiment. In a field near his house, Darwin scattered small pieces of coal. In time, the earthworms had moved so much soil that the pieces of coal had settled deep in the soil proving that the worms were indeed at work turning the soil. With this discovery, Darwin proved that the common earthworm was not a pest but an essential part of the agricultural process.

Narrator: Now get ready to answer the prompt. According to the lecture, how did Charles Darwin revolutionize agricultural science? You have 20 seconds to develop your response and 60 seconds to speak.

Test 2 - Writing - Page 105

Task 1 - *Illegally Downloading Music* - Track 22 - Page 106

Narrator: Task one. Directions. Now listen to a lecture on the same topic.

Prof: 1 → It happens every second of every day all over the world. One click and that new song—the one you didn't pay for—is on your iPod. You may think it's legal. After all, downloading music is fast and easy, right? Think again. It goes without saying that downloading music off the web without paying for it is a crime.

2 → I know. I know. Some will argue that "It's my democratic right to download music without paying for it." Nonsense. The internet might have started out with the intention of being a democracy but believe me, those days are long gone. The internet these days is about two things: information and money. Big money. One of the biggest money makers on the web is music, and music is protected by law. If you download U2's latest album, let's say, and you don't pay for it, then you are breaking the copyright law that says U2 owns that music. It is their

property and you just stole it. If you want to listen to U2, you've got to buy it, no ifs, ands or buts.

3 ➔ Also, the artist has a legal right to get paid for his or her work no matter how or where it is downloaded. How would you like it if somebody were stealing your music? This is exactly what Napster was doing. Napster was the first peer-to-peer music sharing site. Musicians, however, took Napster to court for not paying royalties, money owed each time a song was downloaded via Napster. Napster argued that it was just helping friends share music. The courts disagreed. Napster paid a big fine and is now a pay site.

4 ➔ Moreover, illegally downloading music off the web is not a privacy issue. If you break the law by illegally downloading music, you are a criminal. I'm sorry, but you can't have it both ways. You can't break the law and hide behind the privacy issue. The law is clear. Criminals have no right to privacy. Period.

Narrator: Now get ready to write your response. Summarize the points made in the lecture and show how they cast doubt on the points made in the reading. You have 20 minutes to complete the task.

Test 3 - Listening - Page 124

Task 1 - *Power Point* - Track 23 - Page 125

Narrator: Task one. Directions. Listen as a student talks to a professor, then answer the questions on the next page.

Student: Professor Huston?
Prof: Jill, hi. Come in. I got your email. Thanks. Your presentation is on...
Student: Havaiannas.
Prof: Right. Those famous Brazilian flip flops.
Student: Do you have a pair?
Prof: No. But my daughter has three. She practically lives in them. Right, so how can I help you? In your email, you mentioned you needed help with your presentation. Let me just pull it up here so I can jog my memory.
Student: I don't need help so much as clarification. I understand we have to pick a product and do a ten-minute presentation on it.
Prof: Correct.
Student: But I'm not sure why we can't use PowerPoint. Isn't PowerPoint, you know...
Prof: An integral part of a business presentation? You would think. I mean, how can you give a presentation these days and not use PowerPoint, right?
Student: That's pretty much my thinking.
Prof: Well, since this is your first presentation—I'm assuming it is—I want you to focus on the basics of speaking before an audience and not just flip through a bunch of PowerPoint slides. That's what presenters often do, so much so that PowerPoint takes over. It becomes the presentation while the presenter fades into the background. Not a good thing. As a result, the presentation turns into a slide show with the presenter simply reading bullet points off a screen. At that point, you lose control of your audience. If you lose control, you're no longer in a position to persuade your audience to buy whatever it is you're selling.
Student: And it could get pretty boring, just reading slides.
Prof: Very. Your audience will start checking their cell phones, start yawning, even walk out. Remember: you are pitching your product with the purpose of persuading your audience that your product will change their lives.

Student: I see. So it's all about me being up front and center persuading an audience.
Prof: Bingo. And the way to persuade an audience is to be continually in contact with them. That means making constant eye contact. Body language is critical too. Were you in class when I handed out the guidelines for the presentation?
Student: Yes, I got them. Thanks. In the hand out, you said we could bring a product sample. Now, I don't want to beat a dead horse, but wouldn't it be easier to just take a photo of the product and make a PowerPoint slide?
Prof: Like I said, you've got to walk before you can run. Walking means learning the basics of a good presentation, and a good presentation is all about using personality to persuade. Believe me, some of the best presentations I've seen have not used PowerPoint. That said, I will allow a product sample. Just one.
Student: Got it. Product sample. No PowerPoint.
Prof: Good. Anything else?
Student: What if I get nervous? What if I just, you know, blank out.
Prof: Don't worry. There are ways to handle nerves. Take a look at this other handout.
Student: Thanks. We will eventually use PowerPoint?
Prof: Ah, yeah. Next semester. But even then, the point to remember is this: PowerPoint is not the presentation. It is simply a support tool.

Narrator: Now get ready to answer the questions. Answer each question based on what is stated or implied in the conversation.

1. What is the topic of the conversation?
2. Why does the student visit the professor?

3. Why does the professor say this?

Prof: PowerPoint is not the presentation. It is simply a support tool.

4. According to the professor, what will an audience do if the presenter loses control of a presentation? Select three. This is a 2-point question.

5. Listen again to part of the conversation, then answer the question.

Prof: Like I said, you've got to walk before you can run. Walking means learning the basics of a good presentation, and a good presentation is all about using personality to persuade. Believe me, some of the best presentations I've seen have not used PowerPoint. That said, I will allow a product sample. Just one.

Narrator: What does the professor imply when he says this?

Prof: Like I said, you've got to walk before you can run.

Task 2 - Housing...Middle Ages - Track 24 - Page 127

Narrator: Task two. Directions. Listen to part of a lecture in a history class, then answer the questions on the next page.

Prof: 1 ➔ During the Middle Ages, peasant families lived in rural houses close to the fields in which they worked, land which was controlled by a lord in a castle. A typical peasant house, usually built by the family themselves, was a primitive shelter that provided little more than a place to eat and sleep. Construction materials included earth and wood for the walls, and thatching for the roof. The most common rural structure was the longhouse or house-barn. Rectangular in shape, this dwelling had doors on opposite ends and on the sides thus ensuring cross ventilation. Inside, the floor plan was divided in half with one end forming the hearth, the place where the family prepared and ate their meals and slept. The opposite half was occupied by livestock, typically a cow for milk, chickens for meat and eggs, and a horse that pulled the plow. In winter, the heat rising off the animals kept the structure warm. Because there was no chimney, the interior was often smoky. The exit for the smoke was through holes at either end of the roof. Fire was a constant threat as was the risk of contracting diseases from living in such close proximity to animals.

2 → Those with more money and social status, namely land-owning families, lived in houses separate from the livestock. The house consisted of two floors. The first floor was the hall, the place where the family ate and entertained around a central fireplace. For the landowner, the hall was of central importance, for it was there that the landowner fed his family and his servants, the meals themselves a measure of the landowner's wealth and hospitality. Above the hall was a private family room called the solar. It consisted of beds and a fireplace for heating and was reached by a private staircase. On the ground floor off the hall were the buttery and pantry. The pantry, a name still in use today, was a storage room for dry foodstuffs, such as flour and spices, while the buttery was a cold storage for perishables, such as butter, cheese, and eggs.

3 → Houses built in cities and towns, unlike rural houses, were built in rows and often shared the same walls. As a result, they occupied less horizontal space while rising vertically several floors. On the ground floor facing the street there was often a shop behind which were the living quarters. The kitchen too was located on the ground floor with a small light court separating it from the house. This transitional space prevented odors and fire from spreading from the kitchen to the rest of the house. Because houses were built so close, and made of wood and thatch, they were highly combustible. During the Middle Ages, cities were often engulfed in flames, the source of which was often traceable to a kitchen fire. The city of London experienced two such conflagrations, the Great Fire of 1135 and the Great Fire of 1212.

4 → At the top of the social ladder were the nobility. They resided in fortified residences called castles. Early castles were built of wood and earth, and evolved into massive stone constructions, many of which were surrounded by a water barrier called a moat. Castles were built in places of strategic importance, such as on a trade route or at the mouth of a harbor. Militarily, they provided protection from invaders and offered a base from which raids could be launched. Inside their high stone walls were stables, granaries, and workshops, all of which served the noble, his family, and his staff. The land surrounding the castle was farmed by peasants who, in times of trouble, sought the protection of the lord. In return, the peasants served as soldiers under the lord and paid for the use of his land through taxes and by sharing part of the harvest. Thus the castle also served as a center of administration.

Narrator: Now get ready to answer the questions. Answer each question based on what is stated or implied in the lecture.

1. What is the focus of the lecture?
2. What is the purpose of the lecture?

3. According to the lecture, in whose house did animals do more than provide a food source?

 4. Why does the professor say this?

Prof: Because houses were built so close, and made of wood and thatch, they were highly combustible.

5. Identify which are features of medieval housing and which are not. This is a 3-point question.
6. According to the lecture, a castle had two main purposes. One was military. What was the other?

Task 3 - *Three-Gun Terry* - Track 25 - Page 130

Narrator: Task three. Directions. Listen to a lecture in an American literature class, then answer the questions on the next page.

Prof: 1 ➔ *The Black Mask*, a 128-page illustrated pulp fiction magazine, first hit the newsstands in 1920. Like all pulp magazines, *The Black Mask* was formula writing at its very best or, more often than not, its very worst. But then in May of 1923, a story appeared in *The Black Mask* that would forever change pulp fiction and American culture as a whole. That story was Carroll John Daly's crime novelette *Three Gun Terry*. In the annals of detective fiction, *Three Gun Terry* is indeed a first. Why? Because Terry Mack, the hero of the story, is "the world's first hard-boiled private detective."

2 ➔ With the publication of *Three Gun Terry*, subscriptions to *The Black Mask* soared. Terry Mack was a hit. Then, in October, 1923, six months after the publication of *Three Gun Terry*, *The Black Mask* published a crime story by an aspiring writer named Peter Collinson. The title was *Arson Plus*. The hero was a nameless private-eye who worked for the Continental Detective Agency. In time, the hero of *Arson Plus* would come to be known as the Continental Operative or simply "the Op." *Arson Plus* was so popular Collinson decided to put his real name on subsequent *Black Mask* stories. That name was Dashiell Hammett, a name that would, over time, relegate Carroll John Daly and his seminal *Three Gun Terry* to literary obscurity. Therein lies the question: Whatever happened to *Three Gun Terry*? Moreover, why has Carroll John Daly, a writer whom critics acknowledge as being the originator of an American literary icon—the hard-boiled private-eye—why has his name fallen off the map while Dashiell Hammett went on to receive most of the credit for creating the genre of writing called hard-boiled crime fiction? That is the question we will try to answer in this lecture.

3 ➔ Carroll John Daly was born in Yonkers, New York in 1889. After high school, he attended the American Academy of Dramatic Arts. He went on to run a movie theater in Atlantic City. In May, 1923, when *The Black Mask* published *Three Gun Terry*, Daly was thirty-three and living as a recluse in White Plains, a suburb of New York City. Why was Daly a recluse? Nobody knows. But we do know this: rarely, if ever, did he venture into Manhattan, the setting for *Three Gun Terry*. Once Daly did make the trip into the city. When he returned home, so the story goes, he couldn't find his house. A neighbor had to point it out to him. Once, for the sake of research, Daly decided maybe he should get to know what it was like to handle a gun. Daly bought a gun only to be arrested for carrying a concealed weapon. As one friend observed, "That was the end of Carroll John Daly's research."

4 ➔ Samuel Dashiell Hammett was born in 1894 on a farm in Maryland. At fourteen, guided by "a rebellious temperament," he dropped out of school and went to work for the railroad. In 1915, at the age of twenty-one, he joined the Pinkerton Detective Agency. As a Pinkerton operative, or "Op," Hammett saw everything from "petty theft to murder." In 1918, Hammett left Pinkerton's, joined the army and contracted influenza. Soon after he developed tuberculosis. He left the army and went back to Pinkerton's but poor health forced him to resign. In 1922, weakened by disease and in need of work, Hammett, encouraged by a friend, turned to writing.

5 ➔ As aspiring crime writers, Daly and Hammett couldn't have been more different. By 1923, Hammett had been around the block and then some, whereas Daly never left his house. Yet it was Daly who wrote *Three Gun Terry*, a shocking crime novelette that introduced Terry Mack, the world's first hard-boiled private-eye.

Narrator: Now get ready to answer the questions. Answer each question based on what is stated or implied in the lecture.

1. What does the lecture mainly focus on?
2. What is mentioned about *The Black Mask*? Select three. This is a 2-point question.
3. According to the lecture, what was Peter Collinson's real name?

4. Why does the professor say this?

Prof: By 1923, Hammett had been around the block and then some whereas Daly never left his house.

5. The professor describes the life of Carroll John Daly. Put Daly's early life in the correct order. This is a 2-point question.
6. The professor mentions three dates. Match each date to the corresponding event. This is a 2-point question.

Task 4 - *Knock-offs* - Track 26 - Page 133

Narrator: Task four. Directions. Listen to a discussion in a business class, then answer the questions on the next page.

Prof: We recently talked about factors that can reduce a company's bottomline such as lawsuits, increased taxation, and loss due to natural events, such as hurricanes and earthquakes. Today we're going to look at another factor that can severely impact a company's bottomline. That issue is knock-offs. Now what do I mean by knock-off? Essentially a knock-off is a counterfeit product.

Joe: Professor, you mean like a fake?

Prof: Fake. Knock-off. Bogus. Counterfeit. Call it what you will. At the end of the day, it's all the same thing: a copy of an original, trademarked product or design illegally manufactured for sale and distribution. More importantly, a trademark is a government registered mark that gives a brand its unique identity. A couple of more famous trademarks are, Jill?

Jill: Nike's swoosh and, you know, what's that one? The two letters locked together? You see it on bags and belts. Dino...?

Prof: Dolce and Gabbana, the fashion designers. Very appealing. And very knocked off. Good. Ah, let's push on. Remember: a trademark is a unique mark or symbol that is protected by law. That means the full weight and protection of American

	law stands behind it. Copy that trademark, knock off some Nikes with the Nike symbol on them, and you're breaking the law. The country worst hit by knock-offs is the United States. Annually, the U.S. loses more than $200 billion dollars to foreign-made knock-offs. Now, what we commonly think of as knock-offs are watches and sunglasses, you know, the stuff you see on street, Fifth Avenue being a prime example of what I'm talking about.
Joe:	Professor, why Fifth Avenue? Why sell knock-offs in such a pricey retail district? I could never figure that out.
Prof:	That's a good question. Jill? What do you surmise?
Jill:	My guess is that Fifth Avenue attracts a lot of tourists.
Prof:	Right. So?
Jill:	So a lot of them would love to buy something on Fifth Avenue, but things are not exactly cheap. Your average tourist is not about to shell out five hundred bucks for a Dolce-and-Gabbana belt when just down the street, a tout is selling a knock-off of the same thing for peanuts. The tourist isn't stupid. Who cares if that belt is fake? It looks real. And the price is definitely right.
Prof:	So by being in the right place at the right time, the tout steps in to meet a need.
Jill:	Right. Supply and demand, or in this case, demand and supply.
Prof:	Sounds plausible. I like how you've inverted demand and supply. Of course, the touts could be there simply because there's less competition from other touts or fewer police. Whatever the reason, D-and-G takes a hit. How much is that knocked-off belt? Twenty bucks? And the original? Five hundred? A thousand? And accessories are just the tip of the iceberg. Knock-offs are having the greatest impact on which sector?
Jill:	Pharmaceuticals.
Prof:	Exactly. In fact, today's Wall Street Journal has a front page story on it. Did anyone read it?
Joe:	Yeah. I did. Online.
Prof:	Can you give us the gist?
Joe:	Sure. According to the article, the U.S. population, ah, age 65 and older stands at 40 million or 2.9 percent of the current population. That's about one in every eight Americans. By 2030, that number will double to 80 million.
Prof:	Why are these numbers significant?
Joe:	Why? Because people over 65 need medication for everything from arthritis to cholesterol to cancer. The woman in the article is taking twenty different pills every day. Twenty!
Prof:	So how does this connect with counterfeiting?
Joe:	The problem is the cost. Let's say you're retired, like the woman in the article. You have a fixed monthly income of one thousand dollars. Out of that one thousand you must pay for rent and bills and food. You're also taking a variety of medications, some of which cost a hundred bucks a pop. When you add it up, many retired people can't pay for such expensive medication, especially if you're taking twenty pills a day. So what do you do? They end up buying knock-offs.
Jill:	Which is good. So why is fake pharma so bad? If those pills are saving retired people money, what's the harm in that?
Joe:	The problem is there's no government oversight or quality control on the manufacturing side. As a result, a knock-off manufacturer can simply fill capsules with sugar, put a name like Pfizer or Bayer on them, and the customer thinks they're getting the real deal when they're not.
Prof:	That's exactly it. So let's bring it full circle. How does all this impact the bottomline? Jill?
Jill:	Knock-offs hurt the bottomline for myriad reasons. First off, companies can lose the incentive to innovate.
Prof:	How so? Joe?

Joe: Well, if I'm a drug company, and my products are continually being ripped off, then what's the point in developing new products if I know I'll lose money in the long run? Also, the more my products are knocked off, the more people will begin to suspect my products, particularly the quality. This, in turn, will result in a significant loss of brand equity.

Prof: Anything else?

Jill: If I manufacture drugs, I can lose significant market share to knock-offs that are chemically the same as the drugs I'm producing. The consumer is not stupid. Word gets around. They know what works and what doesn't. If a knock-off sells for fifty bucks, and the original sells for two hundred, it's pretty obvious which one I'm going to buy.

Prof: Even at the risk of your health?

Jill: What value is my health when expensive brand-name drugs are putting me in the poor house?

Prof: Good way to put it. Now let's be clear. Companies are indeed willing to protect their brand equity by taking their cases to court. One such case was Tiffany vs. eBay. Keith, summarize the Tiffany case for us, will you?

Narrator: Now get ready to answer the questions. Answer each question based on what is stated or implied in the discussion.

1. What is the discussion mainly about?
2. What is the point of the discussion?

3. Why does the professor say this?

Prof: And accessories are just the tip of the iceberg.

4. How can knock-offs hurt a company? Select three. This is a 2-point question.
5. From the discussion, we can infer that "touts" on Fifth Avenue are...
6. According to the discussion, what is true about knock-offs? This is a 3-point question.

Task 5 - *eBooks* - Track 27 - Page 136

Narrator: Task five. Directions. Listen as a student talks to a campus employee, then answer the questions on the next page.

Student: Hi. Can you help me?
Admin: Sure. What's up?
Student: I'm having trouble downloading my e-text on this terminal here. I keep entering my information, you know, student ID, password, and the thing keeps denying me access.
Admin: We're still working the kinks out of the system, I'm afraid. They just installed these terminals last week.
Student: Do the other campus bookstores have e-book terminals?
Admin: No. We're the first. Let's try this again. You got your credit card?
Student: Yes.
Admin: Okay, insert it and let's see what happens. Ah, so there's the home screen. Enter your name and password.
Student: Okay. See? It always denies my password and it spits out my card.
Admin: Which one are you using?
Student: Which one what?
Admin: Which password are you using?
Student: The one I always use when I log onto the school's system.

Admin:	That's the problem. This system does not recognize Campus Net passwords.
Student:	Why not?
Admin:	For security.
Student:	So I have to create a new password? Is that it?
Admin:	Didn't you get the email outlining all this?
Student:	There was an email?
Admin:	Like I said, we're still working the kinks out of the system. Let's try it again. We'll go to the home screen. Now enter your new password in this box here. Make sure it's case sensitive and alphanumeric, at least eight characters.
Student:	Okay.
Admin:	Now hit enter. There you go. There's the course page. The required texts are listed by title in the sidebar here. Choose the one you need.
Student:	Done.
Admin:	Now enter your credit card and hit enter.
Student:	Can I pay cash instead?
Admin:	Sure. Just slip the bills into the slot here and you should be good to go.
Student:	Thanks. Ah...Excuse me?
Admin:	Ah, yes?
Student:	Why isn't it giving me change? I put in four twenties. I should get $5.73 back.
Admin:	That's strange. It was working fine this morning.
Student:	Look, I got a class. I really need to get going. Can you just give me my change from the cash register?
Admin:	Sorry.
Student:	Why not?
Admin:	Like I said, these terminals are not on the school's network. They're hooked up to the vendor's system till we get the kinks worked out. I'm going to have to call the vendor and have someone come look at it.
Student:	What about my change?
Admin:	You'll have to settle that with the vendor.
Student:	Great. I prefer the old system. All I had to do was grab a book off a shelf and pay for it.
Admin:	You'd be surprised how many say that.
Narrator:	Now get ready to answer the questions. Answer each question based on what was stated or implied in the conversation.

1. What does the conversation focus on?
2. From the conversation, we can infer that the student...
3. What must the student's new e-book password be? Select three. This is a 2-point question.

 4. What can be inferred when the employee says this?

Admin: Like I said, we're still working the kinks out of the system. Let's try it again.

 5. Listen again to part of the conversation, then answer the question.

Student: So I have to create a new password? Is that it?
Admin: Didn't you get the email outlining all this?
Student: There was an email?

Narrator: Why does the student say this?

Student: There was an email?

Task 6 - *Impressionists...* - Track 28 - Page 138

Narrator: Task six. Directions. Listen to a lecture in an art history class, then answer the questions on the next page.

Prof: 1 ➜ The nineteenth century witnessed many art movements. However, one in particular tends to overshadow all the rest. That art movement is Impressionism, a school of painting that originated in France in the late 1860's.

2 ➜ The Impressionists were a radical group of painters who broke all the rules of academic painting. In Europe at the time, academic painters were traditionalists who gave the public what they wanted: great canvases that depicted heroic figures and ancient scenes painted with brushwork so fine some paintings looked more like photographs. The Impressionists, however, refuted such a conservative approach to painting. Instead of painting indoors, as did the academics, the Impressionists took their easels outside and painted "en plein air," in the open air; instead of painting classical scenes, which glorified a heroic past, the Impressionists painted scenes of every day life, such as sailboats on a river and bustling city streets; instead of spending hours on one painting, the Impressionists strove to capture the moment with broken brush strokes using mixed and unmixed paint as a means of recreating the physical properties of light. Critics were outraged. This new style of painting was not painting in the formal, classical sense but were sketches and impressions hence the term Impressionists.

3 ➜ Initially, the Impressionists and their revolutionary approach to painting were rejected by the French art world, a closed and cliquish world that was dictated by the tastes of the Académie des Beaux-Arts. The academy gave its stamp of approval to those artists it favored while rejecting those it deemed too radical. Those radicals were the Impressionists, men like Edouard Manet and his painting *Dejeuner sur l'herbe* (Luncheon on the Grass), a painting many critics believe represents the start of modernist painting. Evidence of Impressionist influences can be found in the work of Van Gogh, Picasso and Andy Warhol. Yet at the time, the Impressionists outraged the conventional art world. Undaunted, Manet and the Impressionists charted their own course and soon the art world realized that the work of Manet, Renoir, Monet and Degas, among others, was indeed making an impact, one that persists to this day. In fact, Impressionist paintings are so ubiquitous, it would be easy to assume that it was the only art movement of any significance during the nineteenth century. Nothing could be further from the truth. Twenty miles across the English Channel, some twenty years before the Impressionists shook the French art world, the school of painting known as the Pre-Raphaelite Brotherhood was shaking the foundations of the British art world.

4 ➜ The Pre-Raphaelite Brotherhood was formed in 1848 by John Everett Millais, Dante Gabriel Rossetti, and William Holman Hunt. Like all great art movements, it rejected the old in favor of the new. In this light, the Pre-Raphaelite Brotherhood was similar to the Impressionists some twenty years later. However, where the Impressionists captured impressions outside in natural light, the Pre-Raphaelite Brotherhood drew inspiration from romantic poetry and medieval themes, and conveyed them on large canvases painted in studios. The subjects were bathed in a realistic light and were rendered with great attention to detail. This radical new approach to painting, one in which romanticism and naturalism merged, rejected the predominating Mannerist

Narrator:
school in which the human form was exaggerated in settings that were both unreal and filled with hard, unnatural light.

5 → Like the Impressionists, the Pre-Raphaelite Brotherhood outraged the art establishment with their radical new approach to painting. One painting in particular, *Christ in the House of His Parents* by John Millais, caused a firestorm of criticism. Critics, including Charles Dickens, claimed the painting was blasphemous. Worse, Dickens said Mary, the mother of Christ, was ugly when in fact Millais had based her on his sister-in-law, Mary Hodgkinson. The Pre-Raphaelite Brotherhood's love of medieval themes and details also drew sharp rebukes. Yet, like the Impressionists, the Pre-Raphaelite Brotherhood refused to be swayed by popular opinion. Today, paintings, such as Millais's *Ophelia*, Rossetti's *Beata Beatrix*, and Hunt's *Scapegoat* are acknowledged masterpieces. Moreover, the influence of the Pre-Raphaelite Brotherhood can be seen in the protean work of William Morris, a prolific artist and textile designer who founded the decorative art firm William, Marshall and Faulkner, a commercial art house that, in 1860, signaled the beginning of the decorative arts, a movement that spawned the Arts and Crafts movement and Art Nouveau, of which Louis Comfort Tiffany was a central figure.

Narrator: Now get ready to answer the questions. Answer each question based on what was stated or implied in the lecture.

1. On what does the lecture mainly focus?
2. Which three Pre-Raphaelite artists are mentioned? Select three. This is a 2-point question.

3. Why does the professor say this?

Prof: However, where the Impressionists captured impressions outside in natural light, the Pre-Raphaelite Brotherhood drew inspiration from romantic poetry and medieval themes, and conveyed them on large canvases painted in studios.

4. What can we infer about the Impressionists and the Pre-Raphaelites?
5. According to the lecture, Louis Comfort Tiffany was...
6. What is true about the Impressionists and the Pre-Raphaelites? This is a 3-point question.

Test 3 - Speaking - Page 142

Task 3 - *Dress Code* - Track 29 - Page 145

Narrator: Task three. Directions. Now listen as two students discuss the announcement.

Woman: A dress code? Give me a break.
Man: That's the new policy. Starting next semester.
Woman: Where does the school get off telling us what we can or can't wear? Hel-lo. This is the United States. Last I heard it was a democracy. What I wear is none of the school's business. I'm paying them to educate me not to deny me the right to wear shorts.
Man: I can understand the policy. Some students really push the envelope when it comes to fashion. I mean, c'mon, school is not the place to be flashing skin or

	walking around dressed like a rock star. It's distracting. Seriously. This is a university not a club.
Woman:	Where does it stop? That's what I want to know. First clothes, then what? Are they going to tell us what to read? What to eat? What to think? Give them an inch and they'll take a mile, believe me.
Man:	When I went to high school, we all wore the same uniform and nobody complained. Uniforms created greater equality. Also, I didn't have to worry about what I was going to wear every day.
Woman:	Sorry, but that analogy doesn't cut it. High school uniforms are simply a way to control adolescents with way too much energy. This is a university. We're supposed to be responsible adults, remember? By taking away our right to dress as we please, the school no longer trusts us. They're treating us like kids, and I don't like it.
Narrator:	Now get ready to answer the prompt. The woman expresses her opinion about the announcement. State her opinion and explain the reasons she gives for holding that opinion. You have 30 seconds to develop your response and 60 seconds to speak.

Task 4 - *Refining* - Track 30 - Page 147

Narrator:	Task four. Directions. Now listen to a lecture on the same topic.
Prof:	1 ➔ A barrel of crude oil is the oil industry's standard unit of measurement. One barrel contains 42 gallons or 159 liters. Within that barrel of crude is a complex mixture of molecules called hydrocarbons. Hydrocarbons are what's left of plants and animals that lived billions of years ago. This organic matter, deep within the Earth, is heated by the Earth which, over time, turns it into crude oil hence the term fossil fuel. To make consumer petroleum products from a barrel of crude oil, products such as gasoline and diesel fuel, the hydrocarbons must be separated. That separation process is done at a refinery through a process called fractional distillation.
	2 ➔ Fractional distillation starts by boiling raw, unprocessed crude oil. The hydrocarbons in the oil all have different boiling points. This means they can be separated through distillation, a process in which the raw crude oil is changed into its gaseous form through boiling. When a particular hydrocarbon reaches its boiling point, it changes from a solid to a vapor. This vapor is then drained off into a separate holding tank where it is cooled and condensed into liquid form. The lightest products, those which have the lowest boiling point, such as gasoline, exit from the top of the boiler while the heaviest products—those with the highest boiling points, such as lubricating oil—exit from the bottom.
Narrator:	Now get ready to answer the prompt. Refining is a complex and dangerous process. Using information from the reading and lecture, describe this process. You have 30 seconds to develop your response and 60 seconds to speak.

Task 5 - *Job Offer* - Track 31 - Page 149

Narrator: Task five. Directions. Listen to a conversation between two students.

Man: Hey, Sylvia. Did you get the job?
Woman: I did.
Man: Congratulations. You don't look so thrilled.
Woman: I am. Very. But I've got a choice to make. I applied for a part-time position, right?
Man: Right.
Woman: So I go for the interview and before you know it, they're offering me a full-time position with benefits.
Man: Whoa. So what're you going to do?
Woman: That's the $64,000.00 question.
Man: Why don't you tell them you'll work part-time, then do full-time when you graduate? That way you could finish your education and have a job when you graduate. They might even pay for the rest of your education that way.
Woman: Oh, I don't know. Asking them to pay for my education when they've already offered so much seems a bit, you know, greedy.
Man: Okay. So quit school. Serious. You've got a once-in-a-lifetime job offer. With the economy the way it is, you'd be crazy not to take it. Best of all, the pressure of finding a job would be gone just like that.
Woman: But what about my master's degree?
Man: Work for a few years, then finish it part-time in the evening. People do it all the time, work and go to school at the same time. By working, you could pay for your master's if your company won't pay. What was that job again?
Woman: Entertainment director on a cruise ship. It goes all over the world. Miami. Rio. Greece.
Man: Sweet.

Narrator: Now get ready to answer the prompt. The students discuss two solutions to the woman's problem. Identify the problem and the solutions, then state which solution you think is best and why. You have 20 seconds to develop your response and 60 seconds to speak.

Task 6 - *White-Collar Crime* - Track 32 - Page 151

Narrator: Task six. Directions. Listen to a lecture in a sociology class.

Prof: 1 ➔ Most have never heard of Professor Edwin Sutherland yet we've all heard the phrase white collar crime. Sutherland came to define white collar crime as a "crime committed by a person of respectability and high social status in the course of his occupation," a perfect example of which is Bernard L. Madoff.

2 ➔ On December 11, 2008, the business world was rocked by news no one could believe. Even now, people are still shaking their heads. On that December day, Bernard L. Madoff was arrested for securities fraud. Madoff freely confessed that his private investment fund was in fact a Ponzi scheme, a criminal enterprise in which Madoff took money from one party and, instead of investing it as promised, gave it to another party while taking a cut in the process.

3 ➔ How did Madoff get away with it and for so long? The answer is simple. Madoff was one of the most respected men on Wall Street. He'd served as chairman of the Board of Directors of the National Association of Securities Dealers and was one of the first to champion electronic trading. He was active in

high society as well, serving on the boards of prestigious universities and charities. In short, Bernie Madoff commanded so much business and social respect that no one ever suspected that he was running a criminal enterprise. And why would people suspect him? After all, his private investment fund was making people rich, even in bad times. Yet when the stock market crashed in the fall of 2008, Madoff's house of cards crashed with it. With stock prices falling, Madoff investors suddenly wanted their money back. The only problem was Madoff could not return their investments. The money had simply vanished.

Narrator: Now get ready to answer the prompt. How does the lecture define and develop the concept of white-collar crime? You have 20 seconds to develop your response and 60 seconds to speak.

Test 3 - Writing - Page 153

Task 1 - *Global Warming* - Track 33 - Page 154

Narrator: Task one. Directions. Now listen to a lecture on the same topic.

Prof: 1 → It's amazing how some scientists bend the facts to serve their own agendas. That said, let me shed some light on the carbon sink issue. The CO_2 released from carbon sinks has a different isotopic ratio than the CO_2 produced by our burning of fossils fuels. In other words, carbon sink CO_2 and fossil fuel CO_2 have different fingerprints. This fact, ignored by the article, proves that the rise of CO_2 in the atmosphere during the 20th century is indeed man-made, and that global warming will only increase.

2 → Also, one will argue that forecasting climate change on a computer is not always accurate. However, what the article fails to mention is that computer modeling accurately predicts broader trends in climate change, and that these trends all indicate increased warming trends. Measuring the GMST is indeed a critical part of measuring climate change. However, such a detailed analysis is not the only way to gauge future climate change. Remember: 85% of the world's energy needs come from the burning of fossil fuels. Where does all that CO_2 go? Into the atmosphere as greenhouse gases. You don't need a computer model to conclude that all that CO_2 poses a serious problem.

3 → Global warming is a natural phenomena we are just beginning to understand? What is this guy smoking? Researchers at Texas A&M have proven that increased water vapor serves to amplify the warming process. In other words, water vapor is like gasoline poured onto an already raging fire. That fire is those greenhouse gases already present in the atmosphere. How do we stop that fire? By substantially reducing our dependence on fossil fuels.

Narrator: Now get ready to write your response. Summarize the points made in the lecture and show how they cast doubt on the points made in the reading. You have 20 minutes to complete this task.

Test 4 - Listening - Page 172

Task 1 - *Malware* - Track 34 - Page 173

Narrator: Task one. Directions. Listen to part of a discussion in a computer class, then answer the questions on the next page.

Prof: Welcome everybody. Hope you had a good weekend. Today, we're going to start with Ann. Ann was assigned the task of researching malware. Ann? What did you come up with?

Ann: A lot, actually. I'm sure you all know what malware means, but just in case, malware is short for malicious software. It's software designed with the purpose of entering your computer without your permission. It's like somebody suddenly enters your house or apartment and starts checking the place out. By the way, if you have any questions, just stop me. Okay? Great. So where was I? Ah, right. Malware. Malware comes in all shapes and sizes. There are viruses, Trojan horses, spyware, adware, scareware. Most of it is spread by the internet. Here's a great fact I found. According to Symantec, there's more malware being released every year than legitimate software.

Prof: Ann, where did it all start?

Ann: You mean, what was the first piece of malware?

Prof: Yes. Were you able to find out?

Ann: I was. It was a virus, actually. Starting around 1949, computer scientists began writing about computer viruses and how they could reproduce like human viruses. The first computer virus, you know, the first real piece of code, didn't appear until 1972. That was the Creeper Virus.

Betty: 1972? Was the internet even around then?

Ann: No, it wasn't. Not as we know it. Back then they had something called ARPANET. That's short for Advanced Research Projects Agency Network. It all started during the Cold War in the 1950's. The U.S. military needed a way to make sure that its military computers stayed connected if attacked, so the government got all these guys from Harvard and MIT to design an interconnected information system. They did and called it ARPANET. ARPANET is basically the start of the internet as we know it. Anyway, a guy named Bob Thomas was working on ARPANET when he created the Creeper virus. He did it as an experiment to see if it would work, and it did. He sent it to computers on ARPANET and it started reproducing. However, it never left ARPANET and was harmless. Like I said, it was just an experiment. The first computer virus to appear outside a lab was the Elk Clone. It was created by Richard Skrenta in 1981. The Elk Clone attacked Apple computers.

Prof: Ann, how did it get on Apple computers in the first place?

Ann: By floppy disk. Back then, people shared them and that's how the Elk Clone spread. When it infected a computer, it would display a poem. Pretty tame, really. In 1986, the first PC virus, the Brain, was created by the Farooq Alvi Brothers. And get this. They created it as a way of preventing the medical software they'd developed from being pirated. If you copied their software off the internet, or wherever, you'd get a warning saying something like, "Warning! You've just been infected. Call us for the vaccination."

Prof: So what's the difference between a virus and a Trojan horse?

Ann: A computer virus can reproduce just like, say, the flu virus. You know the flu virus is invading your body when you feel really sick. That's because the virus is overwhelming your body's defense system. It's the same with computer viruses. They reproduce and overwhelm the host computer. That's what happened to me once. I got a virus that made all the words on my screen melt.

Betty:	How did you get it?
Ann:	Probably on a flash drive. That's how a lot of viruses travel, by portable media.
Betty:	So what did you do?
Ann:	I had to reformat my hard drive and reload all my programs.
Betty:	Drag.
Ann:	Tell me about it. A Trojan horse, on the other hand, is a piece of malware designed not just to mess up your computer but to control it without your knowing it. Trojan horses often show up as legitimate links in emails. This tricks the user into opening the link just like the Trojan horse the Greeks used to trick the Trojans into opening Troy. And we all know what happened to the Trojans, don't we?
Prof:	And once in a host computer, then what?
Ann:	It can do any number of things, like start sending spam to everyone on your email list or downloading bank files and passwords.
Betty:	So let me see if I've got this straight. A Trojan horse seeks to control or steal from a host computer whereas a virus simply disrupts or crashes a computer. Correct?
Ann:	You got it.
Narrator:	Now get ready to answer the questions. Answer each question based on what is stated or implied in the discussion.

1. What is the discussion mainly about?
2. What is the purpose of the discussion?

 3. Why does the student say this?

Student: And we all know what happened to the Trojans, don't we?

4. The student describes the history of computer viruses. Put that history in order. This is a 2-point question.
5. In the discussion, the student describes Trojan horses and computer viruses. Identify the characteristics of each. This is a 3-point question.

6. Listen to part of the discussion, then answer the question.

Betty: So what did you do?
Tom: I had to reformat my hard drive and reload all my programs.
Betty: Drag.

Narrator: Why does the student say this?

Betty: Drag.

Task 2 - *Panama Canal* - Track 35 - Page 176

Narrator: Task two. Listen to part of a lecture in a history class, then answer the questions on the next page.

Prof: 1 → The Panama Canal is one the great engineering feats of the modern era. Stretching forty miles across the Isthmus of Panama, the canal connects the Atlantic Ocean in the east with the Pacific Ocean in the west. Before the canal opened in 1914, a ship sailing from New York to San Francisco south around South America had to travel fourteen-thousand miles. The Panama Canal cut that distance in half.

2 → Connecting the Atlantic and the Pacific had been envisioned as early 1513. In September of that year, Spanish explorer and conquistador Vasco Núñez de Balboa was the first European to lay eyes on the Pacific Ocean after having crossed the Isthmus of Panama, home to one of the most inhospitable jungles on Earth. However, it wasn't until 1888 that the French, led by Ferdinand de Lesseps, began construction on the canal. By then, de Lesseps was famous the world over for building the Suez Canal, a waterway that connects the Mediterranean Ocean and the Red Sea. In 1856, de Lesseps, a diplomat by trade, was awarded the concession to build the Suez Canal from Said Pasha, the viceroy of Egypt. With that concession, de Lesseps started the Suez Canal Company. The indefatigable de Lesseps gathered a team of international engineers and employed thousands of workers. After ten years of digging, much of it done by forced labor, the Suez Canal opened on November 17, 1869 to much fanfare. With the completion of the Suez Canal, and the completion of the American transcontinental railroad six months earlier, the world could now be traversed without stopping. As for de Lesseps, the man who dug a canal through the desert, his popularity soared. In May 1879, when the Geographical Society in Paris voted to build a canal across the Isthmus of Panama, de Lesseps was chosen to lead the project.

3 → From the outset, construction of the Panama Canal was plagued with problems. Malaria and yellow fever decimated the workers while landslides from torrential rains buried dredges and filled in land that had been excavated. To raise money for the failing project, de Lesseps encouraged the average Frenchman to do his patriotic duty and buy shares in the Panama Canal Company. Banking on his reputation as the man who had built the Suez Canal, de Lesseps raised the necessary capital. Yet scandal soon broke out. De Lesseps and a number of others had bribed journalists and politicians to lie about the failing canal. The value of the company's stock plummeted. Millions of people lost everything overnight. The Panama Canal Scandal, as it was called, marked the end of French construction on the canal, and the end for de Lesseps as a free-wheeling entrepreneur and canal builder. All told, with the canal unfinished, some 20,000 canal workers, the majority of whom had been recruited from the islands in the Caribbean, had succumbed to disease and work-related accidents.

4 → In 1904, the United States government under president Theodore Roosevelt bought the Panama Canal Company from the French. At the time, Panama was Colombian territory. The Americans offered to buy Panama from Colombia but Colombia refused. Panamanian separatists revolted. With the support of the American military, the Panamanians won their independence and the nation of Panama was formed. In return, Panama granted America the right to build a canal and administer it indefinitely. In August, 1914 the canal was finished two years ahead of schedule. Yet the world paid scant attention, for all heads were turned toward Europe where World War One had started that very same month and year.

5 → Despite the political controversy surrounding the Panama Canal even to this day, its construction is notable for many milestones. One was the eradication of yellow fever, a disease that had decimated the French workforce. Scientists identified the mosquito as the carrier of the disease thus living and working quarters were regularly fumigated. The result was a dramatic reduction in yellow fever and malaria deaths. Another milestone lies in the construction of the canal itself. It was the world's first—and remains to this day—an all-electric installation. The raising and the lowering of the locks, and the trains that move

ships into position, are all powered by electric motors designed and built by General Electric, a company started by Thomas Edison.

Narrator: Now get ready to answer the questions. Answer each question based on what is stated or implied in the lecture.

1. What is the topic of the lecture?

 2. Why does the professor say this?

Prof: Connecting the Atlantic and the Pacific had been envisioned as early as 1513.

3. What do we know about the Panama Canal? Select three. This is a 2-point question.

 4. Listen again to part of the lecture, then answer the question.

Prof: With the support of the American military, the Panamanians won their independence and the nation of Panama was formed. In return, Panama granted America the right to build a canal and administer it indefinitely. In August, 1914 the canal was finished two years ahead of schedule. Yet the world paid scant attention, for all heads were turned toward Europe where World War One had started that very same month and year.

Narrator: What does the professor mean when she says this?

Prof: Yet the world paid scant attention, for all heads were turned toward Europe where World War One had started that very same month and year.

5. The professor mentions three dates. Match each date to the corresponding event. This is a 2-point question.
6. After the Panama Canal was built, the time a ship had to travel from New York City to San Francisco was cut by how much?

Task 3 - *Pacific NW Tribes* - Track 36 - Page 179

Narrator: Task three. Directions. Listen to part of a lecture in an anthropology class, then answer the questions on the next page.

Prof: 1 ➔ The indigenous people of the Pacific Northwest are located in the Canadian province of British Columbia and in the American states of Alaska, Washington and Oregon. Surviving on the richness of the Pacific Ocean, particularly salmon, these pre-Columbian Indians were, at one time, the most numerous of all North America's native inhabitants. Their origins trace back over 12,000 years. Based on the evidence, archeologists now believe that the tribes of the Pacific Northwest originally arrived from Asia during the Pleistocene Period. They crossed what today is the Bering Sea. At the time, however, there was no water. Instead, there was a land bridge connecting northeast Asia and today's Alaska. The most likely scenario is that the indigenous people of northeast Asia followed their food supply—grazing herds of bison, deer and mammoth—across the Bering land bridge and down into North America. Those who settled along the rugged, storm-tossed Pacific coast developed highly-complex cultures centered around large coastal villages.

2 ➔ The tribes of the Pacific Northwest were unique in that they did not live in hide-covered dwellings, as did a majority of other North American tribes. Instead, families from the same clan lived together in large wooden houses. These houses were made from cedar, a tall, fast-growing tree with a straight grain, few knots and, most importantly, weather resistant, an essential trait, for the average rainfall in some parts of the Pacific Northwest is equal to that of the Amazon. The cedar was cut into long rectangular boards or planks hence the name plank house. If you look at a picture of a plank house, or chance to visit one, you will notice that the design looks strikingly similar to a modern-day house with the same wooden walls and the same angled-roof and front door. Another distinguishing feature of the plank house is the elaborately carved and painted tribal symbols on the exterior walls. Unfortunately, few plank houses have survived, the often-extreme weather of the area having returned most of this cultural heritage to the soil.

3 ➔ Another unique aspect of Pacific Northwest Indian culture was the totem pole. These highly decorated poles stood separate and in front of houses. The making of a totem pole starts with a cedar tree, some which are over fifty-feet high and twelve feet in diameter. The branches are removed as is the bark. A carver, a highly-respected member of the tribe, then sculpts faces into the pole. The faces are those of animals the native people would have encountered on a daily basis, animals such as ravens, killer whales, eagles, bears, and salmon. Early Christian missionaries had assumed that totem poles were shamanistic symbols and were worshipped as such. However, anthropologists now know that totem poles carry no religious significance. Instead, each totem pole tells the story of the clan that erected it. Those stories might be the recounting of a great battle or a successful hunt.

4 ➔ Another misconception about the totem pole was that the stories were once thought to ascend in a vertical order with the most important character crowning the pole. This, in turn, gave rise to the popular idiom, "The low man on the totem pole," namely, the person residing at the bottom of the hierarchy, such as a junior worker in an office who has little or no authority compared to those above. Research, however, now indicates that the Pacific Northwest tribes place no value on how the brightly-colored faces are arranged.

5 ➔ The origin of the totem pole was once a mystery too. Some have hypothesized that the scarcity of old totem poles, those going back two or three centuries, suggested that the tradition of carving of totem poles started when the tribes of the Pacific Northwest acquired iron tools from the Europeans. However, anthropologists now believe that ancient totem poles are rare due to the climate of the Pacific Northwest. With the area getting so much rain and snow—and because totem poles are made of wood—most of the really old totem poles, and plank houses, have simply rotted away.

6 ➔ One particular kind of totem pole is the shame pole. These poles are erected as reminders to those who neglected to pay their debts. The most famous shame pole depicts former Exxon CEO Lee Raymond. On this pole, Raymond's face is upside down, a constant reminder that Exxon never fully paid the debt the court says it still owes to clean up the oil spill caused by the super tanker the Exxon Valdez, a catastrophic oil spill that destroyed the pristine Alaskan shoreline near the town of Valdez, Alaska.

Narrator: Now get ready to answer the questions. Answer each question based on what is stated or implied in the lecture.

1. What is the lecture about?
2. What is mentioned about totem poles? Select three. This is a 2-point question.

 3. Why does the professor say this?

Prof: Unfortunately, few plank houses have survived, the often-extreme weather of the area having returned most of this cultural heritage to the soil.

4. According to the lecture, which idiom originated with the totem pole?
5. What are the unique features of a plank house? Select three. This is a 2-point question.
6. Why does the most famous shame totem pole remind the world of Lee Raymond?

Task 4 - *Slang vs. Jargon* - Track 37 - Page 181

Narrator: Task four. Listen as a student talks to a professor, then answer the questions on the next page.

Liz: Professor Custer?
Prof: Hi Liz. What's up?
Liz: I missed last class.
Prof: Right. I noticed your seat was empty.
Liz: I had the flu, but I'm feeling much better.
Prof: Great. So what's up? How can I help you?
Liz: I got the notes from class, you know, what I missed and all.
Prof: Good.
Liz: But I'm still not sure about the difference between, you know, slang and jargon.
Prof: Okay. Let's deal with slang first. There are a few things to remember about slang. For starters, it's an invented language, created and shared by a group with shared interests.
Liz: You mean, they just create their own words?
Prof: That's right. Now these invented words—this sociolect—have a specific purpose, which is to exclude non members from the group.
Liz: Can you give me an example?
Prof: Oh, I don't know—rap music. The lyrics are slang in its purest sense. Have you ever listened to a rap song? I mean, really listened to it?
Liz: Yeah. I love rap, but I have no idea what they're talking about.
Prof: Exactly.
Liz: Even when I read the lyrics, most of it makes no sense.
Prof: That's because you don't understand the code, the invented language, the slang. The result is you are on the outside looking in—and that is the purpose of slang.
Liz: So if I want to join the group, I have to learn the code, the slang, right?
Prof: You would think. Don't get me wrong, you can learn all the rap slang you want, but will Fifty Cent or Lil Wayne or Snoop Dog accept you into their group, their gang? After all, you know the language, the code, right? Not likely.
Liz: So slang is like this invisible wall?
Prof: Precisely. For rappers, it's a wall of invented words designed to exclude you from the gang and to keep outsiders—other gangs and, more often than not, the police—from figuring out what your gang is saying. Of course, rap slang is only one kind of slang. Internet slang is also big. Do you know why kids use internet slang, all that abbreviated, seemingly nonsensical code?
Liz: To keep their parents from finding out what their saying?
Prof: You got it.

Liz: So what about jargon?
Prof: Jargon is slang too. Once again, it's an invented language—a sociolect—created by a group with mutual interests. The difference is that you can learn jargon—for example, computer jargon, you know, mouse, keyboard, etc.,—and you can become systems engineers or app designers. Or you can learn car jargon so you can talk to a mechanic when something goes wrong with your car. In other words, you can, by learning jargon, become part of the group.
Liz: So jargon is inclusive whereas slang is exclusive.
Prof: Exactly.
Liz: Are we kind of, you know, speaking jargon now?
Prof: Absolutely. The jargon of English usage. In fact, that's why you're here. Because you missed last class, you've been feeling excluded. You got the notes, the explanations of what I said—the jargon basically—but it wasn't enough. You needed to know more. You wanted to know all the code from last class, so you wouldn't feel left out and left behind. So what did you do?
Liz: I dropped by.
Prof: How do you feel now? Excluded or included?
Liz: Included. Wow. I never thought of it that way. So where do, you know, idioms fit in?

Narrator: Now get ready to answer the questions. Answer each question based on what is stated or implied in the conversation.

1. What is the topic of the conversation?
2. Why does the student visit the professor?

3. Why does the student say this?

Liz: So if I want to join the group, I have to learn the code, the slang, right?

4. The professor mentions three sociolects. What are they? Select three. This is a 2-point question.

5. Listen again to part of the conversation, then answer the question.

Liz: So jargon is inclusive whereas slang is exclusive.
Prof: Exactly.
Liz: Are we kind of, you know, speaking jargon now?
Prof: Absolutely. The jargon of English usage.

Narrator: What does the professor mean when she says this?

Prof: Absolutely.

Task 5 - *Internships* - Track 38 - Page 183

Narrator: Task five. Directions. Listen as a student talks to a campus employee, then answer the questions on the next page.

Admin: Hi, can I help you?
Betty: Is this the careers center?
Admin: It is.
Betty: I'd like to find out about interning.
Admin: Great. What's your major?
Betty: Business.

Admin: Is there a particular area you're focusing on?
Betty: Not yet. I was hoping an internship would help me decide what I want to do after I graduate.
Admin: Okay. Well, over here we have information about internships.
Betty: Wow. So many.
Admin: This one came in just this morning. It's from Apple. The Human Resources Department is offering three-month internships. If you're interested, this is the application form and the name to contact.
Betty: Are there any requirements?
Admin: Requirements?
Betty: You know, like a really high GPA or something?
Admin: No. Just enrollment in a college or a university.
Betty: I see. Where is the Apple internship?
Admin: It's at their headquarters in Cupertino, California.
Betty: Whoa…That's pretty far from Connecticut. Do they offer housing?
Admin: I'm afraid not. Internships don't usually offer housing.
Betty: Do you have anything closer? I'm still living at home.
Admin: General Electric is offering internships in their corporate tax department. This is a great opportunity. GE's tax department is very famous, you know.
Betty: Really? Why?
Admin: Their corporate tax department is very cutting-edge. What GE does tax wise everyone else copies, even the government. This would be a great opportunity to meet the best tax experts around. Also, it's being offered in their Fairfield headquarters.
Betty: That's just down the road.
Admin: GE tax internships are very popular. I suggest you apply. These internships go fast. I've had six in this morning asking about them.
Betty: GE would be really great, and I could drive there, no problem, but I'm not really into tax. Do you have anything like, you know, in marketing?
Admin: Marketing? Let's see, marketing…Where is it? It was here just a minute ago…Ah, here it is. Donny's Discount Donuts. They're offering internships in their marketing department. Have you seen their TV ads?
Betty: Yeah. The one with the monkey is pretty, you know, weird. Totally. Do you have anything else?
Admin: You know, the last person who interned at Donny's was hired full-time.
Betty: Really?
Admin: Did you know that Donny's is one of the fastest growing companies? They posted record profits last year and will soon go public.
Betty: Yeah, but it's still, you know, donuts.
Admin: I realize it's not the most glamorous internship, but at least you would get your foot in the door. And it is local. Would you like to apply?
Betty: Let me think about it.
Admin: Don't think too long. Remember: You snooze, you lose.

Narrator: Now get ready to answer the questions. Answer each question based on what is stated or implied in the conversation.

1. What is the topic of the conversation?
2. What can we infer about the student?
3. Why does the admin say this?

Admin: Their corporate tax department is very cutting-edge.

4. The admin mentions three internships. What are they? Select three. This is a 2-point question.

 5. Listen again to part of the conversation, then answer the question.

Admin: Did you know that Donny's is one of the fastest growing companies? They posted record profits last year and will soon go public.
Betty: Yeah, but it's still, you know, donuts.
Admin: I realize it's not the most glamorous internship, but at least you would get your foot in the door. And it is local. Would you like to apply?
Betty: Let me think about it.
Admin: Don't think too long. Remember: You snooze, you lose.

Narrator: Why does the admin say this?

Admin: Don't think too long. Remember: You snooze, you lose.

Task 6 - *Early Middle Ages* - Track 39 - Page 185

Narrator: Task six. Directions. Listen to part of a lecture in a history class, then answer the questions on the next page.

Prof: 1 ➔ At the height of its power in the second century AD, the Roman empire extended from present-day England in the west to present-day Palestine in the east. It controlled North Africa and the shipping routes on the Mediterranean. These routes were vitally important for they carried produce back to Rome, particularly grain, the supply of which was controlled by the government. In so doing, the government levied a tax against it. It was this money that built the Roman empire and its seemingly invincible legions. Yet in AD 476, the Western Roman Empire, its territories controlled by corrupt and ineffective governors, fell to an invading army of Goths. This event was a turning point in world history, for it marks the end of classical antiquity and the beginning of the Early Middle Ages in Europe.

2 ➔ The Early Middle Ages, circa 500 to 1,000 AD, was a time of social and economic chaos. With the collapse of the Western Roman Empire, long distance trade was abandoned, for the trade routes built by Rome and secured by its once-powerful army were now under the control of myriad German tribes constantly at war with each other. The precipitous decline in trade directly affected manufacturing. Pottery, for example, was an industry that vanished almost overnight, as did the trade in luxury goods, such as silk and spices from the Far East and salt from Africa. With them went the merchant class, men whose money was the tax base upon which Rome had survived.

3 ➔ The Early Middle Ages was in such turmoil that it is often referred to as the Dark Ages. The Roman Empire, which had been a stabilizing economic and cultural force for over five hundred years, had given way to a Europe in which anarchy ruled. Out of the chaos rose Charles Martel, a Frank who was called "The Hammer." Martel, born in 686, was the illegitimate son of duke Pepin II. After his father's death, Martel went on to win a series of battles across Europe, including his defense of Christian Europe against a Muslim army at the Battle of Tours in 732. Historians regard Martel as a great military leader. They also credit him with devising what today is known as the feudal system. In order to wage war, and protect his ever-expanding empire, Martel needed to maintain a large standing army. That army was made up of heavily armored horseman

called vassals. The vassals, who would later on be known as knights, swore allegiance to Martel. In return, Martel, who by 718 was king of present-day France, granted them large tracts of land called fiefs. The vassals then leased their land to peasant farmers. The peasants, little more than slaves, were heavily taxed for their work, the money going to Martel for the purpose of expanding the Frankish empire which, by the 800's, included most of western Europe and was under the control of Martel's grandson, Charlemagne. Charlemagne had by then established a central court in Aachen in present-day Germany. For protecting Pope Leo III, he was crowned the Holy Roman Emperor, for Charlemagne's empire did indeed mirror that of ancient Rome's.

4 → With Charlemagne creating a stable social order, there was a renewed interest in writing, art, architecture, and the study of scripture. This period is known as the Carolingian Renaissance, a period many historians believe was the precursor to the European Renaissance, circa 1,300 to 1,600. When Charlemagne died in 814, he was succeeded by his son, Louis the Pius. Upon his death, his three sons divided the empire into three kingdoms, territories which would eventually evolve into France, Germany and Italy.

Narrator: Now get ready to answer the questions. Answer each question based on what is stated or implied in the lecture.

1. What is the lecture mainly about?
2. What vanished with the fall of Rome? Select three. This is a 2-point question.
3. What does the lecture tell us about Martel? Select three. This is a 2-point question.

4. Why does the professor say this?

Prof: The Roman Empire, which had been a stabilizing economic and cultural force for over five hundred years, had given way to a Europe in which anarchy ruled.

5. What can we infer about Martel?
6. The professor mentions three dates. Match each date to its corresponding topic. This is a 2-point question.

Test 4 - Speaking - Page 189

Task 3 - *School Mascot* - Track 40 - Page 192

Narrator: Task three. Directions. Now listen as two students discuss the announcement.

Woman: So, Phil, what's your pick for the new school mascot?
Man: What are the choices again?
Woman: A bear and a chicken. I'm voting for the chicken.
Man: You want the symbol of our school to be a chicken? You can't be serious.
Woman: I am. Think about it. What other school has a chicken mascot?
Man: Alice....
Woman: Every other school has an eagle, a bear...
Man: I like bears.
Woman: Or some kind of dog. Bor-ing. But a chicken? That would make our school unique.
Man: It'll make everybody laugh at us. The Greenwich College Chickens? No way. No way.

Woman:	But that's the point. Why does a mascot have to be serious? Why can't a mascot be fun, like a chicken, or a goat, or a giraffe even? Education is way too serious.
Man:	Alice...
Woman:	What?
Man:	Earth to Alice.
Woman:	What!
Man:	We eat chickens.
Woman:	Go on.
Man:	Read the announcement. A chicken does not "symbolize the strength and traditions of our three-hundred-year-old institution." A bear, however, represents strength and determination, the school motto, remember? Seriously. Vote for the bear. It's going to win hands down.
Woman:	Yeah, well, don't count your chickens before they're hatched.
Narrator:	Now get ready to answer the prompt. The woman expresses her opinion about the announcement. State her opinion and explain the reasons she gives for holding that opinion. You have 30 seconds to develop your response and 60 seconds to speak.

Task 4 - *Brown-headed Cowbird* - Track 41 - Page 194

Narrator: Task four. Directions. Now listen to a lecture on the same topic.

Prof: 1 ➔ In this lecture, we'll take a closer look at the breeding habits of the brown-headed cowbird. The cowbird is what's called a brood parasite. Let me explain. As mentioned, the cowbird was originally a nomad, travelling with the buffalo and eating whatever the buffalo kicked up, insects, seeds, whatever. In this light, the cowbird was very much an opportunist. Yet the cowbird had a problem. Because they were nomadic, raising a family was a problem. If they stopped to raise a brood, they'd lose their food source, for the buffalo were always on the move. The cowbird, ever the opportunist, resolved this problem in a unique way, one that characterizes the species to this day.

2 ➔ When it comes time to lay her eggs, the female cowbird, instead of building a nest, deposits her eggs in the nest of another, much smaller host bird. The cowbird eggs then hatch. Because the cowbird chicks are much bigger than the host chicks, the host brood dies while the mother bird—unable to tell the difference between her own brood and the cowbird brood—is forced to feed the baby cowbirds till they fly off. This parasitic process—one in which one animal takes advantage of another—makes the brown-headed cowbird a true brood parasite.

Narrator: Now get ready to answer the prompt. The brown-headed cowbird is a brood parasite. How do the reading and the lecture define and develop this classification? You have 30 seconds to develop your response and 60 seconds to speak.

Task 5 - *Plagiarism* - Track 42 - Page 196

Narrator: Task five. Directions. Listen to a conversation between two students.

Man:	Are you sure?
Woman:	Yes. My professor plagiarized my essay, not just a few words, but an entire page verbatim in his last research paper.
Man:	This happened once before. A student accused her professor of plagiarism.
Woman:	And?

Man:	The professor was fired.
Woman:	Great. Maybe I should just forget the whole thing. Maybe I should be flattered that a professor borrowed my work, and just shut up about it.
Man:	Marilynn, the man did not borrow your work. He stole it. If you'd done this, stolen his work, you would've been kicked out of school in two seconds. No. There's no way you can back down. You've got to confront the man. You need to take your essay and his paper to his office, and tell him in no uncertain terms that what he did was wrong.
Woman:	But he's one of the most popular professors.
Man:	He's a thief.
Woman:	He gave me an A+ —for the essay he plagiarized!
Man:	Look, if you don't want to confront him, then you've got to go to the Dean. This is a serious breech of academic ethics. The sooner you confront the man, the better. Who knows how many other student essays he's plagiarized?
Woman:	But if I go to the Dean, it'll be all over the school in no time.
Man:	Yeah, well, I know what I'd do.
Narrator:	Now get ready to answer the prompt. The students discuss two solutions to the woman's problem. Identify the problem and the solutions, then state which solution you think is best and why. You have 20 seconds to develop your response and 60 seconds to speak.

Task 6 - *Homeostasis* - Track 43 - Page 198

Narrator:	Task six. Directions. Listen to part of a lecture in a science class.
Prof:	1 ➔ Homeostasis is a regulating process that helps a system maintain a stable internal balance. That system can be either open or closed. An example of a closed system is the Earth. Like all closed systems, the Earth has a definable border, namely, the atmosphere dividing us from space. Mass, large objects, cannot penetrate that border. Only the sun's energy can. That energy is heat which the Earth absorbs. As the Earth cools, it gives off heat. By doing so, the Earth's temperature is maintained. Within that homeostatic balance, life, as we know it, exists. 2 ➔ An open system is one in which mass and energy can both cross a border. In other words, an open system, to be homeostatic, must be permeable. Countries, for example, are open systems. Take the United States. People and products—mass in the form of products and energy in the form of ideas—flow back and forth across our borders every day. The result is a stable, system-regulating process or society. Economists call this a steady-state economy. 3 ➔ A biological example of an open system is the human body. To survive, to maintain homeostasis, we must constantly take in energy in the form of mass or food. When we're finished processing that food, we get rid of that mass to maintain the balance. Now remember that some parts of the human body are closed systems, for example, the circulatory system. Blood is pumped from the heart, a closed chamber, through a series of closed veins and arteries, and back again. Objects with mass, like food and waste, cannot permeate this system; however, energy, such as oxygen and carbon dioxide, come and go, as well as nutrient-based energy that comes from digested food.
Narrator:	Now get ready to answer the prompt. How does the lecture define and develop the concept of homeostasis? You have 20 seconds to develop your response and 60 seconds to speak.

Test 4 – Writing – Page 200

Task 1 - *Standardized Testing* - Track 44 - Page 201

Narrator: Task one. Directions. Now listen to a lecture on the same topic.

Prof: 1 → Proponents of standardized testing are quick to wave the flag of comparative statistics as being the best way to measure academic performance. Yet what supporters of standardized testing fail to realize is that, in their rush for statistics, they have boiled education down to a game, a game in which there are winners and losers. I'm sorry, but education is not about dividing students into winners and losers. It's about uniting with a focus on equality, the very thing standardized testing destroys by pointing the finger at those schools with lower-than-average scores.

2 → The article goes on to describe how teachers benefit from standardized testing. By using statistics, teachers know which subjects to focus on to increase scores, the example being math. Okay, so math is a problem. But why does it suddenly become a teaching priority? Why should English or history suffer? The reason is clear: this is not about providing students with a balanced education. It's about satisfying administrators and their constant demand for higher scores, for higher scores suggest that all is well when, more often than not, statistics lie, for if too much emphasis is placed on one subject, other subjects will suffer in turn. And who is to blame for that? Teachers trying to please administrators while ignoring the needs of their students.

3 → My biggest complaint with standardized testing is that someone is always to blame. If it's not the student's fault for getting a low score, then it must be the teacher's. If only it were so simple. What if on test day, a student were tired, or sick, or had family problems, or wasn't getting enough to eat? Are teachers to blame for all these variables? If you believe in low-scoring test results, then you have to say yes: bad teaching is to blame for poor student scores. Unfortunately, many excellent teachers have been fired because standardized testing has provided such leaps of logic.

4 → Let's be honest. Standardized testing is a numbers game played by administrators and teachers with the students left out in the cold. The sooner we get rid of standardized testing the better.

Narrator: Now get ready to write your response. Summarize the points made in the lecture and show how they cast doubt on the points made in the reading. You have 20 minutes to complete this task.

Acknowledgements

For their editorial insights and suggestions, the author would like to thank Patricia Stirling, Gretchen Anderson, Kateryna Kucher, Renata C. T. Rabacov, Yosra Ben Chikh Brahim, Oussama Bellaleh, and Jeff Kolby at Nova Press.

For their contributions to the audio CD, the author would like to thank Patricia Stirling, Gretchen Anderson, Jennie Farnell, and Jon Conine.